Eloquent Dissent

Eloquent Dissent

The Writings of James Sledd

edited by
Richard D. Freed

Boynton/Cook Publishers
HEINEMANN
Portsmouth, NH

Boynton/Cook Publishers
A subsidiary of Reed Elsevier Inc.
361 Hanover Street Portsmouth, NH 03801-3912

Offices and agents throughout the world

Library of Congress Cataloging-in-Publication Data
Sledd, James.
    Eloquent dissent : the writings of James Sledd / Richard D. Freed.
        p.   cm.
    Includes bibliographical references (p.).
    ISBN 0-86709-369-2
    1. English philology—Study and teaching (Higher)—United States.
    2. English language—Rhetoric—Study and teaching—United States.
    3. Education, Higher—United States.   4. United States—
Civilization.   I. Freed, Richard D. II. Title.
PE68.U5S58   1995
428'.007'173—dc20   95-36669
                                                           CIP

Acquisitions Editors: Bob Boynton and Peter R. Stillman
Production and Copy Editor: Renee M. Nicholls
Cover designer: Barbara Werden

Printed in the United States of America on acid-free paper
99 98 97 96   VB   1 2 3 4 5 6

*For Michele, loving and patient
far beyond the original deal.*

Contents

Acknowledgments

Thanks to Dennis Letts, who has taught me more than he knows about the important things; to David Ritz for continuing encouragement and friendship that began almost forty years ago; to my wife, Michele, and my children, Adrienne and Greg, who have given a meaning to my life that it would not otherwise have had; and to Jim Sledd, for his wisdom and wit, his patience, and for being a true professor—the one person in The Profession whom I still, after all these years, try to emulate. Thanks also to Bob Boynton and Peter Stillman for offering much valuable help to a novice in the world of making a book, and to Eastern Kentucky University for several grants that helped me in this effort.

Introduction

Why a Book of Essays by James Sledd?

There are, I believe, two kinds of people in the English teaching world: the large and growing number who have never read or heard of James Sledd, and those who would happily welcome the opportunity to reread the best of Sledd's essays. This explains why I receive two kinds of responses from colleagues when I tell them I have gathered Sledd's essays for republication—those who ask me who this man is, and those who are sure I am doing God's work and must in no way be hindered from completing my holy quest. This book is presented happily to the latter group and hopefully to the former. Those who know of Sledd's writings realize full well that they remain as fresh and relevant as they were when first printed. Those who come to these writings for the first time most likely will be happy to discover an honest, angry, witty voice that has been heard for many years and continues to this day to ring out. New readers will surely agree that this voice still ought to be heard—as much, perhaps, today, and possibly more now than ever. Sledd was, and is, a voice calling for truth and justice in education and in American society. Old readers know that James Sledd has always had more fellow travelers than he ever expected or realized.

Over the last forty-plus years, Sledd has been an insightful and severe critic of the status quo in the world of composition instruction—a world that is and has always been badly in need of honest, rational, cogent criticism. To call Sledd both a delightfully witty gadfly and a piercingly angry writer would be to do him and his writings a disservice. Sledd's essays *are* bitingly funny, and they are passionately bitter; they are always provocative in an entertaining way. He is an intelligent and sane revealer of professional self-serving cant, be it collective or individual. Throughout his very active career, Sledd has enthralled readers and listeners by exposing the professional hypocrisy of those on the inside—the "boss compositionists," as he calls them; the ancient idea that power corrupts is never far from his mind. Sledd himself has *always* religiously refused to participate as a Member of the Academy, the "in" power group (I seriously doubt he was ever actually invited). He has remained an insistent loner, a crusty outsider, a voice feared by the "good ole boys" (and "girls") on the inside who have some sellout to hide.

Because most of Sledd's best, most important, provocative and entertaining essays have appeared in professional journals over a period of more than forty years, they are, for all practical purposes, without republication, in danger of being forgotten. I believe strongly that the essays included here, as well as those listed in the bibliography, should be read today by anyone who is in the English teaching profession or about to get in. The writings should also be read, of course, by any reader who enjoys a rare and vital combination of wit, intelligence, outrage, honesty, and, especially, clarity of thought. In the old way, James Sledd is a master of the art of the essay. His words—his remarkable style, his ideas—should remain available to us. This book, then, is for the teaching assistants and graduate students who have worked and drunk beer with Jim, the countless teachers who have read and been inspired by his writings over the years, the students who have been in his classes, the many people who have traveled long distances to hear Sledd read one of his brilliant papers, and for those colleagues who have valued Sledd's opinions throughout the years. It is also, perhaps most of all, for new readers.

Other Voices from Far and Near

The appeal of Sledd's writings turned out to be more widespread than I had originally anticipated. When I first began work on gathering these essays, I showed one of them to an old friend, Philip Maxwell, a successful Texas lawyer with no abiding interest in teaching composition. He insisted on reading more, and then on meeting Sledd. When I introduced Phil as an attorney, Jim instantly raised his hands high overhead and responded, "No need to stay here; I don't have any money!" Phil stayed anyway, and a new Sledd fan was born instantly. Phil, an intelligent nonacademic, asked me to call him when this book comes out.

When I told Dennis Letts, a cherished colleague and friend, about this project, he insisted first on driving three hundred miles to help me cart boxes from Sledd's office and then on helping me begin to sort through the stuff. Rifling through the boxes of papers, we were like kids who had snuck into the attic to rediscover old secrets. We had fun, but Dennis assured me then and often since that this project was serious, important business. Over the years, Dennis Letts's voice has been a strong one in my ear; on this project, there have been many other voices as well, some from unexpected places, all insisting that my effort was more urgently needed than I might have imagined.

When I first met with Bob Boynton, semiretired bossman at Boynton/Cook, I thought I might have to sell the idea of republishing the yellowing pages of Sledd's essays. I was pleasantly surprised to hear Bob begin our conversation with, "It's about time someone has done this for the younger readers who may never have heard of Jim and his ideas. How long do you think it will take to get the edition ready?" When I met Peter Stillman, editor-in-chief of Boynton/Cook, at a 4C's book exhibit, he asked before I could begin to speak, "Where's the Sledd manuscript? You're late."

In June of 1994, I traveled to Saudi Arabia to learn about Arab culture and the Saudi people. While in Riyadh on a visit to King Saud University, I met a young man with a Ph.D. in linguistics, Dr. Al Mozainy. Casually I mentioned that I was working on editing Professor Sledd's writings. Dr. Mozainy responded enthusiastically that he admired Sledd very much for his political acumen and for his witty style. He told me that Sledd's ideas, expressed so effectively in the essays, were much needed in the university education of Saudi students. Radical pedagogy in Saudi Arabia!

A Very Full Plate

I have been working on this project for over two years. Why, I have often wondered, has it taken so long to gather a few essays, do a simple bibliography, and write some brief headnotes? It turns out that the project wasn't so simple.

Having first traveled to Austin, Texas, for the first gathering of "stuff," I had returned home with several full boxes—a basic start in my search. Library detective work then led me to an ever growing body of work. The joke was, as Sledd had promised it would be, on me. The quality of Jim Sledd's writings is so uniformly high that I found myself doing intellectual wheelies trying to decide which essays were the best written, the cleverest, the most effective, the most genuinely current, the most poignantly true. Almost every essay seemed, and seems, to fit all of these criteria.

Nevertheless, I did not succumb to that old composition teachers' tactic of throwing all the papers down the steps and choosing those at the top of the stairway. Ultimately, decisions on what to include were based on attaining a representative sample. I realized that I could hardly miss, no matter which essays I chose; anyone who enjoys the writings presented here will also find the essays listed in the bibliography pertinent, enjoyable, and of equally high quality.

Another problem I had not anticipated was that the longer I waited, the more I had to choose from—Sledd continues to speak publicly and write eloquently about what's wrong with the world and the writing profession of the 1990s. There will almost certainly be entries to add to the bibliography by the time this book gets to print.

The Heart of the Matter:
Selecting and Ordering the Essays

When I first proposed the reprinting of these essays to Sledd, he laughed and refused. I persisted, however, and finally got him to agree, though he continues to find my project amusingly unnecessary and certainly futile. He also agreed to my request to sit down with a tape recorder for an extended interview. In mid-February of 1993, we sat and talked for two days in his office at the University of Texas. His instant response to my initial question of how we would proceed was, "Let's go get a beer." The ninety-five-page transcript of that conversation shows Jim, in some ways, at his acerbic best. A few excerpts from that transcript are quoted in this text.

When I asked Jim to categorize the subjects he had written about that still might have currency (aside from his earlier, more traditional scholarly essays on medieval and eighteenth-century writers), he replied:

> The concerns I *think* that would go together would be these: one, the teaching of the English language in English departments, particularly to prospective teachers. I don't think English teachers know anywhere near what they ought to know about the language in order to teach properly. So that's one thing. Another is the bidialectism struggle. And a third one is the oppression of graduate students and part-timers. Now those three things fit together and would make a sort of reasonable, reasonably unified group.

While this classification gives an idea of the general concerns Sledd has written about, putting the essays into such neat "piles" inevitably oversimplifies his writing. The essays are about these topics, but they always integrate overriding concerns so that they are almost never solely about one single subject.

After a lot of puzzling, I decided to place the essays in their chronological order of publication. Throughout, the overriding concern with integrity in the English teaching profession is a constant, only changing in its specific focus over the years. My argument is not that there are "early concerns" and "the later years," but that the earliest essays in this volume are absolutely as current today as they were the day they were written. Over the years Jim has neither dropped a stitch nor picked up many truly new ones. He always discusses with urgency and élan the essential issues that concerned professionals who teach—especially writing—ought to be worrying about.

Radical or Conservative?

James Sledd has spent much of his time arguing passionately about what a modern American university ought to be and do, and complaining bitterly that most institutions continually fail to live up to their stated commitments. Known widely as a radical leftist, Sledd offers surprisingly traditional arguments: universities should not be controlled by external economic and political pressures; administrations should treat professors, especially younger colleagues who are not able to protect themselves, fairly; departments should treat beginning college students, who are allowed and even encouraged to enroll, decently, particularly over how they use the English language. Professors and administrators ought not exploit graduate students and part-time teachers by employing them as "slaves" to teach difficult and time-consuming freshman writing courses, and students should not be used as economic fodder—to people lower-division classes that are taught by slave labor.

Sledd's most basic premises are as simple, as conventional, as traditional as can be: he claims that people involved in a university (as well as those in any position of authority over others in our society) should be competent and honest; they should avoid self-aggrandizement. Sledd argues that no university can exist in isolation from the rest of society—from the body politic. With this clearly expressed belief, James Sledd has gotten himself into a lot of trouble—there is disturbing irony in the fact that his views are seen to be and are, in a literal way, radical. Sledd's criticisms often go to the root of what is wrong; yet many of his values are conservative. He simply tries to tell the truth as he sees it about what is so terribly wrong and dishonest in academia, and how that is related to what is wrong and dishonest at the centers of power in American society.

Where James Sledd can rightly be called radical is in his criticism of a society based on the greed of capitalism. In "Reflections," Sledd concludes, "if you really dream about language arts for all children, learn how an acquisitive society frustrates education, not how educationists propose to cure social cancer with pedagogic placebos." Teaching students that they should plan to use education to move up an economic or social ladder, Sledd argues, is dishonest and evil. The downtrodden, he argues with a sense of fatalism, are not likely to be allowed to move very far up any socio-economic ladder. Sledd was, in fact, early to foresee that the ladder is and has been made of rotten rungs, and he wants nothing whatever to do with encouraging students to try to climb it.

The idea of teachers using "upward mobility" as a carrot for educational motivation and pedagogy, Sledd cries bitterly, was and is largely fraudulent. More important, the idea that education *should* be used for such a purpose flies in the face of our oldest humanistic traditions. Even if we are really able to help students achieve material well-being by learning to speak and write in standard English, Sledd argues with passionate eloquence, then we would simply be morally wrong for trying to do so. We ought not try to encourage our students to join a corrupt system.

Thus, when the radical rapscallion James Sledd proclaims in a tone of customary self-mockery that he is a "Southern, conservative, paleo-Methodist," most people chuckle, but he makes the claim nevertheless. When I asked him about this, Sledd responded, "Basically, I am altogether a conservative. I don't think I've ever spoken a radical word. I call myself a paleo-Methodist. There was a story going around the department, once, that I was a neo-Marxist, and I replied, 'I am a paleo-Methodist,' and I meant it. I am."

Yet in his criticism of teachers who put self-interest over their students' interest, in his intense dislike of greed and hypocrisy fostered by the overarching capitalist system, Sledd has indeed always been clearly radical. From our conversation:

FREED: But of course you also think there is something radically wrong with many of the stated values of our society? To that degree you are a radical, no?

SLEDD: Well, in that case, I think all of the organized religions of the world would have to be called radical.

FREED: Yeah, of course. They are too. So you have good company. You and Jesus Christ.

SLEDD: Well, Richard, things do worry me like that. Shelly Sachs and I were the very best of friends. And the notion that he would look down on me because I was a Southern Methodist, and I would look down on him because his father was a Jewish immigrant from Russia was totally impossible . . . this isn't radical, this is . . . "go ye into all the world and preach the gospel to every creature."

FREED: But in any serious sense, surely Christianity is radical, in its idea that people should be treated equally?

SLEDD: I think Christianity is wrong in its claims to divinity, but I accept the ethics.

FREED: Well, when you say reform, how would you bring about reform? What would you do?

SLEDD: The basic thing is to realize that you cannot change the educational system without first changing the society. So I think a primary duty of academics is to attack the structure of American society as it exists today. Now, in many ways it's like pissing in the wind; you'll just get your face wet, but that's no reason not to do it. People talk about the failure of socialism; I don't think socialism's ever been tried. To call the Russian system a socialist system is a jest. But I still believe, "from each according to his ability, to each according to his needs." I see nothing wrong with that.

Sledd is radical primarily in his insistence on integrity, regardless of the consequences, though his basic values are as traditional as humanism itself. Because this kind of honesty in our society and in the university teaching profession is rare, especially in matters of self-interest, Sledd seems quite rightly to be designated a radical. Humanist values are always radical when seen as the opponent of existing societal values.

This Above All

In his professional career James Sledd has changed courses whenever he felt compelled to do so by the logic of his thinking. In the 1960s, for example, after he had become a prominent structural linguist, he suddenly ceased to write in this field. As he explains:

> I was also asked to teach some linguistics courses, and so I had to do an awful lot of scrambling to learn the current fashions in American linguistics. Just as I had learned one set of fashions, Noam Chomsky came along and I had to throw all that away and learn what he was up to. Then, after about the '60s, I learned that I really couldn't keep up in two departments. I had tried to be both literary man and linguist, and I decided I couldn't do that any longer. So I directed the freshman comp course for a couple of years.

When Sledd felt he could no longer contribute meaningfully, he had the integrity to stop trying, even though his writings on linguistics were eagerly awaited by his colleagues. Sledd has always applied the basic standards of being responsible for what one says and does, being a responsible, careful, and thorough researcher and writer, and above all speaking the truth as one sees it, to himself as well as to others.

Sledd's attacks have been almost entirely directed to those in power because he cannot excuse their abuse of that power, their desire to serve themselves. He condemns those who are ignorant in spite of their social, political and economic advantages and who should know better. Rather than criticize the economically impoverished, he ridicules those who scorn the underclasses for not acting like "we" do. He doesn't attack teachers of writing; he condemns the writing research "gang" who control professional organizations and write about teaching writing while they teach no writing classes. He criticizes administrators—from department chairs up. Not surprisingly, his attacks have taken the form of savage letters to local newspapers and national literary magazines, bitterly funny departmental memos, brilliantly delivered papers, and some of the liveliest professional writing read by those of his generation. He does not condemn students; he condemns those who use or misuse students for their own ends. He writes in defense of those who have no power. His actions and writings have not made James Sledd the world's most popular individual among research scholars, the "boss compositionists."

Sledd as Lecturer

If you have had the good fortune to hear Jim Sledd read a paper at a professional meeting—something that he does less often now that he is approaching his eightieth year—you will undoubtedly hear him complain about precisely the same societal ills and destructive professional practices that he has ranted and raved about for over forty years. A brilliant reader, Sledd has often been asked for manuscripts of delivered papers for later publication. Many of the essays included in this collection were first heard by a live audience. Sledd's tone is clear, polished and easy; he speaks the way he writes and writes the way he speaks. This conversational quality has much to do with the readability of the essays. The reader often feels that Sledd is speaking directly. I think he is.

I remember going to Tuscaloosa in 1979 to hear Jim do battle with E. D. Hirsch. Feeling like a camp follower, I think it was the first time I realized how widespread his reputation for public oratory had become. For those of us who had come to watch the battle with the then respected Hirsch, it had seemed like an opportunity of a lifetime. It was. The battlefield was tilted against Hirsch because the intellectual onslaught against his ideas had already begun to destroy his credibility. Sledd made easy work of his opponent (though Hirsch's *Cultural Literacy* cottage industry continues to collect ever larger royalty checks). The Sleddite camp followers, like so many before and after, were treated to the unforgettable fireworks of a brilliant thinker, a speaker having fun with an easy target. I would urge anyone who enjoys looking at these essays to take advantage of any opportunity to listen to Jim read one of his papers.

No one I have ever read or heard is able to begin an essay or lecture as effectively as Jim Sledd. Had there been space in this collection, I would have included a section entitled "Beginnings." I would also have included in the bibliography a list of the multitude of papers he has read over the years. Like the opening paragraphs he reads and writes, Sledd's titles are marvels of rhetorical, pungent wit. What is included in the bibliography here will have to do.

Jim read a paper at the 1993 4C's meeting in Nashville. Having known him for over twenty-five years, having read his essays with special attention, and having heard him deliver many, many lectures, I went to Nashville with some apprehension. Could Jim, after all these years, slouching slowly and deliberately toward octogenarianism, still deliver the goods? His doctor now prohibits him from drinking friends under the table, and he is certainly no longer able to wrastle with would-be muggers, as he did twenty years ago. Thus I was worried that Sledd might be losing some of the razor sharp edge that has made him such a remarkable public speaker and the most insightful critic to be heard at any given meeting. However, in 1993 Jim's mind and his words were as sharp as ever; I had been foolish to think they might be otherwise.

Then, Now, Tomorrow . . .

Jim will be the first to assert that not much has changed since he first started complaining. Yet he continues with unabated vigor to attack the "prestigious" professionals who write about teaching writing while they teach no writing; he also remains outraged at the dishonesty of the larger political powers that seem always to be around. In spite of his vitriolic sarcasm and his humorous self-effacing pessimism, he continues to care deeply about the role of language in human affairs; he continues to care about the relationship between language teachers and language users. He is wise enough to realize that his writings will not solve the ills of the profession or bring about vast changes in the world. But he remains too much an active member of the community to simply shut up and fade away. I believe he cannot choose to do otherwise.

During our conversations in Austin in February, Jim was more open with me than ever before in talking frankly about his personal life and feelings about his long career. At one point, in speaking about his personal attitudes, he recalled the profoundly influential years he spent at Oxford as a Rhodes Scholar in the late 1930s. Jim talked about having a larger perspective in a way that I will always remember:

FREED: I'm looking for your feelings about it all. To this point you have always been pretty pessimistic about what can be done. Do you retain that pessimism? Are you thinking, this is a nice project, but . . . ?

SLEDD: Richard, at Oxford I was placed at the top of the second class. If I had written one more Alpha paper and one less Beta paper, I would probably have been given a First Class. But I didn't. I think I was properly placed at the top of the second class. I've never forgotten something my father said to me. All of his children who went to college, and we all went, except the one who died too young, were Phi Beta Kappa. And he said to me one night on the front porch, "Jim, there's nothing special about us. We're pretty much what ordinary people ought to be." I am a respectable second class person. Given the advantages I had and the opportunities that were thrust upon me, I should have done one hell of a lot more than I did. I'm not weeping into my beer or anything. It seems to me *essential to keep your standards clear*. And I've known only a handful of people in my life who I think are really first class.

FREED: Who would those be?

SLEDD: A man at Chicago, Elder Olson, who's dead now. Noam Chomsky, whom I knew fairly well back in the '60s and haven't seen or spoken to since. There are very few of them. And it's essential, I think, that we recognize the really first rate, the really top notch people and judge ourselves against them.

These are the words of a man many people during the last forty years have felt strongly to be a writer of genuine importance, a thinker of high rate who has influenced many people.

He is also fun to read.

Reflections
(1980)

This brief statement reveals traits that exist throughout Jim Sledd's writings: sharp wit, clarity of thought, and a burning anger with the powers that be. Because of its succinct elegance, this essay is the only one placed out of chronological order.

Language arts for ALL children? In the unlucky words of an upwardly mobile female, "Not bloody likely!"

I won't stop to argue that reading, writing, speaking, and listening aren't language arts but arts of which language is the medium. The difference matters, partly because the label *language arts* limits our subject too narrowly, invites the depredations of linguists on the make, and discourages social and political concern; but other things need saying more.

There's not the slightest chance that the school system of the United States, the nation that propped up the shah and Somoza for so long, will do any more than talk about meeting the needs of all our children. State-supported schools support the state. John Stuart Mill said that, long before the NCTE appointed a committee to milk the bureaucracy in the national interest; and it shouldn't be necessary—and anyway isn't possible in five hundred words—to argue the point with school-teachers (not bureaucrats) who are systematically beaten down by censorship, accountability, competency tests devised by the incompetent, and a variety of other repressive instruments (including professors). If I did want to build an argument, I would show how our professional societies have served the cause of domination by making the goal of American education

1

"upward mobility in the mainstream culture." Upward mobility means the continued irresponsible conspicuous waste of irreplaceable resources, the continued exploitation of the "undeveloped" countries by the United States, and the perpetuation of a class structure which presupposes that the despised and rejected must be always with us as the foundation of our self-esteem. Yes, hypocritical reader: I'd rather be a nigger than po' white trash.

To me, then, the most significant development of the apathetic, reactionary '70s has been the mindless unwillingness of English teachers at all levels to recognize that as a group we are DOWNWARDLY mobile and that our interests are NOT the nation's interest—that is, not the interest of the multinational corporations which run ours among other nations. You don't believe it? Then ask yourself if your raises for the past year or so have matched the obscene growth of corporate profits; and when you've enjoyed the resultant self-pity for a moment, think about the condition of the really poor. What do they do as prices really rise but wages really fall?

Socially and politically, we English teachers have just been plain stupid. I'll never forget the misleader of children who answered my criticism of upward mobility as a goal with her own profession of faith in avarice, pride, envy, gluttony, *et sim.* "I've made it to steak," she said. "I've made it to steak, I'm headed for lobster, and I want to take my pupils with me." For people who feel like that, three references are essential reading: reports on conditions among Blacks, Hispanics, and native Americans; reports on corporate profits in the *Wall Street Journal;* and especially their own income tax returns. The dim hope for the '80s is that even teachers will realize, as they slip from lobster to catfish or from steak to stew, which side their bread is no longer buttered on. Nobody lives by the loaves and fishes that he hasn't got.

So. . . . If you really dream about language arts for all children, learn how an acquisitive society frustrates education, not how educationists propose to cure social cancer with pedagogic placebos.

Prejudice: In Three Parts
(1961)

This essay is clearly James Sledd's most autobiographical writing. It reveals Sledd's lifelong insistence on being honest with himself and his readers in trying to uncover the truth. Here, he deals with the conflict between some of the values of his southern upbringing and his urgent belief in the obligation of the privileged and powerful to defend the rights of the oppressed. Life, Sledd argues, is complex. This may be the only essay Sledd ever wrote that is wholly devoid of cutting irony. It is an early plea for universal equal opportunity.

I.

I am a middle-aged Southerner. More specifically, I am a middle-aged conservative white Southern academic from an educated middle-class Protestant Christian family. I grew up, like most Southerners of my kind, in the calm unspoken assurance that I belonged to a superior race. Nobody told me I did, and if I had been conscious enough of the assumption to state it openly, my mother would have made me hush. Children did not talk about such things. Indeed, our old-fashioned family really believed in equality before God and the law, and we children escaped some prejudices so luckily that national and religious differences had, and still have, small meaning for us. What was more, our father as a young man had sacrificed his job and possibly risked his life in defense of what he considered justice for the Negro. He carefully taught us to be polite and kind and to take no unfair advantage of those whose dark skins condemned them to be laborers and servants. We were proud of him; and with a mildly pleasant consciousness of virtue, we did as we were told. We have continued to behave so for half a century. But the lesson learned without teaching was not forgotten either. I at least, in those same fifty years, have never escaped the consequences of a childhood in a land of white supremacy. I can never have, with a Negro, the same easy, unplanned, intuitive relationship that I can have with whites; for I can never have it again on the only terms that my childhood left possible for me.

The good old woman who helped my mother raise us loved us dearly, and we loved her. Her father and mother had served my mother's mother, so that she was one of us before I was born. She dressed us, fed us, laughed and sang and played with us, corrected us, called us her children and made the saying true. She followed my grandmother's and my mother's coffins, she has held my children in her arms and kissed them, and when I last met her at Five Points in Atlanta ten years ago, she kissed me too and I was glad she did. Yet Julie was always a servant, born so and destined to remain so. She never entered or left our house but by the back door, and she ate her meals in the kitchen there alone. She kissed me in the street, but I could not take her with my wife and children into a hotel or restaurant. We sat on the staircase in the lobby of an office-building after five o'clock and ate popcorn together.

If I could ever think of Julie as degraded, I would say that that is the real argument against racial discrimination—that it degrades its victims on both sides. Uninstitutionalized rudeness to her, if we as children had been capable of it, would of course have been instantly punished, just as cruelty or arrogance to any Negro, whether family servant or total stranger, would have been: we were the kind of children who never said *nigger*. But we also assumed that Negroes lived in shacks in a separate part of town, that they wore old clothes and chopped our wood or delivered our ice and coal, that they did not go to white hotels or eat in white restaurants or sit beside white people on the streetcar, that their children went to separate schools, that they worshipped God in separate churches and at last were separately committed to God's earth. Those things we saw all around us and simply accepted, as children do, because they were familiar. The lesson we learned without teaching was that ours was a white man's world. We did not make that world; it was there when we were born, and we tried, in our way, to alleviate its cruelty. We still were in it and of it, and it left its mark. It left in the deepest part of my mind a set of attitudes which I repudiate intellectually but which remain as a lasting source of conflict and self-distrust.

Some of the consequent humiliations have been so painful that I can hardly describe them truthfully. I remember one in particular.

I had left Atlanta, for the first time really, to go to Oxford. In my college there was a Negro prince from Africa. That was the first time that I had had a Negro as a fellow-student, and I was rather proud of myself for not resenting it. I used to argue about "the Negro problem" with a boy from Texas. "Man is one," I said as I had been taught to say; "civilizations are many." Nyabongo soon put me in my place. He was writing a book of his people's folk-tales, and since I was reading English and he did not trust his composition, he asked me to polish the manuscript for him. It was not enough for me to agree and do the favor unobtrusively (I would never have dreamed of saying "no"). When Nyabongo brought the manuscript to my rooms, I had to explain that although I was a Southerner, I did not share the usual Southern prejudice. "Yes," Nyabongo said coldly, "I assumed that you were a civilized man." If his book was ever published, it has some of my blood on it: the exploited have their own ways of exploitation.

The intelligent white Southern Christian of a generation or two ago could not have been knifed so easily. His Christianity and his fatherly tradition guaranteed decency in his conduct, and he had not learned to doubt his feelings. It was in 1902, in an article in the *Atlantic,* that my father made a Southern Christian's case for better treatment for the Southern Negro. Writing from a little college town in central Georgia, he bitterly denounced lynching as a "wild and diabolic carnival of blood" conducted by "our lower and lowest classes," whose nature "is hardly comprehensible to one who has not lived among them and dealt with them"; and he attacked the constant petty humiliations to which Negroes of every class were subject—separate and inferior waiting rooms and Jim Crow cars, separate and inferior hotels and restaurants, rudeness in stores and on the street, different churches for the worship of the same God. Without sentiment and without mercy, he proposed that human law should be enforced so that divine law might be obeyed: "our lower classes must be *made* to realize, by whatever means, that the black man has rights which they are *bound* to respect." There was no alternative to justice.

That was strong talk from a man whom the mob burned in effigy but preferred not to face in person, but it was also the language of a man who called himself, quite literally and without melodrama, "an unreconstructed rebel." The two "facts" on which his argument was based were bluntly stated and with equal emphasis: "the Negro has inalienable rights," but he "belongs to an inferior race." From my father's second statement, it followed that all plans to give the Negro social equality were wrong because they proposed to tamper artificially with the natural bases of society; it did not follow, from his first statement, that direct efforts should be made to deliver the Negro from poverty and ignorance. The proposal was only that the Southern white should recognize "the equality of the fundamental rights of human creatures." The Negro should simply be given his simple due: the chance to "work out his destiny among us" with no special favors but under no peculiar disabilities. If then his position should remain inferior, the fault would be his. The exercise of his "inalienable rights" could not remove "the limitations of the race."

I envy the clarity and simplicity of my father's convictions. His heart and his head were at one. He never doubted the superiority of his class and race; and, just as he demanded that every man accept the responsibilities of his position, so he accepted the responsibilities of his own. He could speak and act decisively and could contemplate the results of his speech and action without fear and without regret. I can do no such thing. With no great faith in divine or natural law and with even less in governments, I share my father's belief in "the equality of the fundamental rights of human creatures," but I cannot use his arguments in defending that belief. Intellectually, I reject my father's notions of superior and inferior races, yet I am my father's son. Clarity and simplicity, in these matters, died with a generation whose innocence, perhaps, was guilt but whose minds were whole. I and others like me must govern a whole set of human relations by will and conscious thought. It is a hard and painful thing to do.

II.

In 1945 I finished my graduate work at the University of Texas and accepted an instructorship at the University of Chicago. Race and region were not issues there, for equality of basic rights was so much a matter of course that no one needed to fuss about it. Nobody gave a second thought to the fact that my speech, my background, and my beliefs were Southern, and nobody wondered how I would get along with Negro students or how they would get along with me. It was just assumed that we would treat one another as human beings. The one discrimination that I practised was to be a little more lenient, a little more consciously polite, to Negro students than I was to others; their one answering discrimination was to be sometimes a little more demanding, a little less friendly, than their classmates. These slight deviations from humaneness did not affect Southerners only. Once in a while I thought I sensed a faint suggestion that it might be wise to give better grades to Negro students than they might deserve; and our chairman told us once of the remark which a tough and wittily perceptive Negro had made to him. "You can't treat me like all the other students," the young man had said; "you've got to treat me better." But that was the limit of discrimination on the Midway when I first went there.

For ten years, then, my wife and children and I lived in Hyde Park. It was a noisy, dirty, decaying neighborhood, and housing was unbelievably bad; yet in many ways it was an exciting place, and we were happy that our boys were growing up in a United Nations of small playmates. The children, it seemed, were quite unconscious of racial, religious, or national distinctions. For several years their classes, their Cub packs, their baseball and football teams were happy small-scale models of a society where tolerance could be no virtue because friendship had forestalled it. A birthday party for a child meant invitations to Northerner and Southerner, Christian and Jew, Japanese and German, Negro and white; and a cocktail party could be much the same with noisier personnel. We were luckier than we knew.

We realized what luck we had had when the luck changed. We had come to Chicago at the end of a great era, and steadily the neighborhood was declining. Decent people were eager to make and keep it stably multiracial, but criminality was an increasing threat to order. The criminals too were drawn from a multiracial group— at first from low-class whites, then from Negroes, Puerto Ricans, white laborers out of the nearer South; but Negroes were not the least numerous. Crime increased; the well-kept areas shrank before the spreading slums; the streets grew more and more dangerous at night; law-abiding residents of all races puzzled over leaving the community or staying to make a fight for it. We stayed, for a while; but finally we left.

One reason—not the strongest among several, but still a reason—was the slow realization that the fight was not just a fight between disorder and the law. It was several fights at once, some of them open, some unrecognized or even officially denied; and the rules were not the same for everyone. Attempts to preserve or restore the neighborhood meant attempts to drive out present trouble-makers and to prevent others from coming in; but among the trouble-makers were many Negroes. An unbroken multiracial front against disorder grew hard to maintain. Whites were afraid of seeming prejudiced, Negroes uncertain of their first allegiance; and the double-talk and indecision that resulted made a perfect opening for the single-minded predator of either race.

Ironically, it was in the courtroom that we had our introduction to the Race Man, the resolute Negro racist who dislikes whites because they are whites and who uses the white man's sense of guilt as a weapon of guerilla warfare. My wife one day had sent our two oldest sons, who were still in grammar school, to the grocery store. On their way home they were robbed at knife-point by some Negro boys. We were not surprised into comic indignation. We had seen a little and heard more of purse-snatching, burglary, robbery, and assault by white and black alike, and we knew that our boys had been the victims of petty thieves, not the white aristocrats of Chicago crime. Mainly we wanted to recover the ten dollars which we could not afford to lose. After asking some questions at the store, we had a fairly strong suspicion who the culprits were; and though I told the police, when we reported the incident, that I would not make a case against children, I asked them to go with me to the children's house to see if I could get my money back. The officers assigned were Negroes, and with their help I reached an agreement with the children's mother. When they came home, she said, she would find out if they had taken the money, and if they had she would return it. Then a higher police officer intervened. He said I would have to take the matter to court, since the suspected boys came from a notorious family which had terrorized the local storekeepers. Negro witnesses were afraid to talk, and storekeepers lost less through pilfering than they would through the smashing of a plate-glass window. The officer left me no choice. If I did not go to court willingly he would use the law to make me. The police arrested the young suspects, our children identified them, and we went to court as we were told to do.

It was I who went on trial. Neither the defense lawyer nor the probation officer, to whom the accused youngsters were quite familiar, made any effort to talk to me or to my sons; and in court the lawyer's questioning was designed entirely to suggest that the whole business was a frame-up which I had engineered. He failed, but he made the effort; and the stingingly funny result of my effort to be a good citizen was that I lost my ten dollars, wasted two working days, and had to stand quietly while a man whom the law protected suggested that I was contemptibly dishonest. Apparently, that lawyer was not concerned to get at the truth or to enforce the law. For him, it seemed enough that whites had made a case against blacks; he was in court to see the whites discomfited. As we left the courtroom, I asked an observer for a civic group who the man was. He was not a shyster, I was told, but one of the more prominent Negro lawyers in the city. The observer then told me to keep our children in the house after five o'clock if we wanted them to be safe. Later, we learned from the principal of the neighborhood grammar school that the suspects' brothers had been in trouble for threatening other children with knives on the school playground, and we followed the further adventures of the clan through crime reports, including a murder case, in the daily papers.

Our experience was not atypical, people told me, of the South Side of Chicago; but it was a small thing, and not for a moment to be compared with the systematic denial of civil and human rights to whole communities for generations. I have profited from knowing how it feels to be pushed around; and in our travels since, our children have profited from living in a foreign country where they belonged to a minority race. It would be laughable if I should try to dramatize one small injustice in a world of infinitely larger ones just because the small injustice was directed against my family and me. But the effect of many such experiences on many people is not laughable, and since we left Chicago I have seen more instances of the same injustice. In mixed schools in Berkeley, California, where we went to escape the dirt and violence of Hyde Park, our sons again met open conflict between races. Just as their friends had been beaten on the street or in their own backyards on the South Side, a schoolmate and good friend of theirs was beaten on a Berkeley street by a roving Negro gang. The boy's parents seemed almost afraid to mention the beating, as if they thought that to conceal it was the best way to avoid trouble. In the junior high school and in the high school, our sons and their friends told me of the protection racket: when a white boy was asked for a nickel, he risked a beating if he refused. More than once, the police had to patrol both school-grounds to prevent gang fights, which Negro boys would try to provoke. If by repeated insults they could goad a white boy to hit first, the gang would beat him and then complain to the authorities that he had struck the first blow. The white child was subjected, in a small way, to the kind of treatment that the Negro suffers on a much larger scale; but there was no public indignation to protect the white. People seemed to believe that the wrongs of the Negro minority were somehow righted if its lowest members were allowed to inflict similar wrongs on innocent members of the majority.

I saw the effect of this reversed discrimination both on my sons and on the boys I worked with in a Berkeley Scout troop. The more friendly and level-headed boys still kept their ideals of social justice and still knew that their discomforts were comparatively slight. The high-school social clubs were traditionally for whites only; I knew one seventeen-year-old who conducted a one-man campaign to get Orientals and Negroes admitted to the club of which he was president. None of the boys, however, would ever again be simply unconscious of racial differences. They drew a sharp distinction between the decent Negroes who were their friends and the thugs whom they despised; and for the thugs they had no sympathy. They insisted that social responsibility should work both ways. The less idealistic and levelheaded were grossly intolerant. Many of them, children of prosperous and educated families, were outspokenly scornful of their Negro classmates, more so than the boys from similar families whom I remember from my own youth in Atlanta. Discrimination multiplies and perpetuates itself. Among Negro teenagers in American cities, there has come to be a good deal of generalized hostility to all whites, whether friendly or unfriendly; and the minority of troublemakers among the Negro boys know how to take advantage of their color. White parents and white teachers are often afraid to make a strong stand against them; for they have learned, as I have, how quickly liberals and Race Men may come to the defense of the trouble-makers with charges of discrimination. As a result, the decent white boy, like the decent Negro, is at a disadvantage; and his response to the hostility of the Negro and to its protection by public sentiment and public authority is disillusionment and anger. My impression is that the rising generation in America may have worse race relations than mine has had.

III.

In 1960, after a year on an assignment in Ceylon, I accepted a professorship at Northwestern University and returned to the Middle West, this time to pleasant, wealthy, half-suburban Evanston. In Kandy and Colombo I had seen more than enough of the backwash of empire and the indigenous corruption which succeeded it. I had met gay, warm people whose kindly grace shamed me for my harsh clumsiness, but I had also seen race prejudice as bad as I had seen it anywhere except in Hitler's Germany. The Sinhalese are the majority group in Ceylon; the Tamils are the largest minority. In 1958, there were race riots. Demagogic politicians did a good deal to cause them, and hundreds of people were killed; yet in 1960 the politicians were still at it. In the two general elections that resulted from the assassination of the Prime Minister late in 1959, they tried again to set fire to racial and religious hatred. Sane people said the mobs would be worse than ever if they did break loose, but the politicians and even some intellectuals and ordinary citizens often seemed to enjoy the vilification. Known leaders of racial mobs campaigned successfully, and violence seemed still so close that Tamils in Sinhalese areas were afraid for their lives. In the meanwhile, newspapers and government officials kept up the profitable old indignant outcry against the West.

I was not unhappy, then, to be back home, with no great satisfaction in the work I had done abroad but free at least from the label *expert* and from the necessity of representing anything and comfortably settled in a better job than I deserved. Two things mainly bothered me, aside from middle age and the high cost of living. One was the discovery that I could not write an essay about my year in Ceylon that I had been asked to write. The essay kept turning into a discussion of race conflict. It sounded phony, and I could neither finish it nor leave it alone. The other bother was the growing realization that in the fifteen years since I first came to Chicago, the status of the Southerner in the academic community had changed. Simply as a Southerner, it seemed to me, he had now become an object of automatic suspicion and dislike to a good many of his colleagues. Discrimination in reverse had finally established itself in the universities too.

I reached this conclusion after talking and listening to a good many people. Among other things, we talked about the qualifications for university teaching. I believe that if a man is not grossly immoral or flagrantly subversive, the primary qualifications are learning and the ability to teach and write; and I should think that I had disgraced myself if I demanded that my colleagues should belong to racial or regional groups or should hold political opinions which were popular and congenial to me. Some of my companions seemed to think differently. If I understood them, some thought that in a Northern university a Southern scholar who rejected Northern liberalism would for that reason be less qualified to teach than a Northern liberal would be. Others would themselves not pass that judgment but thought that liberals would. Academic competence, I decided, was once more being given a political definition.

My decision may of course be wrong. I may have mistaken the matey self-congratulation of a pride of liberals for the roaring of real lions, and a better sense of humor might let me enjoy the comedy of the pharisee. But I cannot pretend to such detachment. A surfeit of holy conversation determined me at last to finish my essay. I knew it might exhibit the frustrated ridiculous turkey-cock indignation of an ineffective little man who had occasionally tried to do good and who thought he had been kicked in the teeth for his pains. I also knew it would contain some truth. The uniformity of what I have seen and known in the last ten years makes me think that my experience must at least be fairly representative; and as for the objection that of course my conclusions from these facts are wrong because I am a Southerner, I should say that the objection would prove me right. A theoretical egalitarian cannot defend his positions by claiming superiority.

I have been misunderstood, then, if my essay has been read as a penitent Southerner's confession. I have not described my own limitations and their causes in such detail because they interest me. I think they are so typical that they distress me. By moving, one can escape dirt and violence, but not prejudice. A real estate man tells me with furtive pride that in this or that Evanston school there are no Negro children, a high-school student complains of teen-age anti-Semitism, colleagues sneer at the South, and I can get more indignant at that rudeness than at the frenzy of white supremacists in Louisiana. If all of us believed in original sin, none of us would shake another's faith. The Bible Belt where I grew up has been ridiculed for keeping that old doctrine after it has abandoned so much of the old theology, and indeed the conservative Southerner might describe himself, when he feels dramatic, as a puzzled and self-distrustful man who shares the Christian's aspiration and his despair of human nature but cannot reconcile the two since he has neither the Christian's humble faith in God nor the liberal's arrogant faith in man. But belief in original sin is only the recognition of evil, not its cause. It may be a deterrent. A man's recognition that his deepest feelings may be corrupted will prevent him from translating those feelings, in any direct and obvious way, into corrupt behavior. I hope I am not just comforting myself when I say that every argument concerning race relations should rightly be qualified, as mine must be, by the limitations of its maker.

The consequence of my belief is not relativism, which is inconsistent with belief. If the relativist were logical, he would be incapable of argument. His action would be governed only by caprice, and his final appeal would have to be to force or successful fraud. Actually he is devoted to unconsidered dogmas and often drops his relativism as soon as it has served to justify one group or discredit another. Belief in original sin is not for me a theological dogma but a recognition and confession of a fact of experience, and it is only the argument *ad hominem* that is cancelled by being generalized. If no one can claim all wisdom, everyone must be heard for the insight which may possibly be his.

It is, however, a consequence of my belief that I cannot hope for the spectacular emergence of brave new worlds. I have to recognize the value of stability, the frailness of order, as well as the necessity for change; and the obligation to take decisions and act on them is balanced by the limitations of human knowledge and wisdom. My Northern liberal friends are very sure of their goodness. Perhaps such self-confidence might lead to rather more consistency. All decent men would agree that the full rights of citizenship should be granted on an equal basis to every citizen in every state, including

Negroes in Louisiana and Kentuckians in Illinois; and the timidest official should be prepared to enforce the law against anyone who denies such rights. I am not attacking those propositions. I assume them and go on to insist that *every* really means *every*, "each and all," and that a man should either quite frankly disclaim any concern with racial problems and concentrate on getting through his own life as best he can or else should extend his dislike of prejudice to all its forms. I could content myself with the first alternative; I do not see how a liberal can refuse the second.

And yet he sometimes does. There are people who attack racism only as it is practised by others, not as it is practised by themselves. One can live complacently in a snow-white suburb, support the NAACP, attend indignant meetings, denigrate Southerners, and be esteemed a very respectable citizen. Such behavior is personally hypocritical and socially harmful. To hate Southerners because they are Southern, or white men because they are white, is just as vicious as to hate Jews because they are Jewish, or black men because they are black: if a black thug can be forgiven his thuggery because he is the product of past slavery and present slums, a white thug can be forgiven his whips and fiery crosses because he is the grandson of slave-owners and a citizen of Georgia. It is not right, or even possible, to buy friendship by denying civilization, or peace of mind by examining only our neighbor's conscience. Murderers in the Congo are as guilty as stone-throwing mobs in Georgia, and a colored man's hatred for the white is not less hateful than a white man's hatred for the colored. White men have little to be proud of in the history of their dealings with the colored races; the colored heirs to the white man's power have often learned to hate the whites but not to tolerate one another. Men of all races are parties now, in one way or another, to the conflicts of race against race that divide us more deeply than class conflicts have ever done. The guilt is universal, and the responsibility is universal; but the honest recognition of guilt and the serious acceptance of responsibility are rare.

My own guilt has crystallized in balanced sentences. If I cannot accept responsibility seriously, I will at least accept it trivially by citing Scripture and throwing back those illiberally liberal stones.

The Profession of Letters as Confidence Game

(1966)

Relying on a traditional definition of humanism as the entire body of human knowledge, Sledd attacks both academic scientists and humanists for focusing more on money than on knowledge. Any reader of this essay will understand why Sledd has not been the most popular member of the academic community—he has always made colleagues uncomfortable by speaking his mind with a sharp tongue, a nasty tone of voice. In this essay, for the first time, Sledd begins to analyze the exploitation of graduate and part-time instructors. The third part of the essay is an eloquent discussion of the dilemma faced by any honest teacher of language trying to deal with the issue of how best to teach students English—ethically.

I.

Our Commissars on the Humanities, in their *Report*, have given a new twist to the economic interpretation of American culture: there is nothing wrong with heathens or materialists which more money for the humanities will not cure.[1] Humane cash will prevail against the heathen, since English professors are priests and a National Humanities Foundation an adequate temple for a New Jerusalem; and cash will cure materialism, since disease is not disease if all men are infected. Meanwhile the scientific heart need not be troubled, though a chief motive for the *Report* is jealousy of the prosperity of scientists. The labmen too may have their part in the scienties, the new synthesis which emerges from the Commissars'

14

pronouncement "that science, as a technique and expression of intellect, is in fact closely affiliated with the humanities." On a higher level, indeed, the humanities *are* science, and science is the humanities; for "science . . . embraces in its broadest sense all efforts to achieve valid and coherent views of reality," while humanists "offer their fellow countrymen whatever understanding can be attained by fallible humanity of such enduring values as justice, freedom, virtue, beauty, and truth."

Science is humanism, truth beauty—which is all the Congress needs to know before it votes the money; and the Commissars deal just as glibly with the danger that men may be dragooned by a Humanities Foundation claiming all those countries of the mind where the Science Foundation has not set up a flag. Federal grants for the sciences, the argument runs, have so upset our colleges and universities that only federal grants for the humanities can restore the balance; but the colonialism of the scientists will be beneficent. Federal control of federal control is not federal control; and besides, the NHF will get its cash not just from the government but "from the widest range of sources—foundations, corporations, individuals." The surest protection, that is, against the abuse of the Foundation's power will be to give more power to the Foundation. "Plurality of support," in the words of the Commissars, "will generally strengthen the freedom and variety of scholarship in a democratic society"—as indeed it might if the Foundation were not itself an instrument to make the plural singular.

I propose an impolite translation from the Commissionese:

Professors of the humanities want money and status; the manipulators of the humanistic world want power to impose their schemes; both Punch and showman think they can get what they want through a Scientities Foundation; and both are thus enabled to believe that the Foundation will be their truest church and the bulwark of human freedom.

Small images of the larger life around us, we play our version of the Great Confidence Game.

II.

The committee which spoke for the MLA to the humaniteers is bluffing for high stakes with a small pair.

"A majority of college students," our representatives admitted, "do not speak, write, or read their own language well. Graduate instructors who direct master's essays and doctoral dissertations are shocked at the extent to which they must become teachers of 'hospital' English. Yet we are aware that many of these candidates are already engaged in part-time teaching of freshman English. If they cannot recognize and correct their own egregious errors, what is happening to the end-products of their teaching?''

An unkind echo might inquire who taught these beginning teachers, or who let them into graduate school if they cannot read and write, or who is ready to let them out of graduate school as illiterate as they came, or who sits with a handful of students in his seminar while a teaching assistant misleads a roomful in the composition course. An insistently unkind echo would ask how we square our priestly claims for literature with our representatives' confession. Because we teach literature, we have argued, we deserve society's support; but our literary criticism in this century has been largely concerned with diction, and now our representatives admit that we have nourished verbal cripples on verbal ingenuities. We believe in literature for people who cannot read.

The way of escape from that dilemma is clear enough—a real commitment to elementary teaching by all of us, so that we may touch the lives of more than a fraction of a fraction of our country's youth; but our representatives denied that call to a hard duty without waiting for the cock to crow. They proposed to pass the buck, as usual, to the schools. "Whatever the causes," they announced, of our students' ineptitude, "correction must come at the lower levels, since by the time students enter college, any bad habits in speaking, writing, and reading have become so fixed and ingrained that colleges can do little more than stress 'remedial work.'" The remedies will be administered, presumably, by the same graduate students whose hospital English tells us that they need them, and "correction at the lower levels" will be the task of overburdened teachers no better prepared (because we have refused to train them) than our hospitalers in the colleges.

The MLA's committee must believe that a senator is born every minute.

III.

It is easier to declaim about hospital English than to talk usefully about healthy language. Discussion of correctness and goodness in English usage is sometimes best interpreted as a claim to special status and a device for enhancing the Confidence Man's importance; sometimes it enacts a foolish and affected alienation; sometimes it is an expression of hostility to the natural and social sciences; usually it deals with nothing more serious than the choice among disputed synonyms as indices of prestige. Usage in this sense, this fragment of class-conscious synonymy, is not much more important for the teacher of composition than the choice of neckties. For the linguist it is; but his problems are sociological, not literary.

I will say nothing of the Confidence Man as Name-giver, though most students and many teachers do believe that some disputed synonyms are bad in themselves, without qualification, for any purpose on any occasion. The Rules Man is vicious. Unjustified rules are a flat denial of the free choice that no man can escape and still be human.

Some linguists give the Name-giver the chance to say that for them, anything goes in language, and whatever is is right. They should speak more plainly. The statement that native speakers make no mistakes is often just a linguist's resolution that in his grammar he will describe every piece of some sample of real talk. Bad grammars follow from such resolutions, but no literary consequences. Some other linguists, in contradiction to their professional relativism, purvey an unsophisticated but somewhat dogmatic equalitarian philosophy; yet they cannot be justly accused of having no standards for the use of language. The Confidence Man means only that they have standards which he dislikes.

To the standard of Taste unrationalized, both good writers and Confidence Men subscribe, and no harm would be done if they would delete the *non* from *de gustibus.* Good writers and good editors and the best teachers have learned by long experience to know when a sentence or a paragraph has been put together just as it ought to be for them. They should also have learned that they are not Everyman. Good taste is best if we know why it is good; bad taste will never be exposed if reason is denied; and the imposition of any taste as a puzzling dogma is intellectual violence. Like the insistence on the usage of the best speakers and writers, imposed taste makes men follow blindly when they might see where they ought to go.

Linguistic Engineers will have no truck with individual taste. They define correct English, and sometimes good English too, either by the actual practice of the ruling class or by the shared linguistic prejudice of the status-seeking community, which Washington will eagerly help them to impose. For these manipulators, no question of the fitness of means to ends arises, unless the end is status. Justice demands that the culturally deprived should be given the choice of competing, if they wish, with the culturally depraved—and of going to hell for choosing so; since the ordinary questions about usage are really questions about indices of prestige, they should be answered in those terms; but conformity for its own sake never made book, man, or nation great.

Compassion is not the only motive for linguistic engineering. The prestige dialect may be taught for the good of the state and not the individual, on the grounds that a standardized language is a necessity for an industrial society. Individuality must be reserved for alphas. The betas and gammas, in return for cake, commissions, and soul-butter about democracy, must speak and write as much alike as they can be made to, so that the IBM machines will not break down or the computers get hysterics. Men who can so unwish themselves are indeed most tedious beings and, as it were, abortions.

Literarily inclined linguistic engineers teach us that we should choose our diction in such a way that the English language itself will stay good or get better. I would agree, if they would tell me, clearly, either the means or the meaning of improving the language, for which I think I have probably done my best if I use it myself, and help my students use it, as well as we know how. Though the aging idealize the language as they learned it, I cannot sacrifice my students' present for the emotional satisfaction of preserving some fragments of my past.

I cannot even deny that, like all English teachers, I am also, in some degree, a Linguistic Engineer, and committed to the disparagement of what endures from yesterday—namely, those features of my students' language which I correct. To recommend old forms instead of new, or new forms instead of old, or to recommend a different form instead of its coeval, is in each case to recommend a change. I refuse to say that whatever is is right in this present best of possible worlds.

So much for seven possible standards by which we might choose among synonymous expressions and teach our students either to choose or at least accept our choice: the Rules, Permissiveness, Taste, Status, the Brave New World, English Immaculate, and the Inscription for the Entrance to a Pigsty. I value taste, especially when it is rationalized; but I do not believe in permissiveness, I cannot define a good language, and the other four standards are excuses, of one kind or another, for subhuman conformity. I have to try to frame a different answer.

I do believe in knowledge, and in reason, and in the scantiness of man's supply of both. Hence I want my students to know what pairs of synonyms are disputed, and for what reasons, and what choices would be made by different groups. Open-eyed conformity in inessentials saves energy for non-conformity which is worth the effort, and most questions of usage are piddling. Serious linguistic choices, the choice of language for creation or inquiry or persuasion, will always involve much more than *ain't* or *different than.*

If that is so, we will never agree on a single standard unless we first agree (as I hope we never will) on a single poetics and rhetoric and indeed philosophy. One man's totally unphilosophic notion is that his use of language must be judged by its effectiveness for his purposes and that his purposes themselves must also be judged in appropriate ways. In rhetorical writing, the only kind I am moderately competent to teach, I tell my victims to choose language which will do what a better man than I, in their situation, would want his language to get done.

That simple-minded advice leaves all their problems unsolved, both the moral problems (which I am unfit to deal with) and the rhetorical problems of adjusting means to ends. Reasoned particular linguistic choices are never easy, since the best available argument is the inductive one, that what has worked in similar situations in the past will work again, and since rhetorical situations involve a great many variables—the subject, the audience, the character of the writer, his relation to his readers, his purpose, his medium of publication, and so on. Nobody ever writes well who has not read well, and a good rhetorician at his best is only playing well-educated hunches.

Still my simple-minded standard has some consequences that I like. It reminds my students that good writing is purposeful, that there are no pat answers to a writer's questions, that the largest collection of citations will never prove that a particular sentence is either good or bad, that it is still necessary to consider precedents so that principles may be inductively established, and that good writing requires the exercise of their best taste and reasoned judgment as individual free men.

On these terms, though the game of teaching cannot be played with easy confidence, at least it cannot be easily played as a confidence game.

Notes

1. This paper was read at the Christmas meeting of the Modern Language Association in New York in 1964. An invitation to talk about some current notions of correctness and goodness in the use of English produced not an essay but three fragments which refused to coalesce. Perhaps they are variations on a common theme. At least the arguments are not so time-bound as they may look, for the issues involved are more abiding than the decision to spend or not to spend a certain portion of the public funds.

A Talking—For the Love of God
(1968)[1]

Sledd's advice on integrating language study into the high school curriculum is as sane and sound now as it was when this essay first appeared. As he has done often, Sledd rails here against those in linguistics and literature who take themselves so very seriously, especially the "rogues' gallery at the NCTE." Sledd shifted his research focus from linguistics shortly after writing this essay.

I.

Next to the student, the most important person in an educational system is the teacher, and the American teacher's worst enemy is the educational system. It's a big, expensive machine and it's supposed to turn out educated men and women, but a good while ago somebody made a mistake, and now it turns out about half and half—men and women and IBM cards; and every year it grinds up a lot of teachers. That's really what I want to talk about, indirectly— about how to teach in spite of the anti-teaching machine; but because I'm very limited I'll have to talk directly about the teaching of my own subject (if I can claim to have a subject), the English language. In the announced title there's a mistake which I'm sure I made; but nobody worries any more about wrong titles: I've been called a linguist, and that place in Washington is called the Office of Education. I call my ten acres in the Montana mountains Credibility Gap.

I could have talked to you with a lot more confidence a year ago than I can now: I was a lot smarter in August than I am in April. In between I've learned at M.I.T. that I'm a good five years behind the bright young men, and at Newton High School I've learned that often, when I've talked to high-school teachers about high-school teaching, I must have sounded like a little green man from a vagrant UFO. Probably I still do. Just a few weeks ago, I was talking to some teachers in another part of the forest. They had been told they ought to do something about linguistics, and because I didn't want to be tagged as interplanetary, I was mainly asking them leading questions: What is it that we should do? Who's to decide? Where can competent teachers be discovered? Which staff shall teach the linguistics if any does? What is linguistics anyway? Which of the many irreconcilable doctrines shall we choose? Why bother? And so on. I was being pretty cagey, as I've said, and I left lots of questions open; but on one or two things I did take definite stands. Competent *teachers,* I insisted, should decide what we ought to do and how to do it, and they "should never be insulted with a demand that they teach a prescribed set of lessons in a prescribed sequence and a prescribed way. Teachers who surrender to such demands should be fired immediately."

Well, you already know that when I said *that,* my spaceman suit was shining brightest green, and sparks were crackling from the antennae behind my ears. I had insisted on freedom for competent teachers. In the discussion afterward, the headmaster of an expensive private school let me know what *he* thought about freedom. His teachers hadn't made any decisions, he said, and he hadn't even discussed the problem with them. He had simply told them, one morning, that they were going to teach structural linguistics; his new program was confined to the first six grades because after the sixth grade, teaching grammar is pointless; and the program was so successful that the students were now calling prepositional phrases P-groups. At the end of the meeting, when the chairman asked me for concluding remarks, I didn't make any: after the headmaster I had heard the teachers, who had heard me. Grammar was utter boredom, one woman said, and anyway usage took all her time: she had to spend three weeks on *he don't.* She raised the question of how to counter the influence of bad grammar from teachers in other departments, and somebody else wanted to know whether children should be urged to correct their parents: opinion was divided. After forty-five minutes the conversation shifted to literature, and I heard about a thematic approach in the eighth grade, about teaching the Bible, the relative merits of Greek and Norse mythology, and the success of an experimental unit on *Dracula.* I retracted my antennae and flew back to Boston.

Not that I'm the only candidate for membership in the Worshipful Company of Martians. Plenty of my linguistic colleagues don't know yet that they *have* antennae, and a lot of their propaganda would be dangerous if it weren't so plainly interstellar. With solemn benevolence they offer us the latest analysis of relative clauses, which they made in the last half-hour. After more protracted meditation, they offer us a poetic theory analogized from structural phonemics, or a strictly verbal rhetoric of expression analogized from transformational grammar, or a rhetoric-cum-poetic in which the terms *particle, wave,* and *field* are first kidnapped from newspaper physics and then sold down the river for literary abuses. They provide new linguistic histories of our language which aren't in the same league with philological ancients like Professor Baugh, or big books full of confusion about linguistics and English grammar, or little books full of emptiness about linguistics and the teaching of English. Then they announce a revolution in teaching, and urge us to make a mishmash of structural and transformational grammar the center of a new curriculum.

And the linguistic branch of our profession doesn't have a monopoly on nonsense: nobody does. A random glance at the rogues' gallery of the NCTE shows us there are people who say that the colleges don't need to teach composition any more because the students already write so well, and there are people who hold cumulative, integrated, and sequential conferences about the New English, and there are people who think that sitting at a big desk does wonders for the brain, and there are people who say that literature taught as we teach it makes pregnant teen-agers wise and good by showing them that "love is best," and there are people who think the government can appropriate enough money to buy at least a little bit of wisdom and goodness for everybody, and there are people—young people—who say English *has* no subject matter and they don't care *what* students do in their classes so long as they go out swinging, and in general we're all people together and the world is full of us.

So I finish my year at Newton and M.I.T. a lot more ignorant than when I began it, and a lot more troubled, and hurting with the knowledge that reality and our profession are hardly on speaking terms and that the machine men, the administrative types, don't care about reality but about the machine and their place at the controls. I heard a psychologist talk the other night about living in "temporary systems." He was a machine man, I decided, and before long I tuned him out; but he did raise the big old question how a man can keep the stability which saves him from dissolving into fifty men and can yet change fast enough and often enough to keep within sight of the accelerating world. Since 1937—if you can forgive me a second catastrophic enumeration—since 1937 we've seen the Munich agreement, the extermination of the German Jews, the second World War, the Bomb, the Cold War, the end of colonialism, the war in Korea, Sputnik, the collapse of order and the emergence of murderous tribalism in the new nations, our conflict over Civil Rights, the flight from our decaying cities, war in Viet Nam and the Middle East, insanity in China, the increasing centralization of power in our Federal government, the failure of communication between the generations, the Chicago Cubs in first place, and such complete denial of our political ideals that nobody noticed when government with the consent of us governed died of the plague and was secretly buried at night.

That's the world that has made our youngsters what they are— disorganized, baffled, eager for friendship, suspicious of friendliness, self-pitying, looking for something for nothing, looking for unselfish causes, long-haired, pretentious, contemptuous of phonies—a whole roomful of people in each of their young persons. We've lived in the same world, but we lived in an earlier one too, and one reason why we've managed to get through the past thirty years is that we *aren't* youngsters: we can still sometimes feel and think and act like our parents and grandparents, who had nothing worse to put up with than the Civil War. Part of our heritage is the comforting trivialities of a less catastrophic age: my grandfather taught Latin, my father taught New Testament Greek, and when the Bomb fell on Hiroshima I was teaching naval cadets by day but writing a dissertation on Renaissance lexicography at night. Now, in a world already infinitely distant from the world of Henry Adams, how do we help our children through the shattering present and into their unimagined future when we live on the strength of our vanished past? If you laugh and say that the first of the Adams asked Eve that, the answer is that God didn't bomb him out of the Garden of Eden—he and Eve left in a dignified walk while the angel only waved a sword.

Take a case in point, the "functional bidialectalism" by which not just respectable but really generous white adults try to persuade the disrespectful children of the black ghetto to use the language of our past. The lower-class black youngsters who now live in Northern cities instead of on Southern farms don't talk like middle-class white Northern businessmen, so middle-class white Northern businessmen won't give them jobs. In those circumstances, the interplanetary observer untroubled with an earthly history would recommend that white people should give up their prejudice and that if anybody should learn to talk two ways the white Yankees should because they've had all the educational advantages and lots of practice talking out of both sides of their mouths. The little green man from outside of time would burn out a transistor when he learned that in fact the educational machine and all the middle-aged, middle-class white altruists, whom I honestly admire, have decided just the opposite. White prejudice can't be changed. It has to be reinforced. Black youngsters will be allowed to talk their kind of talk among themselves, and nobody will tell them that it's *bad* talk; but they'll learn that healthy lesson without teaching, because when they deal with the white man's world they've got to talk like the white man. The precious hours of their schooling, when they might learn something about themselves and about *their* world, will be spent in studying white man's English.

Even without my antennae, that sounds all mixed up to me, as if we schoolteachers couldn't tell yesterday from tomorrow; and it gets nuttier still when it occurs to me that "functional bidialectalism" is like Black Power in that *both* are reflections of the white man's past. Our revolutionaries themselves seem to think that the piratical system we live by would be pretty good as it is if only the color of a man's skin didn't keep him from getting his share of the loot, just as the makers of the new countries want to industrialize them too so that steel mills will poison the air and tankers foul the beaches everywhere. Somehow my antennae don't tingle at the thought. Predators and scavengers of all colors have never helped anybody but themselves, no matter how closely they've observed the real to find their own advantage; and the machine men would only issue a new report by the engineer's union or add a false smokestack with a louder whistle if somebody asked them how to be one but many, the same yet different, how to hold on to a little being while becoming all the time.

So I end this introduction that turned into a bit more than half my speech by saying that I've got lots of questions and not many answers and that I can't get answers from the machine. The machine would have made Adam take a linguistics course before he named the beasts of the field. When I think of the machine, I think of the principal of a famous school who wrote me a letter once. He had read something I wrote—or he pretended he had: I didn't believe him because he thought I believed what I'd spent twenty years denying, that linguistics can be the center of the intellectual world. Anyway, he wanted to talk about linguistics, and he began by saying that he was ignorant of the subject and ended by fixing its place in the curriculum. In between he said the suggestion was meaningless that *teachers* should make the first recommendation.

Well, I don't *know* the place of linguistics in the school curriculum any longer, if I ever did. I guess probably the study of our language could have many different places in different schools, and maybe none in some; and as I finally get around to my real subject (it was "Schoolroom Linguistics: The Hazardous Transformation")—as I finally get around to my real subject, I have to emphasize both a mundane scepticism and a starry faith. First, it's entirely possible that the whole campaign for schoolroom linguistics may quietly subside because it's become a machine campaign and the machine is phony and maybe the study of the English language isn't close enough to our students' living needs. I don't think that's going to happen. If it does, there'll be some fine accounting for wasted time at Judgment Day. But the possibility's still there. Second, despite my principal and my headmaster, it *is* teachers, and maybe especially the young teachers, who ought to decide such things: arrogant administrators only get in the way of intelligent decision-making. In that faith, and I hope for the benefit of teachers, I'll say now the few familiar things that I still can say.

II.

More and more of our Operators have begun to plug linguistics in the last ten or twenty years. Generally, that's been a good thing, because English departments are mainly inhabited by literary people who've never seriously studied their own language. Partly in rebellion, however, against the literary dictatorship, the propagandists for linguistics have been inclined to claim too much; and one might gather, from the general tenor of their pronouncements, that English linguistics is a unified, uncontroversial body of revolutionary new doctrine, that the new doctrine is presented in new textbooks which are far better than any we have had before, and that textbooks and doctrine together make a fit center for a glorious new curriculum.

Bright young teachers will know, and ordinary young teachers should be told, that the world isn't as simple as all that. Linguistics is about as free from controversy as the Security Council. Though the transformationists shot down the structuralists ten years back, some of the structuralists keep flapping their arms and making bird-like noises; scholarly grammarians like Long and Zandvoort keep writing long after being told that they are dead; and in the Church of the New Light ancient converts who struggled through *Syntactic Structures* and even kept up their courage through *Aspects of the Theory of Syntax* now have to find out what a new crop of graduate students have just said to one another over their coffee and what the sound pattern of English is this year, and how much faith a believer in good standing is allowed to put in various apostles and schismatics and hangers-on. As for the textbooks, I won't say much, since I know how easy it is to make a bad one; but I haven't burned my copy of Jespersen's *Essentials.*

The big trouble, however, with the propaganda for the language-centered curriculum is neither the controversies among linguists nor the quality of the new texts: the controversies are a sign of life, and the textbooks have been getting better and more numerous. The big trouble is that a language-centered curriculum in English is in principle impossible. The entire campaign for curricula integrated about language rests on an equivocation between linguistics imagined as the universal science of man, the study of anything and everything in which language is involved, and linguistics as it exists, the specialized study of language and languages; and not all the fancy talk has changed the patent fact that most of our problems in literature and composition can't even be stated in linguistic terms if by linguistics we mean any body of real knowledge and method that professed linguists can really make available. On this point people should have either to put up or shut up, particularly if they're anthropologists or the like who've never taught composition or literature, can't write themselves, and don't enjoy reading. What has Shakespeare got to do with the *Linguistic Atlas,* and what can phonologists say about *Middlemarch?* How can a linguist tell me where in a speech to place a refutation or how to develop an argument by analogy? Why should a grammarian pretend that he's an expert in the teaching of reading when the essence of good reading is drawing inferences and forming judgments? Except in the imaginations of Educational Agencies and instituteers, linguistics is not a universal science of man but, like every other humanistic study, a partial and limited inquiry, troubled by controversy, yet offering us some insights which as teachers we would be wrong, I think, to ignore.

My own simple arguments for that mild concluding affirmation have been much the same for a good long time. When catechized, I've given a stock recital of some practical reasons—that we need the history of English to understand our older writers, that we can't talk happily about prosody without phonology, that for stylistic discussions we need a grammar, that we need both a grammar and defensible standards of good English in teaching composition, that "in an age when much of literary criticism is essentially linguistic" we need some knowledge of language to protect ourselves from nonsense. But my chief reasons haven't been practical. Instead, I've tried to take higher ground, and have said that "the deep reason for teaching the English language must be the old conviction that man should understand himself" as the speaking animal. That sounds pretty good, particularly when I add a bit about "the vehicle of our culture and the foundation of our humanity." It may even be true. I'd just feel more comfortable about it if I learned as much about myself from a painful week with a good grammar as I sometimes seem to learn from a happy morning with a good poem or if I never suspected, when I looked in the mirror, that the ungainliness of linguists is contagious.

Anyway, I can't give any *better* arguments, and I can't tell you anything you don't already know about the conditions of your teaching or the students whom you teach. When the Polonius Professor of English at Ivy State challenges you to work miracles five times a day, he's only blowing the loud whistle on the false smokestack. He doesn't know, first hand, what a teacher faces, and I don't know either, of course, since my tiny experience is limited to selected students in top schools like Newton and like Evanston Township on Chicago's rich North Shore. Even there I've learned that we can't teach all students alike and that a good argument for letting *teachers* decide what to teach is that they do meet their particular students every day and can judge their needs. We shouldn't be satisfied with a single curriculum for all the schools of a city, we ought to be horrified at the thought of a single curriculum for all the schools of a state, and if abstract arguments break up on concrete facts, we must respect live reality not the dead theory.

There's another reason, too, for cultivating the diversity that machine men disapprove. We want free education, with maximum liberty for the individual teacher in his individual classroom, and we want really inquiring and experimental education; but if we try something like the hazardous transformation and it doesn't work, we have to be able to get rid of it without catastrophic loss. That means, I think, that we should begin our experiments, in limited ways—a *plurality* of experiments in a variety of ways—and that the worst thing we can do about schoolroom linguistics is to make a general adoption of some publisher's big new series, which leaves a teacher with nothing to do but to smile triumphantly in the proper places. We'd get a lot better teaching if textbook-makers and state supervisors didn't assume that teachers are morons and if appointive bodies didn't assume that morons should be supervisors. I'd like to see the time when a good teacher could make his own linguistics program by choosing independently from a good list of small paperbacks, just as he often does when he teaches literature. Maybe to some extent that's already possible.

The rest of my remarks, I'm afraid, are going to be pretty scrappy, since my introduction got out of hand and I've already talked too long without saying much. Saying nothing at all about the grade where linguistic work could or should begin or about the kind of student who could most profit from it, in passing I'll just remind myself and you that there's no reason in the nature of things why that work should be the unique concern of our departments of English, and there's every reason why it should not be parrotry. English might teach some linguistics, but it might be the foreign language people, or perhaps a group drawn from different staffs; and whoever takes the responsibility, if anyone, the course or courses should be so taught that the students will see why they're studying them and how they're related to other courses. It's much too easy, for example, in a course in grammar, to do derivations and draw trees, or to concoct sentences which illustrate particular transformations, without asking what the point is, why it's all worth doing. We can be sure, I think, that the details of our grammatical descriptions will continue changing with disconcerting speed, so that what we must teach, if we can, are the insights, the best available answers to the big abiding questions, and not manipulation for the sake of manipulation. A student who just memorizes a rule about auxiliaries or determiners will likely have to unmemorize it before he's much older. He may have something of permanent value if he can be brought to see why the rule is stated as it is, what it does and what it leaves undone, and where the whole study of language fits into his total education, so far as it does fit.

I'm assuming, of course, not just the logical priority of grammar in whatever work may be done with the English language, but a particular kind of grammar—a transformational grammar, a particular kind of teaching—as nearly inductive, to use a term loosely, as we can make it, and a particular kind of teacher—the teacher who has the time and the knowledge to plan his own lessons and even make up a good many of his own exercises. Where those assumptions are impossibly astronautical, something less ambitious might be attempted, for certainly teachers should teach nothing that they don't securely understand about the language and nothing whose demands for time would weaken the teaching of composition and literature; but in the few curricula I've seen there's enough waste, or enough time already assigned for language-study, to make it at least conceivable that a high-school student should get a better introduction to English linguistics than I got in college. That introduction should not consist of grammar alone. A familiar pattern includes something about the lexicon as well, something about dialects, and something about linguistic history. A logical sequence would probably put some few shaping generalities first, then the syntax, the lexicon, and either the dialectology or the history, with phonology getting the short end of the stick. We English teachers should resist our temptation to put the history of the language first. We like to put the history first, if the truth were told, because we think it's easier than those way-out grammars and because it lets us sneak away from linguistics to talk about the Norman Conquest and Chaucer and Shakespeare; but the history is really tougher than the grammar, which it presupposes. In fact, the history is *so* tough that we don't have any good big new treatments of it. When we leave the grammar, we'll have to do even more catch-as-catch-can.

One more point before I quit. I've tried to be sceptical in this paper—sceptical of myself and sceptical of others; and I've insisted for a long time that the average school ought not to attempt a shiny program in "The New Linguistics" until the colleges and universities have provided a bigger supply of linguistically competent teachers. You still may think that in my last few paragraphs I've finally gone into orbit and that an "introduction to English linguistics" is a galactic ambition for a high school. For some schools, I'm sure it's not just galactic but stupid, and since I'm not trying to sell any shiny new programs, I wouldn't argue with a teacher who thought so. But shiny new programs are not what makes schools better anyway. Schools get better when they hire good teachers and give them a chance to teach, freely. There are plenty of schools, now, with better teachers than I've found myself to be this year; and any teacher who seriously wants to do something about teaching the English language can make a start right off, without waiting for an in-service course or an institute or a new *summa linguistica* approved by *Good Housekeeping* and the NCTE. The way to start, for the teacher who wants to, is just to start—start in his own class, with whatever textbooks he can get, whatever he really knows and his kids should learn. It doesn't have to be grammar, though grammar does have priority: it could be dictionaries and the vocabulary, or pronunciation and dialects, or the language of Shakespeare, or any of a good many other things. And if it does turn out to be grammar, it doesn't have to be transformational grammar, though that's probably the best choice: Kittredge and Farley is still available in some libraries, and most bookrooms have a set of Warriner. My scepticism, in short, mustn't make the best advice I can give unclear or hesitant. I'm still willing to risk the hazardous transformation.

Let me finish with a story.

I had an errand to do, one day this spring, at a famous New England school. It's a rich school, in a rich town, with fine buildings and lots of expensive equipment. As I waited outside a lecture hall, I could hear the sound-track of a film that a teacher was showing. Some bedroom-voiced soprano was mutilating "Melancholy Baby."

"Smile, my honey dear," she burbled, "as I wipe away each tear"—
and then, in a gush of amorous grammaticality— "or else I SHALL be
melancholy too!" Pretty soon the students came out, swinging and
singing, and I did my errand and went home. I had seen American
education.

Notes

1. This paper was presented at the Annual Spring Conference of the New
York State English Council at the Hotel Syracuse, April 28, 1967. Mr. Sledd
has a nasty feeling that he's said it all before.

Bi-Dialectalism
The Linguistics of White Supremacy
(1969)

Bi-dialectalism, the attempt to teach nonstandard speakers to use standard spoken and written English as a second dialect, was touted as a way of helping economically deprived students move up the financial and social ladder. Sledd never bought into the scheme, claiming it was doomed to failure and ethically misdirected from start to finish. This essay and the one that follows are Sledd's most well-known; they assure him a place among the high-minded iconoclasts who insist on pointing out that the emperor is wearing no clothes—in this case, that our society and the teaching profession are radically flawed.

When I asked Sledd how he felt about the issue of bi-dialectalism in 1993, nearly twenty-five years after this essay first appeared, he responded in the following way:

SLEDD: There are some changes, but basically the same things are going on. The NCTE's little newsletter, *The Council Chronicle*, quoted a woman the other day who said that essentially, unless students learn the language of power, they will never get status among the powerful. Now that's a give-away statement because it shows that that woman accepts the values of this society. To me that's always been the great problem with attempts to deal with the language of black people, black students.

FREED: You agree with that statement, in a certain sense—pragmatically —right? Not the moral issues, of course.

SLEDD: It's certainly true, but her aim, apparently, is to introduce her students into what's called "The American Way," and I would say it's wiser to teach standard English as a weapon, both defensive and offensive. Climbing the ladder of success—that metaphor is the bottom line. Now think what it says about a society. It reduces everything to profit. We can't live that way. That's why we're in the mess we're in now.

FREED: Do you think this issue is still a concern?

SLEDD: People say, "oh, that's old hat," but basically, nothing much has changed. You still have people teaching the old handbooks. You still have people making "upward mobility in the mainstream culture" their basic aim for themselves and for their students. I remember I talked once in an education class here, and someone said, "I've made it to steak, I'm headed for lobster, and I want to take my students with me." Now that, to me, is the essence of stupidity.

FREED: The teacher said that?

SLEDD: No, the pupil in the class. Those pupils were all teachers. It was a course for teachers. But the teacher has been a big wheel in the NCTE, and as best as I could make out, she thoroughly approved of that statement. "Onward and upward to Maine lobster?" Hah, downward and backward to Georgia catfish!

FREED: Well, aren't you, in a way, as a teacher, helping them to have choices: whether or not to learn standard English, whether or not to try to climb the ladder? Don't they get to choose? Isn't the flip side of the freedom issue that if students choose to learn standard English as a means of trying to climb a ladder, then you have to go along?

SLEDD: I can help them to learn standard English, telling them all along "upward mobility" is a crock. I'm not going to help them in the struggle for upward mobility. I will do all I can to help them get food, clothing, shelter, medical care, a job that won't destroy their soul, some leisure. But upward mobility simply means putting your neighbor's nose out of joint by wasting more than your neighbor can, and . . . no, . . . never.

FREED: Is the purpose of a writing class to be determined by the person who takes it?

SLEDD: There's no point in talking about THE purpose of a writing class. There'll be a lot of purposes. I can't control student purposes. I will advise them. But they have their purposes; I have my purpose.

FREED: So your reasons for teaching standard English can conflict with your students' reasons for learning it?

SLEDD: Well, I've always said the basic questions are motives, methods, and policy toward the students who don't learn. On that last point, an eminence at NCTE said, and I can almost quote it verbatim, "if students fail to learn standard English, they will be forever denied economic opportunity and social acceptance." To begin with, that's factually a lie. George Herbert Walker Bush could never meet the College Board's demands for entering freshmen. And you have lots and lots of Texas millionaires who are only mildly literate. So it's not true, to begin with. But if one tried to enforce such a policy, it would be freezing a two-tiered society—haves and have-nots—and I won't go for that. As for methods, there's a lot of room for discussion there. I would always resist any of the mechanical methods which linguists back in the '60s favored—mimicry and memorization. And for motives, as far as I can see, the main motive of the professional societies in these matters has been upward mobility in the mainstream culture. I'm not interested in that.

Because people who rarely talk together will talk differently, differences in speech tell what groups a man belongs to. He uses them to claim and proclaim his identity, and society uses them to keep him under control. The person who talks right, as we do, is one of us. The person who talks wrong is an outsider, strange and suspicious, and we must make him feel inferior if we can. That is one purpose of education. In a school system run like ours by white businessmen, instruction in the mother tongue includes formal initiation into the linguistic prejudices of the middle class.

Making children who talk wrong get right with the world has traditionally been the work of English teachers, and more recently of teachers of that strange conglomerate subject which we call speech. The English teacher in the role of linguistic censor was once a kind of folk heroine (or anti-heroine), the Miss Fidditch of the linguists' diatribes. Miss Fidditch believed in taking a strong stand. It never occurred to her that her main job was making the lower classes feel so low that they would try to climb higher. Instead, Miss Fidditch taught generations of schoolchildren, including future linguists, to avoid *ain't* and double negatives and *used to could* and *hadn't ought,* not because *ain't* would keep them from getting ahead in the world, but because *ain't* was wrong, no matter who used it, and deserved no encouragement from decent people who valued the English language. She did her job all the better for thinking that she was doing something else.

Miss Fidditch is not popular any longer among educators. Though the world at large is still inclined to agree with her, the vulgarizers of linguistics drove her out of the academic fashion years ago, when they replaced her misguided idealism with open-eyed hypocrisy. To the popular linguists, one kind of English is as good as another, and judgments to the contrary are only folklore; but since the object of life in the U.S.A. is for everybody to get ahead of everybody else, and since linguistic prejudice can keep a man from moving up to Schlitz, the linguists still teach that people who want to be decision-makers had better talk and write like the people who make decisions. The schools must therefore continue to cultivate the linguistic insecurity which is already a national characteristic but must teach the youngsters to manipulate that as they manipulate everything else; for neither Miss Fidditch's dream of a language intrinsically good, nor a humbler idea of realizing the various potentialities of the existing language in its responsible use, can get in the way of the citizenry in its upward anguish through the pecking order. The linguists think that people who do knowingly what Miss Fidditch did in her innocence, will do it more efficiently, as if eating the apple made a skilled worker out of Eve.

As long as most people agreed that up is toward Schlitz and another TV set, and as long as they could pretend that every American eaglet can soar to those great heights, Fidditch McFidditch the dialectologist could enforce the speech-taboos of the great white middle class without complaint: either the child learned the taboos and observed them, or he was systematically penalized. But the damage done to the Wasps' nest by World War II made difficulties. People who talked all wrong, and especially black people, began to ask for their share of the loot in a world that had given them an argument by calling itself free, while a minority of the people who talked right began to bad-mouth respectability and joined the blacks in arguing that it was time for a real change. Some black people burned up the black parts of town, and some students made study impossible at the universities, and in general there was a Crisis. Optimists even talked of a revolution.

The predictable response of the frightened white businessman's society was to go right on doing what it had done before—which had caused the crisis—but to do it harder and to spend more money at it. Education was no exception. Government and the foundations began to spray money over the academic landscape like liquid fertilizer, and the professional societies began to bray and paw at the rich new grass. In that proud hour, any teacher who could dream up an expensive scheme for keeping things as they were while pretending to make a change was sure of becoming the director of a project or a center and of flying first-class to Washington twice a month. The white businessman strengthened his control of the educational system while giving the impression of vast humanitarian activity.

Black English provided the most lucrative new industry for white linguists, who found the mother lode when they discovered the interesting locutions which the less protected employ to the detriment of their chances for upward mobility. In the annals of free enterprise, the early sixties will be memorable for the invention of functional bi-dialectalism, a scheme best described by an elderly and unregenerate Southern dame as "turning black trash into white trash." Despite some signs of wear, this cloak for white supremacy has kept its shape for almost a decade now, and it is best described in the inimitable words of those who made it. Otherwise the description might be dismissed as a malicious caricature.

The basic assumption of bi-dialectalism is that the prejudices of middle-class whites cannot be changed but must be accepted and indeed enforced on lesser breeds. Upward mobility, it is assumed, is the end of education, but white power will deny upward mobility to speakers of black English, who must therefore be made to talk white English in their contacts with the white world.

An adequate florilegium may be assembled from a volume entitled *Social Dialects and Language Learning* (NCTE, 1964), the proceedings of a conference of bi-dialectalists which was held in 1964. William A. Stewart of the Center for Applied Linguistics begins the chorus (p. 13) by observing among our educators "a commendable desire to emphasize the potential of the Negro to be identical to white Americans"—a desire which is apparently not overwhelming, however, among the Black Muslims or among the young men who have enjoyed pot-shooting policemen for the past few summers. Editor Roger W. Shuy next speaks up (p. 53) for social climbing by our American Indians, who have been notably reluctant, throughout their unfortunate association with their conquerors, to adopt our conquering ways. Our linguistic studies, Shuy remarks in the purest accents of fidditchery, "should reveal those elements, both in speech and writing, which prevent Indians from attaining the social status which, with socially acceptable language, they might otherwise attain." A similar desire to be at peace with status-holders is suggested (p. 66) by Ruth I. Golden, who opines that "a human being wants most of all to be recognized as an individual, to be accepted, and to be approved." Since Southern speech brings "negative reactions when heard by employers in Detroit," where Dr. Golden labors in the schools, she devotes herself to stamping out /i/ for /e/ in *penny* and to restoring /l/ in *help* (pp. 63 f.).

An admirable scholar from New York, William Labov, then agrees (p. 88) that "recognition of an external standard of correctness is an inevitable accompaniment of upward social aspirations and upward social mobility," and advises that people who (like Jesus) prefer not to take excessive thought for the morrow can probably be made to. In Labov's own words, "since the homes of many lower class and working people do not provide the pressures toward upward social mobility that middle-class homes provide," and since adults in those lower reaches are sometimes resistant to middle-class values, we must "build into the community a tolerance for style shifting which is helpful in educational and occupational advancement," and we must build into the children, "starting from a level not so much above the nursery school and going on through high school, a tolerance for practice in second role playing" (pp. 94–97, 104).

Presumably, Labov sees nothing wrong in thus initiating children into the world of hypercorrection, insecurity, and "linguistic self-hatred" which marks, as he has said elsewhere, "the average New Yorker" (*The Social Stratification of English in New York City*, Center for Applied Linguistics, 1966, Chapter XIII); and Charles Ferguson, the eminent ex-director of the Center for Applied Linguistics, is equally confident of *his* right and duty to remake his fellow men in his directorial image. Talking about the Negroes in our Northern cities, Ferguson says that "we have to face a rather difficult decision as to whether we want to make these people bi-dialectal . . . [please to remark Ferguson's choice of verbs] or whether we want . . . to impose some kind of standard English on these people and to eradicate the kind of substandard English they speak" (p. 116). To cite another NCTE volume (*Language Programs for the Disadvantaged* [NCTE, 1965], p. 222), if the black children of the ghetto "do not learn a second kind of dialect, they will be forever prevented from access to economic opportunity and social acceptance." Middle-class white prejudice will rule eternally.

The bi-dialectalists, of course, would not be so popular with government and the foundations if they spoke openly of the supremacy of white prejudice; but they make it perfectly clear that what they are dealing with deserves no better name. No dialect, they keep repeating, is better than any other—yet poor and ignorant children must change theirs unless they want to stay poor and ignorant. When an NCTE "Task Force" set out to devise *Language Programs for the Disadvantaged* (NCTE, 1965), it laid down a perfect smoke screen of such hypocrisy, as one would expect from persons who felt called upon to inform the world that "without the experience of literature, the individual is denied the very dignity that makes him human" (p. v) but that not "all disadvantaged children are apathetic or dull" (pp. 24f.).

"In this report" (p. 117), "teachers are asked to begin by accepting the dialect of their students for what it is, one form of oral communication. . . ." Teachers are warned particularly that they "need to accept the language which Negro children bring to school, to recognize that it is a perfectly appropriate vehicle for communicating ideas in the Negro home and subculture" (p. 215), that it is "essentially respectable and good" (p. 227). But though teachers must not attack "the dialect which children associate with their homes and their identity as Negroes" (p. 215), they must still use all the adult authority of the school to "teach standard informal English as a second dialect" (p. 137), because the youngster who cannot speak standard informal English "will not be able to get certain kinds of jobs" (p. 228).

The most common result of such teaching will be that white middle-class Midwestern speech will be imposed as mandatory for all those situations which middle-class white businessmen think it worth their while to regulate. In the words of Chicago's Professors Austin and McDavid (p. 245), "future educational programs should be developed in terms of substituting for the grammatical system of lower-class Southern speech [read: black Chicago speech] that of middle-class Chicago white speech—at least for those economic and social situations where grammatical norms are important." Labov goes so far as to ask (*Social Dialects and Language Learning*, p. 102) whether Northern schools should tolerate Southern speech at all—whether they should not also correct the "cultivated Southern speech" of privileged children who move North.

The description of compulsory bi-dialectalism may be completed by examining the methods which its proponents advocate for perpetuating the supremacy of white prejudice. Essentially, those methods are derived by analogy from structuralist methods of teaching foreign languages—methods whose superiority has been claimed but never demonstrated and whose intellectual foundations vanished with the demise of structuralist ideas. As an eminent grammarian privately observed after a recent conference, "The achievements of the operators will continue to lie in the field of getting and spending government money. . . . They seem to have an unerring instinct for finding ways of spending it unprofitably—on conferences at which they listen to each other, for example. Now they're out to teach standard English as a second dialect through techniques that have served very poorly in teaching second languages."

High on the list of those techniques is incessant drill on inessentials. In theory, the drills are the end-product of a long process of systematic comparison of the children's nonstandard dialects with the standard dialect which they are to be taught; but since the systematic comparisons have never been made, the bi-dialectalists fall back on a simple enumeration of a few dozen "features of pronunciation, grammar, and vocabulary which can be considered indices of social stratification" (Roger Shuy, "Detroit Speech," in A. L. Davis, ed., *On the Dialects of Children*, p. 13). Professor Rudolph Troike of the University of Texas was thus simply platitudinizing piously when he told the TESOL convention in 1968 that "any instructional program . . . must begin with as full an *objective* knowledge as possible" of both or all the dialects involved. The escape hatch in Troike's statement is the phrase *as full as possible.* What is usually possible is an unsystematic list of shibboleths—the simplification of consonant clusters, the Southern pronunciations of *walk* and *right, ax* for *ask,* the dropping of post-vocalic /r/, *ain't* and *fixin' to, bofe* and *mouf* for *both* and *mouth,* and the like. These innocent usages, which are as familiar as the sun in the late Confederacy, are apparently the terror of Northern employers, who the bi-dialectalists assume are almost suicidally unconcerned with such details as character, intelligence, and training for the job. The fact is, of course, that Northern employers and labor leaders dislike black faces but use black English as an excuse.

Having established, however, that a child of darkness under her tutelage says *mouf,* the pretty white lady sets out to rescue his soul. First she plays tapes of Southern speech to convince her victims, who understand Southern speech far better than they understand hers, that Southern speech often makes "complete understanding of content . . . difficult," "not readily comprehensible"—as is demonstrated by the fact that the pretty white lady would never have detected her victim's four-letter word just by listening and without watching his lips (New York Board of Education, *Nonstandard Dialect,* pp. 1, 14, 17). The difficulty of detecting him is all the more reason for fearing the iniquitous *mouf*-sayer: it proves he is a cunning devil who probably says *dentissoffice* too and who perpetrates such subversive "malapropisms" as "The food in the lunch room is not fitting to eat" (*On the Dialects of Children,* p. 23). How else *would* he spell *fitten*? But for such a hardened rogue, a good many "motivational activities" are likely to be necessary before the pretty white lady can really start twisting the thumbscrew with her drills.

Yet the drills are available, and the pretty white lady will use them when she sees her time. She has drills of all kinds—repetition drills, substitution drills, replacement drills, conversion drills, cued answer drills, the reading in unison of long lists of words like *teeth / reef, toothbrush / waffle, bathtub / alphabet, weather / weaver.* To get rid of *dentissoffice,* she may have students debate such propositions as "Ghosts do exist" or "Formal school tests should be eliminated"; and before a really "culminating activity" like playing "Pack the Trunk" she may "divide the class into consonant-cluster committees to seek out words containing" clusters like *sks, sps,* or *kt* (*Nonstandard Dialect, passim*). At this point the class might be invited to suggest a context for a replacement drill—maybe something like "Teacher! teacher! Billy Joe say that Tommy _____ Bessy!" This last suggestion, it must be confessed, has not yet been made in the literature, but it seems considerably more stimulating than choral recitation of Poe's "Bells" (*ibid.,* p. 35).

* * *

Perhaps it need not be added that existing tests and evaluations of such "instructional materials" are something of a farce. If bi-dialectalism is really harder to acquire than bilingualism (Einar Haugen in *Social Dialects and Language Learning*, p. 125), teachers and texts ought surely to be superb, and judgments on them ought to be severe; but New York City's curriculum developers can give "highest priority" to making the children change *a* to *an* before nouns beginning with a vowel (*Nonstandard Dialect*, p. 14), and Texas' Professor Troike can argue the success of his methods by showing that after six months of drills a little black girl could repeat *his hat* after her teacher, instead of translating automatically to *he hat*. Unfortunately, tapes do not record psychological damage, or compare the effectiveness of other ways of teaching, or show what might better have been learned in the same time instead of learning to repeat *his hat*.

So much for a description of mandatory bi-dialectalism, a bit enlivened (since the subject is dreary) by irreverent comment, but not distorted in any essential way. In the U.S.A., we are being told, everybody wants approval—not approval for doing anything worth approving, but approval for doing whatever happens to be approved. Because approval goes to upward mobility, everybody should be upwardly mobile; and because upward mobility is impossible for underdogs who have not learned middle-dog barking, we must teach it to them for use in their excursions into the middle-dog world. There is no possibility either that the present middle class can be brought to tolerate lower-class English or that upward mobility, as a national aspiration, will be questioned. Those are the pillars on which the state is built, and the compassionate teacher, knowing the ways of his society, will change the color of his students' vowels although he cannot change the color of their skins.

It is not at all certain that the bi-dialectalists, for all their absurdities, can be dislodged from their well-carpeted offices. They are supported by the National Council of Teachers of English, the Modern Language Association of America, the Center for Applied Linguistics, the federal government, the foundations, the governments of a number of major cities, and by black people who have made it into the middle class and so despise their origins and their less efficient fellows. In the best of times our top dogs are pleased by docility, if not mobility, among the beasts below; and in 1969 a new ice age is beginning. Newspaper headlines tell us that the Department of Health, Education, and Welfare has been urged to relax its requirements for desegregation of schools immediately but quietly, and President Nixon loses his Miami tan at the thought that militant students will "politicize" our universities—as if government grants to upwardly mobile faculty had not politicized them long ago. In Lyndon Johnson's Texas the citizens of Austin vote down an open housing law, their board of education then justifies segregated schooling by the established pattern of segregated housing, and the governor of the state praises the state university as the source of brain-power to assist the businessman in the lucrative exploitation of what the governor proudly calls the "insatiable appetite" of Texans. The only revolution we are likely to see is the continued subversion, by the dominant white businessman, of the political and religious principles on which the nation was founded.

Yet though the times are bad, they are not hopeless, at least not in the small, undramatic world of English education; and the bi-dialectalists are so gorgeously absurd that the breath of laughter may collapse their card-house if only enough people can be brought to see it as it is. It is not simply quixotic, then, to add to a laughing description of imposed bi-dialectalism a more serious statement of reasons why it cannot succeed and should not be tolerated even if it could—a statement which can lead, in conclusion, to the proposing of an alternative policy.

The argument that bi-dialectalism cannot be forced is easy to make out, even, in part, from the reluctant admissions of some of its proponents. Two principal reasons have already been suggested, the ignorance and unproved methods of the bi-dialectalists. The term *ignorance* is used literally, and in all fairness. Whatever one thinks of teaching standard English by methods like those for teaching foreign languages, contrastive analyses of our different dialects are a prerequisite—but a prerequisite which has not yet been supplied. Until very recently, the principal sources of information were the collections for the *Linguistic Atlas;* but they are unsystematic, partially out-of-date, and in some respects inaccurate and superficial. Where, for example, should one go for descriptions of intonation and its dialectal variants, for accurate accounts of the system or systems of verbal auxiliaries, for analyses of the speech of ghetto children instead of rustic ancients? Such minimal essentials are simply lacking. In fact, it might be said that for all the talk about revolutionary advances in linguistics, neither the structural nor the generative grammarians have yet produced a satisfactory basic description of even standard English.

The best descriptions of all our kinds of English would still not be enough to make coercive bi-dialectalism a success. The English teacher's forty-five minutes a day for five days in the week will never counteract the influence, and sometimes the hostility, of playmates and friends and family during much of the larger part of the student's time. Formal education could produce real bi-dialectals only in a vast system of state nurseries and boarding schools to which the children of the poor and ignorant would be consigned at an early age; but such establishments would be prohibitively expensive, intolerable to the people, and still not absolutely certain of success, because the most essential of all conditions might not be met—namely, the desire of the children to talk like the white middle class.

When one thinks about it in these realistic terms, the whole argument about bi-dialectalism begins to look schizophrenic, as out-of-this-world as an argument about whether Lee should surrender at Appomattox or fight back. There is no evidence that the bi-dialectalists, if they actually had good textbooks, better teachers, and as much money as the country is spending to devastate Vietnam, would really know what to do with those fictional resources. Instead of clear ideas, they offer clichés, like the familiar attacks on "traditional methods and approaches" or the protected pedagogue's arrogant assurance that illiterates can have no human dignity. They fly off quickly into high-sounding vaguenesses, talking (for example) about "differences in social dialect and associated versions of reality" (*Social Dialects and Language Learning,* p. 68), as if metaphysics rested on a preconsonantal /r/. At their most precise, they suggest the prudential avoidance of Southern pronunciations of *walk* and *cough* in Washington because Negroes there look down on new arrivals from Georgia and the Carolinas. They happily assume what they should prove—that intensive training in "standard informal English as a second dialect" has produced or can produce large numbers of psychologically undamaged bi-dialectals, whose new accomplishment has won them or will win them jobs that otherwise would have been impossible for them to get. When their guard is down, the bi-dialectalists actually confess that they *have* no concrete program, since "no one program at any level yet seems applicable to a significant number of other classes at the respective level" (*Language Programs for the Disadvantaged,* pp. 30ff.).

Some awareness of their difficulties, and some uncertainty about priorities, seem indeed to be spreading among the bi-dialectalists (though it would be too much to hope that if their present bandwagon falls apart they will consider themselves discredited and resign their membership in the Society of Mandarins). For one thing, they have become aware of the significance of reading, which William A. Stewart, as late as 1964, could reduce to the level of "socially desirable embellishments" (*Social Dialects and Language Learning*, p. 10). In his latest book, however, *Teaching Black Children to Read*, Editor Shuy announces "the simple truth that speaking standard English, however desirable it may be, is not as important as learning to read" (p. 118). His colleagues Walter A. Wolfram and Ralph W. Fasold are even closer to enlightenment. In the same new volume (p. 143), they hesitantly admit that "there is some question about the degree to which Standard English can be taught to the ghetto child in the classroom at all"; and Fasold meant what he said, for he had said it before at the Milwaukee convention of the NCTE. Though that august body was still congratulating itself on its concern with "a language component for the so-called culturally divergent," it had to bear with Fasold's embarrassing confession: "Because of the operation of social forces in the use of language," he said, "forces which are only poorly understood, it may not be possible to teach Standard English as a second language to Black English speaking children unless they are interacting with Standard English speakers in a meaningful way out-side the classroom" (*Convention Concerns—1968*, p. 10). The Cen-ter's linguistician came as close as standard English would allow to saying that it is segregation which makes black people talk different and that there would be no slum children if there were no slums.

No doubt the most important of Fasold's poorly understood social forces is one which everybody but white linguists has under-stood for a long time: black people may just not want to talk white English. Several years ago, Labov observed that some of his more rebellious New York subjects were deliberately turning away from social-climbing New York speech toward a black Southern model (*Social Dialects and Language Learning*, pp. 96f.), and today com-ment on "the new feeling of racial pride among black Americans" (*Teaching Black Children to Read*, p. 142) is a platitude. Wolfram and Fasold go on to the quite unsurprising speculation that that pride may even extend to the Negro's speech. "If a realization develops that this dialect, an important part of black culture, is as distinctively Afro-American as anything in the culture, the result may well be a new respect for Black English within the commu-nity" (p. 143). More plainly, condescending middle-class white charity is not wanted any more, if it ever was, in language-teaching or anywhere else. We should learn from the example of the British: the social cataclysm of the Second World War, and the achievement of political power by labor, did more to give the "disadvantaged" English youngster an equal chance than charitable bi-dialectalism ever did. We are past the stage when white teachers, whether Afri-cans or Caucasians, can think well of themselves for trying to turn black people into uneasy imitations of the whites.

* * *

The immorality of that effort is the chief reason why enforced bi-dialectalism should not be tolerated even if it were possible. Predators can and do use dialect differences to exploit and oppress, because ordinary people can be made to doubt their own value and to accept subservience if they can be made to despise the speech of their fathers. Obligatory bi-dialectalism for minorities is only another mode of exploitation, another way of making blacks behave as whites would like them to. It is unnecessary for communication, since the ability to understand other dialects is easily attained, as the black child shows when she translates her teacher's prissy white model "*his* hat" into "*he* hat." Its psychological consequences are likely to be nervous affectation, self-distrust, dislike for everyone not equally afflicted with the itch to get ahead, and eventual frustration by the discovery that the reward for so much suffering is intolerably small. At best the altered student will get a somewhat better job and will move up a few places in the rat-race of the underlings. At worst he will be cut off from other blacks, still not accepted among whites, and economically no better off than he was before.

White teachers should hope, then, that their black students will be recalcitrant, so that bi-dialectalism as a unilateral condition for employment can be forgotten. It would make better sense, if pedagogues insist on living in a fantasy world, to require whites to speak black English in their dealings with blacks, since the whites have more advantages than the blacks and consider themselves more intelligent; or perhaps we should be hard-headedly consistent in our brutalities and try to eradicate the vices which really do enrage employers—like intellectual questioning, or the suspicion that ours is not the best of possible worlds.

Indeed, the educationists' faith in education would be touching if it were not their way of keeping up their wages. Nothing the schools can do about black English or white English either will do much for racial peace and social justice as long as the black and white worlds are separate and hostile. The measure of our educational absurdity is the necessity of saying once again that regimented bi-dialectalism is no substitute for sweeping social change —*necessity* being defined by the alternative of dropping out and waiting quietly for destruction if the white businessman continues to have his way.

The reply that the educational system should not be politicized is impossible for bi-dialectalists, since bi-dialectalism is itself a political instrument. They may purge themselves of inconsistency, and do what little good is possible for English teachers as political reformers, if instead of teaching standard English as a second dialect they teach getting out of Vietnam, getting out of the missile race, and stopping the deadly pollution of the one world we have, as horribly exemplified by the current vandalism in Alaska.

One use for a small fraction of the resources that would thus be saved would be to improve the teaching of the English language. Bi-dialectalism would never have been invented if our society were not divided into the dominant white majority and the exploited minorities. Children should be taught that. They should be taught the relations between group differences and speech differences, and the good and bad uses of speech differences by groups and by individuals. The teaching would require a more serious study of grammar, lexicography, dialectology, and linguistic history than our educational system now provides—require it at least of prospective English teachers.

In the immediate present, the time and money now wasted on bi-dialectalism should be spent on teaching the children of the minorities to read. Already some of the universal experts among the linguists have boarded this new bandwagon, and the next round of government grants may very well be for programs in reading and writing in black English. That might be a good thing, particularly if we could somehow get rid of the tired little clique of operators who have run the professional societies of English teachers for so long. Anyway, the direct attack on minority language, the attempt to compel bi-dialectalism, should be abandoned for an attempt to open the minds and enhance the lives of the poor and ignorant. At the same time, every attempt should be made to teach the majority to understand the life and language of the oppressed. Linguistic change is the effect and not the cause of social change. If the majority can rid itself of its prejudices, and if the minorities can get or be given an education, differences between dialects are unlikely to hurt anybody much.

(The phoniest objections to this proposal will be those that talk about social realism, about the necessity for doing something even—or should one say particularly?—if it's wrong. That kind of talk makes real change impossible, but makes money for bi-dialectalists.)

Doublespeak
Dialectology in the Service of Big Brother
(1972)

The title here indicates clearly that in the three years after the previous essay appeared, Sledd had not become more tolerant of those who espoused bi-dialectal education, or of the society that fosters economic oppression of its nonstandard English–speaking citizens. Specifically, here he criticizes the condescending attitude of teachers who read standard English texts in order to teach bidialectalism. Once again, Sledd abhors the arrogant hypocrisy of "crusader" linguists; the language of these language doctors, he argues, is more offensive by far than the language of their patients. Sledd's discussion of African-American English is applicable equally to all stigmatized dialects of English.

A Short History of Doublespeak

It was only a few years ago that Prof. Dr. Roger W. Shuy, then of Michigan State University, discovered American dialects.[1] In a little book which James R. Squire, Executive Secretary of the National Council of Teachers of English, described as "a valuable resource" for teachers increasingly concerned with "the study of the English language in our schools" (Shuy, "Foreword"), Dr. Shuy informed the profession that in Illinois "a male sheep was known as a *buck* only to farmers who had at some time raised sheep" (p. 15) and that "the Minneapolis term *rubber-binder* (for rubber band)" was spreading into Wisconsin (pp. 36–37). He also declared that Southerners pronounce *marry* as if it were spelled *merry;* that they pronounce *fog* and *hog* like *fawg* and *hawg;* that they have a final /r/ in *humor;* that they make *which* identical with *witch* and rhyme *Miss* with *his;* etc. (pp. 12–13).

But one does not expect high scholarship from a popularizing textbook, and though Dr. Shuy's discoveries made no great noise in the world of dialectology, the fault was not his alone. As he himself pointed out, American dialect studies were becoming "both more complex and more interesting," and new questions were being asked.

> Twenty or thirty years ago dialect geographers were mainly concerned with relating current pronunciations, vocabulary, and grammar to settlement history and geography. In the sixties, the problems of urban living have attracted attention, including social dialects and styles which need to be learned and used to meet different situations. We need more precise information about the dialects which set one social group apart from another. (Shuy, p. 63)

One might say metaphorically that the dialectologists, like millions of their compatriots, had left the farm for the big city. There they had discovered the blacks—and were making the best of it. In September, 1967, Dr. Roger W. Shuy was no longer a teacher in East Lansing, Michigan, but a Director of Urban Language Study in Washington, D.C.

The trouble with the blacks, as it seemed to the nabobs of the National Council, was that they didn't talk right and weren't doing very well in school. But they were also raising considerable hell with the police; and since the traditional self-righteous pontification against the South showed little promise of quelling riots in Chicago, Detroit, or New York, the greater Powers of the North had assumed a beneficent air and (as one stratagem) had employed a band of linguists and quasi-linguists who would pretend to help black folks talk like white folks on all occasions which the Northern Powers thought it worth their while to regulate. This was the origin of bi-dialectalism, biloquialism, or—in "good plain Anglo-Saxon"—doublespeak. No missionary enterprise of recent times has been more profitable—for the evangelists.

Readers in search of a longer and more reverential history may find it in many sources, including at least six volumes in the Urban Language Series, under the general editorship of Dr. Roger W. Shuy, now Director of the Sociolinguistics Program of the Center for Applied Linguistics. They are particularly directed to the volume entitled *Teaching Standard English in the Inner City,* which Dr.

Shuy has edited with his colleague Ralph W. Fasold (Washington, D.C.: Center for Applied Linguistics, 1970). Further light is shed by other collections of essays, notably the special anthology issue of *The Florida FL Reporter* which appeared in 1969 under the title *Linguistic-Cultural Differences and American Education;* the report of the twentieth annual Round Table Meeting at Georgetown, *Linguistics and the Teaching of Standard English to Speakers of Other Languages or Dialects;* and Frederick Williams' anthology *Language and Poverty: Perspectives on a Theme.* Professor Williams includes a recent essay by the British sociologist Basil Bernstein, who in his own way is also somewhat critical of doublespeak; and readers interested in Bernstein's earlier work will find it reviewed by Denis Lawton in *Social Class, Language and Education.* By all odds the best of the bi-dialectalists is the genuinely distinguished linguist William Labov of Columbia University, whose little book *The Study of Nonstandard English* includes a selected bibliography. Recently, the apostles of doublespeak have been vexed by more numerous and more vocal objectors, and perhaps there is just a hint of admitted failure in the shifting of attention by some biloquialists from doublespeak to the teaching of reading. Linguists, educationists, and others have addressed themselves to reading problems in memorial volumes like *Reading for the Disadvantaged,* edited by Thomas D. Horn, and *Language & Reading,* compiled by Doris V. Gunderson.[2]

The Moneyed Bankrupt

It is sad to report that the results of such vast activity have been disproportionately small. The biloquialists themselves do not claim to have produced substantial numbers of psychologically undamaged doublespeakers, whose mastery of whitey's talk has won them jobs which otherwise would have been denied them. In fact, the complete bi-dialectal, with undiminished control of his vernacular and a good mastery of the standard language, is apparently as mythical as the unicorn: no authenticated specimens have been reported.[3] Even the means to approximate the ideal of doublespeaking are admittedly lacking, for "the need for teaching materials preceded any strongly felt need for theoretical bases or empirical research upon which such materials could be based" (Fasold and Shuy, *op. cit.,* p. 126). Consequently, there are relatively few teaching materials available (*ibid.,* p. 128), and those that do exist differ in theory, method, content, and arrangement (Walt Wolfram, in Fasold and Shuy, p. 105). In the words of Director Dr. Shuy,

A majority of the materials currently available for teaching standard English to nonstandard speakers rest on the uneasy assumption that TESOL techniques [for teaching English as a second language] are valid for learning a second dialect. They do this without any solid proof. We do not have a viable evaluation tool at this time nor are we likely to get one until the linguists complete their analysis of the language system of nonstandard speakers. Most current materials deal with pronunciations although it has long been accepted that grammatical differences count more heavily toward social judgments than phonological or lexical differences.[4]

Taken literally, that confession would mean that the biloquialists will never be able to tell their patrons whether or not their costly teaching materials are any good, because a complete analysis of any language, standard or nonstandard, is another unattainable ideal. The best of existing descriptions of what is called Black English are only fragments, sketches of bits and pieces which have caught the eye of Northern linguists unfamiliar with Southern speech.[5] Advocates of doublespeak must therefore admit that they have still not produced the "absolutely necessary prerequisite to English teaching in such situations, . . . the linguistic analysis and description of the nonstandard dialect."[6]

Causes of Failure

At this juncture the irreverent might be tempted to ask a question. If happy, accomplished, and fully employed doublespeakers are not swarming in Northern cities, if tried and tested materials for teaching more of them remain scarce, and if complete descriptions of the relevant dialects are not going to exist while we do, then one might ask just what the biloquialists have been doing with the money and manpower which the Establishment has provided them or whether (more suspiciously) the Establishment really wants them to do anything or just to give the impression of a great society on the march toward new frontiers.

One naughty answer would be that the biloquialists have been so busy convening, conferring, organizing, advertising, and asking for more that their intellectual activities have suffered. There is even some expert testimony to this effect:

A recent national conference on educating the disadvantaged devoted less than 5% of its attention during the two days of meetings to the content of such education. Practically all of the papers and discussion centered on funding such programs, administrating them and evaluating them. (Shuy, in Fasold and Shuy, p. 127)

But so elementary a naughtiness is only a partial answer, and in part unfair. It is unfair specifically to William Labov and his associates, who have taught us a great deal, not just about current American English, but about the theory and practice of descriptive and historical grammar; and it does not sufficiently emphasize the extenuating circumstance that well-meaning sloganeers may be trapped by their own slogans as they try to do in a few years a job that would take a generation.

Since the Powers prefer the appearance of social change to the reality, it was not hard to hook governments and foundations on the alleged potentialities of doublespeak as if those potentialities had been realized already or would be on a bright tomorrow; but when the advertisements had brought the customers, the delivery of the actual goods turned out impossible. Nobody knows what the biloquialists admit they would have to know about dialects of English to make doublespeak succeed; and besides this general ignorance (which some of them have manfully attacked), the biloquialists are working under some special disadvantages. It is always hard for people who have not taught much to talk about teaching (though ingenious youths like Dr. Peter S. Rosenbaum can sometimes manage it),[7] and it is hard for linguists who have not heard much Southern speech to talk about speech which is basically Southern: they are constantly discovering distinctive characteristics of "the Negro vernacular," like "dummy *it* for *there,*" which the most benighted caucasian Christian spinster in Milledgeville, Georgia, could assure them are commonplace among poor whites.[8]

There are other difficulties, too, which hamper not only the biloquialists but all practitioners of large-scale linguistic engineering (the jargon is contagious). Linguistics in the '60s and early '70s has been unsettled by new theories, whose advocates are openly skeptical of oversold "applications"; and even in favorable circumstances "interdisciplinary" efforts like biloquialism are always slow to take effect, often hampered by disagreements among the congregation of prima donnas, and sometimes disappointingly unproductive.

Quite as loud as the general lamentation over the failure of "interventionist" programs for the disadvantaged are the debates among the interveners. Thus, to the devotees of applied linguistics, both the Englishman Bernstein and the American partners Engelmann and Bereiter are sinners against the light,[9] but neither Bernstein nor Engelmann has rushed headlong to confession. On the contrary, both are recalcitrant.

For all his talk about restricted and elaborated codes (talk which has won him a retinue of American disciples), Bernstein still sees no reason to interfere with nonstandard dialects:

That the culture or subculture through its forms of social integra-
tion generates a restricted code, does not mean that the resultant
speech and meaning system is linguistically or culturally deprived, that its children have nothing to offer the school, that their
imaginings are not significant. It does not mean that we have to
teach these children formal grammar, nor does it mean that we
have to interfere with their dialect. There is nothing, but nothing,
in dialect as such, which prevents a child from internalizing and
learning to use universalistic meanings.[10]

Obviously, Bernstein has little in common with the biloquialists
except the tendency to talk smugly about *we* and *they* and what *we*
have to do to *them*. Engelmann, equally godlike, ranks "The Linguistic and Psycholinguistic Approaches" under "Abuses in Program Construction" and dismisses both:

It is not possible to imply statements about teaching from the premises upon which the linguist and the psycholinguist operate.
Attempts to use linguistic analysis as the basis for teaching reading have produced the full range of programs, from paragraph
reading to single-sound variations. The linguist's entire theoretical
preamble, in other words, is nothing more than an appeal used to
sanction an approach that derives from personal preferences, not
from linguistic principles.[11]

Unless the Powers are willing to subsidize all interveners
equally, such disagreement indicates that at least some seekers of
funds should get no more funding for the evaluating of their administrating; and the unfunded (to close this selective catalogue of disagreements) are likely to include some linguists, for linguist can
differ with linguist as vigorously as with psychologist or sociologist.
Marvin D. Loflin, for example, transmogrifies all Southern whites to
pluriglots when he finds "Nonstandard Negro English" so unlike the
standard speech of whites "that a fuller description . . . will show a
grammatical system which must be treated as a foreign language."[12]
Similarly, William A. Stewart finds enough "unique . . . structural
characteristics" in "American Negro dialects" to justify the bold
historical speculation that the Negro dialects "probably derived from
a creolized form of English, once spoken on American plantations by
Negro slaves and seemingly related to creolized forms of English
which are still spoken by Negroes in Jamaica and other parts of the
Caribbean."[13]
Perhaps it may be so. At any rate, when Stewart's theory is questioned he is quick to denounce what he calls "the blatant intrusion
of sociopolitical issues into the scientific study of Negro speech";[14]
and his sociopolitical rhetoric, if not his linguistic evidence, has

been so convincing that his conclusions are sometimes confidently repeated by persons whose linguistic sophistication is considerably less than his.[15]

Yet Loflin and Stewart have not had everything their own way among linguists. Raven McDavid is presumably one of Stewart's blatant intruders of sociopolitical issues into virginal science:

> Even where a particular feature is popularly assigned to one racial group, like the uninflected third-singular present (*he do, she have, it make*)—a shibboleth for Negro nonstandard speech in urban areas—it often turns out to be old in the British dialects, and to be widely distributed in the eastern United States among speakers of all races. It is only the accidents of cultural, economic, and educational history that have made such older linguistic features more common in the South than in the Midland and the North, and more common among Negro speakers than among whites.[16]

William Labov is equally firm in rejecting Loflin's theory of nonstandard Negro English as a foreign language:

> In dealing with the structure of NNE, we do not find a foreign language with syntax and semantics radically different from SE [Standard English]: instead, we find a dialect of English, with certain extensions and modifications of rules to be found in other dialects. . . . Striking differences in surface structure were frequently the result of late phonological and transformational rules.[17]

No amount of funding can conceal the fact that somebody, in arguments like these, has got to be wrong.

The Shift to Reading

If the shift from doublespeak to interdisciplinary assaults on reading does hint at some sense of failure among the disunited sloganeers of overambitious biloquialism, their choice of a second front will not redeem their reputation as skillful strategists. The familiar tactic of concealing the failure to keep one promise by making another is unlikely to succeed if the second promise is less plausible than the first; and promises to give everyone "the right to read" are notoriously hard to make good on, even for the linguist in his favorite role of universal expert.

The perusal of books on reading like those edited by Horn and Gunderson leaves one considerably sadder, therefore, but little wiser, than when he began. The inquisitive amateur soon accepts the experts' repeated assertion that little is known—and gets tired of their plea for more research and full employment:

After decades of debate and expenditures of millions of research dollars, the teaching of reading remains on questionable psychological and linguistic grounds.

When one looks at the research on reading over the past half century, the sheer volume of the literature and the welter of topics and findings (and lack of findings) is incredible. Yet, we are sore put to name even a few trustworthy generalizations or research based guides to educational practice.

Eleven widely different methods, represented by a variety of materials, were tested in some five hundred classrooms of first grade children during 1964–1965. Summary reports . . . revealed that by and large methods and materials were not the crucial elements in teaching first grade children to read.

At the present time we need research into every aspect of the education of the disadvantaged.[18]

If the amateur educationist is already an amateur linguist, he probably already knows Labov's opinion that "the major problem responsible for reading failure" in the ghettos "is a cultural conflict," not dialect interference.[19] He is thus surprised only by the source of Dr. Roger W. Shuy's quite unsurprising statement "that learning to read has little or nothing to do with a child's ability to handle Standard English phonology."[20] A Southern amateur who has consorted with Australians, for example, or vacationed among Lake Country farmers, hardly needs linguistic enlightenment to know that the oddest speech is perfectly compatible with the reading of internationally acceptable English. And the mere happy innocent who cares nothing for either linguistics or pedagogy, if he has reflected at all on what he does when he reads, will know that reading is not just a "language art." The essential processes, even in reading parrot-like without understanding, are inference and judgment in what Kenneth S. Goodman has called "a psycholinguistic guessing game";[21] and most of the linguistic entrepreneurs can claim no special competence in such matters.

Somnigraphy and Euphemism

To anyone with a normal dislike for solemn inanity, the contribution of linguistics to the teaching of reading is thus a less promising subject than the sleep-writing and professional euphemism which mark the work of the biloquialists and the inhabitants of schools of education. The name *biloquialism* is itself as fine an instance of verbal magic as one could want. Because nobody likes to admit that his speech makes other people laugh at him or despise him, *dialect* has become a dirty word. Hence its compounds and derivatives, like the older *bi-dialectalism,* must go too—the hope being, one imagines, that if the name goes the thing will vanish with it. For such wizardry, *doublespeak* is the perfect label.

Educationists make as much fuss over the euphemism *the disadvantaged* as the linguists do over *biloquialism.* They have not contented themselves with the one weasel-word, but have matched it with a number of others: *the culturally different, the linguistically different, the culturally deprived, the intellectually deprived, the culturally antagonized* (Horn, *Reading for the Disadvantaged,* pp. v, 11). It is a touch of genius that after choosing a word to obscure his meaning, a writer can then debate what he means by it. Thomas D. Horn concludes that anybody can be disadvantaged, even when he thinks he is in the catbird seat:

> Any individual may be disadvantaged socially, economically, psychologically, and/or linguistically, depending upon the particular social milieu in which he is attempting to function at a given time. Indeed, he may be completely oblivious to his disadvantaged condition and perceive others in the group as being disadvantaged rather than himself.[22]

Horn's readers will not deny their intellectual deprivation.

Somnigraphy, the art of writing as if one were asleep, is as zealously cultivated by biloquialists and educationists as euphemism. Sleep-writing must be distinguished from New High Bureaucratian (NHB), which is grammatical and has a meaning but obscures it by jargon. At its best, somnigraphy is neither grammatical nor meaningful; but no sentence can qualify as somnigraphic unless either its meaning or its grammar is somehow deviant. The following statement approaches the degree of vacuity necessary to somnigraphy; but since its distinctive feature is pompous scientism, it is probably to be treated as NHB:

> Commands or requests for action are essentially instructions from a person A to a person B to carry out some action X at a time T.
> $A \rightarrow B : X ! / T$

Somnigraphy in the pure state is more easily recognizable:

> Illogical comparison: "The selection of informants in this study is more rigid than the original study."

> Tautology rampant: "Before a non-consonantal environment the presence of the cluster-final stop, for all practical purposes, is categorically present in SE."

Failure of agreement: "The difference between the Negro classes appear to be largely quantitative for monomorphemic clusters."

The dying fall: "That we see linguists, psychologists, sociologists, educators, and others exercising varying definitions of language and language behavior, is important to know."

Chaos and Old Night: "Much of the attention given to the sociocultural aspects of poverty can be seen in the kinds of causes and cures for poverty which are often linked as parts of an overall *poverty cycle* (Figure 1)." [But neither the attention to poverty, nor the cures for it, can be found in the cycle itself.]

The *like/as* syndrome: "English, as most languages, has a variety of dialects."

Self-contradiction: "The nativist position carries with it the concept of a distinction between a child's linguistic knowledge and all of the varied facets and factors of his actual speaking and listening behaviors, one factor of which is the aforementioned knowledge." [That is, the child's knowledge both is and is not a part of his behavior.]

Scrambled metaphor: "In brief the strategy is to prepare the child for candidacy into the economic mainstream." [Sooner or later, we will read about the aridity of the mainstream culture—probably sooner.]

Fractured idiom: "Goodman (1965) and Bailey (1965), along with Stewart (esp. 1969), have all discussed the possibility of interference from the dialect on acquiring the ability to read." [And let no man interfere on their discussion.]

The unconscious absurd: ". . . both the linguists and sociologists . . . were relatively free from . . . cross-fertilization. . . ."

Lexical indiscretion: "As long as one operates in terms of languages and cultures conceived as isolates, internally discreet, . . ."

Flatus: "Middle-class children emitted a larger number of . . . self-corrections than the lower-class children did."

The cancerous modifier: "Mrs. Golden's program, as with most of the teaching English as a second language to Negro non-standard English speakers programs, relies on pattern practice. . . ." [Sounds like somebody needs it.]

Confusion of map with territory: "The rule for the absence of *d* occurs more frequently when *d* is followed by a consonant than when followed by a vowel."

The genteel thing: "To improve one's social acceptability to a middle class society, working class people should focus primarily on vocabulary development."

The intense inane: "Reading is a process of recognizing that printed words represent spoken words and is a part of the total language spectrum."

The shipwrecked question: "How do the separate and disparate experiences of individuals lead to a common acceptance of general meaning but which also permit differences of interpretation?" [God only knows.]

Circumblundering a meaning: "The educational world has generally thought of language as lexicon and it is not surprising that they would equate cultural adjustment to the words of the city. . . ."

The undefining definition: "By underlying structure here I mean that ability which even beginning readers have which enables them to avoid misreading via any other manner than by the phonological, and grammatical rules of their native language."

The arresting title: "Economic, Geographic, and Ethnic Breakdown of Disadvantaged Children."

Opposites reconciled: "One obstacle, lack of skill in the use of standard American English, has increasingly been recognized as a major contributing factor to the success of a child beginning his formal education."

Why the Powers Pay

That exhibit, which could be enlarged at will, is neither cruel nor insolent nor joking. The insolence is that the perpetrators of such writing should set themselves up as linguists and teachers of standard English. The cruelty is that people who think and write so badly should be turned loose upon children. The level of simple competence in the use of words is simply low among biloquialists, and to the old-fashioned English professor who still believes that a man's sentences (not his dialect) are a good index to his intelligence, that fact demands an explanation.

The obvious answer is that governments and foundations have put up so much money for doublespeak that they have not been able to find good people to spend it; but that answer simply shifts the question to another level. Why do our rulers act like that? Why should they employ verbicides in the impossible and immoral pursuit of biloquialism? Well-meaning incompetence may characterize many biloquialists; but incompetence has no direction, follows no party line unless some other force is guiding—and the drift of biloquialism is too plain to be accidental. There must be, somewhere, an inhumanity that shapes its ends.

The explanation does not require that inhumanity should be reified in a body of conspirators or that the making of educational policy, at any level, should be viewed as the conscious, intelligent adaptation of public means to private ends. In their dealings with black people, most middle-class white linguists in the United States may be expected to act like most other middle-class whites. Their probable motivations include a real desire to do good, some hidden dislike, some fear, and the love of money and status. Foundation men, bureaucrats, and politicians may be expected to share those foibles; and precisely because the whole conglomerate is shaped and moved by the same forces, it cannot move beyond its limits.

The appeal of doublespeak is that it promises beneficent change without threat to existing power or privilege. If doublespeak were to succeed, the restive communities of the poor and ignorant would be tamed; for potential revolutionaries would be transformed into the subservient, scrambling, anxious underlings who constitute the lower middle class in a technological society. Their children, if there should be a next generation, would rise to be its linguists, its English teachers, and its petty bureaucrats; and doublespeak would be justified by Progress. If doublespeak should fail, as it must, large numbers of young blacks can still be assured that it was they who failed, and not their white superiors; and the blacks' presumed failure in not doing what they could not and should not do can be used against them as a psychological and political weapon.[23] In either event, the white Powers have nothing to lose by their exercise in cosmetology. Both their conscience and their supremacy will be clear.

The Form of the Argument

The essential argument for such an explanation should be stated formally enough to keep the issues plain. As a hypothetical syllogism, the argument would look like this:

> Unless the biloquialists and their sponsors were misled by their presumed self-interest, they would not pursue the impossible and immoral end of doublespeak so vigorously—or defend themselves for doing it.

But they do pursue, etc.
Therefore they are misled. . . .

Less pedantically, nobody insists on trying to do what he can't and shouldn't do unless there's something in it for him somewhere.

It is the consequent of the major premise that needs attention.

The Impossibility of Doublespeak

The impossibility of establishing doublespeak in the real world has already been argued: the necessary descriptions of standard and nonstandard dialects are nonexistent, and materials and methods of teaching are dubious at best. It may be added here that competent teachers of doublespeak are a contradiction in terms. For tough young blacks, the worst possible teacher is a middle-class white female; and a middle-class black female may not be much better, since she is nearly as likely as her white counterpart to look down on her lower-class students. Such condescending culture-vendors have no chance whatever of neutralizing the influence of the world outside the classroom, a world where ghetto youngsters have few occasions to use such standard English as they may have learned and where, if they did use it, they might find the effort unrewarding. Their peers would blame them for trying to talk like white people, and they would hardly be compensated for such isolation by any real increase in "upward mobility." The black college graduate who makes less money than a white dropout is a sad familiar figure.

Teachers of standard English may be sure, then, of resistance from teen-age students in the ghettos, and unless they are more tactful than the biloquialists, they may be sure of resistance from black adults as well. On the issue of doublespeak the black community is undoubtedly divided. Blacks who have made it into the middle and upper classes, and many black parents, want to see young people make it too. They consider the ability to use "good English" a part of making it (though in reality good English is far less important to success on the job than a great many other qualifications). At the other extreme are the tough teen-agers, the adults who secretly or openly share their values, and some of the more militant community leaders; while in between there are probably a good many blacks of various ages for whom the white world's insistence on its standard English sets off an internal conflict between pride and self-hate.

But the black community is not at all divided in its opposition to doctrines of white supremacy, whether politely veiled or publicly announced. No black of any age is likely to be much pleased by condescension and the calm assumption of superiority:

> First, there has been the general attitude, common even among some linguists, that nonstandard speech is less worthy of interest and study than varieties of speech with high prestige. . . . As this relates to the speech of Negroes, it has been reinforced by a commendable desire to emphasize the potential of the Negro to be identical to white Americans. . . .[24]

> Even if it were possible to "stamp out" nonstandard English, changing the students' language behavior completely might be detrimental to their social well-being. They may need the nonstandard for social situations in which it is appropriate.[25]

> More than the foreign-language student, more than the native speaker of Standard English, the second-dialect student needs to know his teacher considers him truly "worth revising."[26]

The neighbor-loving speech which ended with the last quotation was soon followed, understandably, by an angry outburst from a black auditor:

> I am outraged and insulted by this meeting. . . . I would like to know why white people can determine for black people what is standard and what is nonstandard.

But two of the linguists present did not get the message—the plain message that it must no longer be whites only who "conduct the important affairs of the community." The first of them rebuked the young lady rudely, once in the meeting and once in a "subsequent written comment": he rapped about "rapping" on sociolinguists and using phony ploys "in political confrontations." The second, in a display of Caucasian tact, congratulated her on expressing herself "in perfectly standard grammar."

If those who set themselves up as teachers of teachers behave like that, they may succeed in uniting the divided black community —uniting it against the advocates of doublespeak. Whatever the black community does want, it does not want to be led by the nose.

The Immorality of Doublespeak

The biloquialist, of course, makes a great fuss about giving the child of the poor and ignorant, whether black or white, the choice of using or not using standard English. "He should be allowed to make that decision as he shapes his decisions in life."[27] But the biloquialist obviously sees himself as the determiner of the decisions which other people may decide, and the choice he deigns to give is really not much choice after all. In the name of social realism, he begins by imposing a false scheme of values, of which "upward mobility" is the highest; and he then sets out to make the child "upwardly mobile" by requiring hours of stultifying drill on arbitrary matters of usage, so that in situations where standard English is deemed appropriate the child may choose between "Ain't nobody gon' love you" and "Nobody is going to love you." *Appropriate* will be defined by the white world, which will also fix the punishment if the liberated doublespeaker prefers his own definition. Ain't nobody gon' love him if he does that.

The immorality of biloquialism is amply illustrated by such hypocrisy. Assuring the child that his speech is as good as anybody else's, publicly forswearing all attempts to eradicate it, and vigorously defending the individual's free choice, the biloquialist would actually force the speech and values of the middle-class white world on children of every class and color. By *upward mobility* he means getting and spending more money, wasting more of the world's irreplaceable resources in unnecessary display, and turning one's back on family and friends who are unable or unwilling to join in that high enterprise. Every day, by his loud-voiced actions, the biloquialist would tell the child to build his life on that rotten foundation.

But *tell* is too mild a word: *force* is more accurate. *Force* is more accurate because the schoolchild would not have a choice between wasting his precious days (with the biloquialists) in the study of socially graded synonyms and (with intelligent teachers) learning something serious about himself and the world he lives in; and besides, when schooldays were over, the young doublespeaker could not really choose between his vernacular and his imperfectly mastered standard English. In every serious transaction of an upwardly mobile life, the use of standard English would be enforced by the giving or withholding of the social and economic goodies which define upward mobility. The upwardly mobile doublespeaker would be expected to eradicate his vernacular except in some darkly secret areas of his private life, of which eventually he would learn to be ashamed; and his likely reward for such self-mutilation would be just enough mobility to get him stranded between the worlds of white and black. There he could happily reflect on the humanitarianism of the Great White Expert, who saves the oppressed from militancy and sends them in pursuit of money and status, which literature, philosophy, religion, and the millennial experience of mankind have exposed as unfit ends for human life. "That doesn't seem very humane from where I sit."[28]

On Not Loving Big Brother

But the present argument against biloquialism is not a militant argument (though biloquialists have called it one in the attempt to discredit it with a label they think is frightening), and it is not primarily a humanitarian argument (though biloquialists have called it inhumane). Our new teachers of reading cannot read well enough to tell Mill from a militant. The argument here is the argument of an unashamed conservative individualist. With his own eyes the arguer has seen British working people, and Chicanos, and black Americans humiliated by contempt for their language and twisted by their own unhappy efforts to talk like their exploiters. An expert is no more needed to prove that such humiliation is damaging or such efforts an expense of spirit than a meteorologist is needed to warn of the dangers of urinating against the wind; but the weight of the argument rests mainly on the fact that if any man can be so shamed and bullied for so intimate a part of his own being as his language, then every man is fully subject to the unhampered tyrants of the materialist majority. To resist the biloquialist is to resist Big Brother, and to resist him for oneself as well as others. Big Brother is not always white.

In all the variety of his disguises, Big Brother is very near at hand today. In one form he is Basil Bernstein, whose notions about restricted and elaborated codes (as they are interpreted or misinterpreted by Bernstein's American disciples) might vulgarly be taken as supporting an injunction to get the pickaninnies away from their black mammies; in another form he is the arrogant dogmatist Siegfried Engelmann, the amoral educational technologist with a big stick.

The biloquialist follows neither Engelmann nor Bernstein, but his own high-sounding talk should not be taken at face value, either. Doublespeak is not necessary to communication between users of different dialects, since speakers of nonstandard English generally have passive control of standard, if only through their exposure to television; the biloquialist himself assures us that no dialect is intrinsically better than any other; and his announced devotion to freedom of choice has already been exposed as phony, like his promise of social mobility through unnatural speech. When the biloquialist's guard is down, he too can talk the language of dialect-eradication, which he officially abhors:

. . . attempting to eliminate this kind of auxiliary deletion from the speech of inner-city Negro children would be a low-priority task.[29]

Behind the mandarin's jargon and self-praise lies the quiet assumption that it is his right and duty to run other people's lives.

The mandarin will go a long way to make other people see that his good is theirs, so that his values may prevail among the faceless multitude. As educator, his aims are not always educational, but may be as simple as keeping young people off the labor market by keeping them in school, though he tacitly admits that he has planned nothing to teach them there:

> The problems of finding suitable programs will be complicated if, as educators anticipate, education is made compulsory for students until they reach the age of eighteen. Educators will be forced to adapt programs for the group of young people from sixteen to eighteen who under the present system have dropped out of school.[30]

Yet the mandarin's ends, he thinks, justify almost any means.

> Intelligence and verbal skills within the culture of the street is prized just as highly as it is within the school:—but the use of such skills is more often to manipulate and control other people than to convey information to them. Of course it is the school's task to emphasize the value of language in cognitive purposes. But in order to motivate adolescent and pre-adolescent children to learn standard English, it would be wise to emphasize its value for handling social situations, avoiding conflict (or provoking conflict when desired), for influencing and controlling other people.[31]
>
> Between 5 and 10 percent of the 62,000 school children in this city in the American midlands are taking "behavior modification" drugs prescribed by local doctors to improve classroom deportment and increase learning potential. The children being given the drugs have been identified by their teachers as "hyper-active" and unmanageable to the point of disrupting regular classroom activity.[32]
>
> Bettye M. Caldwell . . . has proposed "educationally oriented day care for culturally deprived children between six months and three years of age." The children are returned home each evening to "maintain primary emotional relationships with their own families," but during the day they are removed to "hopefully prevent the deceleration in rate of development which seems to occur in many deprived children around the age of two to three years."[33]
>
> The Defense Department has been quietly effective in educating some of the casualties of our present public schools. It is hereby suggested that they now go into the business of repairing hundreds of thousands of these human casualties with affirmation

rather than apology. Schools for adolescent dropouts or educational rejects could be set up by the Defense Department adjacent
to camps—but not necessarily as an integral part of the military. If
this is necessary, it should not block the attainment of the goal of
rescuing as many of these young people as possible.[34]

In June the Camden (N.J.) Board of Education hired *Radio
Corporation of America* to reorganize its entire school system.
According to *Education Summary* (July 17, 1970), the management
contract for the first year of the USOE pilot project requires that
RCA "be responsible for identifying Camden's educational needs;
specifying priorities; organizing demonstration projects; training
school personnel for functions they can't perform adequately now;
organizing the system on a cost-effectiveness basis; and arranging
for objective valuation of results."[35]

There is not much doubt that the use of such means will corrupt
whatever end is said to justify them. It is not, for example, a super-
abundance of new teachers which now keeps them from finding
jobs, but the government's decision to pay for war in Viet Nam and
not for education. To solve this financial problem, school boards are
encouraged to choose education on the cheap. When they make
their bargains with the big corporations, the corporations get direct
control both of education and of whatever money the school boards
do spend. The corporations can thus keep up their profits; teachers
are made subservient automatons; and the country is delivered
from the danger that either teachers or students might occasionally
think. Disrupted families, drugged students, schools run by business or the military—these are the typical products of Big Brother's
machinations.

The role of the biloquialist in our educational skin-flick is not
outstanding: he is not a madam, just a working girl. His commitment, however, to the corrupt values of a corrupt society makes him
quite at house with the other manipulators, and his particular
manipulations have their special dangers because a standard language can be made a dangerous weapon in class warfare.

Standard English in the United States is a principal means of
preserving the existing power structure, for it builds the system of
class distinctions into the most inward reaches of each child's
humanity: the language whose mastery makes the child human
makes him also a member of a social class. Even rebellion demands
a kind of allegiance to the class system, because effective rebellion,
as the world goes now, requires the use of the standard language,
and the rebel is not likely to master the standard language without
absorbing some of the prejudice that it embodies. In the United
States, the child "knows his place" before he knows he knows it,

and the rebellious adult is either co-opted into the ruling class or has to fight to get a hearing. Biloquialism makes capital of this situation.

Big Brother and his flunkies are in control now; there is no doubt of that. But they have not won the last battle as long as resistance is possible, and resistance is possible until Big Brother makes us love him—if he can. If resistance saves nothing else, it saves the manhood of the unbrainwashed resister. The conservative individualist opposes biloquialism just because he does believe in individuality, to which liberty is prerequisite. "Tell the English," a bad poem says, "that man is a spirit." He is; and he does not live by beer alone; and the *radix malorum* is the businessman's morality of "getting ahead," which the biloquialist espouses when he argues that "right now, tomorrow, the youngster needs tools to 'make it' in the larger world."[36]

Both physically and spiritually, *that* "larger world" is unfit for human habitation.

What to Do

The biloquialist's favorite counter-punch, when he is backed into a corner, is the question "If not biloquialism, what?" and he pretends, if his critic does not spin out a detailed scheme for curing all the ills of education, that in the absence of such a scheme doublespeak remains the best available policy for English teachers. The pretense is foolish, like doublespeak itself. Whatever English teachers ought to do, they ought not to follow the biloquialist, and the mere establishment of that fact is a positive contribution. To know what's not good is part of knowing what is.

The cornered biloquialist will often make his question more specific. It's all very well, he will concede, to expose linguistic prejudice as an instrument of repression and to work for social justice, though he himself may not be notably active in either cause; but in the meantime, he asks, what will become of students who don't learn standard English?

The beginning of a sufficient reply is that the advocate of doublespeak must answer the question too, since there are probably more biloquialists than doublespeakers whom they have trained. In the foreseeable future there will always be distinctions in speech between leaders and followers, between workers at different jobs, residents of different areas. And in a healthy society there would be no great harm in that. Millions of people in this country today do not speak standard English, and millions of them, if they are white, have very good incomes. But in job-hunting in America, pigmentation is more important than pronunciation.

There is not, moreover, and there never has been, a serious proposal that standard English should not be taught at all, if for no other reason than because its teaching is inevitable. Most teachers of English speak it (or try to speak it); most books are written in it (somnigraphy being sadly typical); and since every child, if it is possible, should learn to read, schoolchildren will see and hear standard English in the schools as they also see and hear it on TV. Inevitably their own linguistic competence will be affected.

The effect will be best if teachers consciously recognize the frustrations and contradictions which life in a sick world imposes on them. Because our ruling class is unfit to rule, our standard language lacks authority; and because our society has been corrupted by the profit-seeking of technology run wild, an honest teacher cannot exercise his normal function of transmitting to the young the knowledge and values of their elders. In fact, the time may come, and soon come, when an honest teacher can't keep his honesty and keep teaching. At that point, he must make his choice—and take the consequences. So long, however, as he stays in the classroom, he must do his imperfect best while recognizing its imperfection, and must find in that effort itself his escape from alienation.

Specifically, and without pretense:

1. We English teachers must have—and teach—some higher ambition than to "get ahead." We have the whole body of the world's best thought to draw on. The daringly old-fashioned amongst us might even recommend the Ten Commandments.

2. We should do all we can to decentralize power, to demand for ourselves and for other common men some voice in shaping our own lives. Reason enough to say so is the truism that men are not men unless they are free; but if the practical must have practical reasons, we all can see that in education as in everything else, conditions vary so much from state to state, from city to city, from city to country, from neighborhood to neighborhood, that no one policy for the whole nation can possibly work. Decisions about our teaching must *not* be passed down, as they now are, from a tired little mediocre in-group, who in the best of circumstances are so involved in the operation of the professional machinery that they can't see beyond its operation. A useful rule of thumb might be to never trust a "leader in the profession."

3. As politically active citizens, we must do whatever we can to end the social isolation of "substandard speakers," so that differences

in speech, if they do not disappear of themselves, will lose their stigmatizing quality.[37]

4. As English teachers we should teach our students (and if necessary, our colleagues) how society uses language as its most insidious means of control, how we are led to judge others—and ourselves—by criteria which have no real bearing on actual worth. We must stigmatize people who use dialects as stigmatizing; and if that means that we as correctness-mongers get blasted too, then we deserve it.[38]

5. We should teach ourselves and our white students something about the lives and language of black people. For communication between dialects, receptive control is what matters. In the United States, most black children are already likely to understand most kinds of English that they hear from whites. Presumably white people have the intelligence to learn to understand the blacks. The Center for Applied Linguistics may even be capable of learning that white ignorance is a bigger obstacle to social justice than black English is.

6. In teaching our students to read and write, our aim should be to educate them, to open and enrich their minds, not to make them into usefully interchangeable parts in the materialists' insane machine. We should know and respect our children's language as we demand that they know and respect our own. And we should make no harsh, head-on attempt to *change* their language, to make them speak and write like us. If they value our world and what it offers, then they will take the initiative in change, and we can cautiously help them. But we must stop acting as the watch-dogs of middle-class correctness and start barking at somnigraphy.

7. As teachers and as citizens, we must defend the freedom of inquiry and the freedom of expression. Neither is absolute, and it is often hard to strike a balance between the demands of the society that pays us and the intellectual duties of our calling. It is clear, however, that subservience to government and indifference to social need will alike corrupt inquirer and inquiry and thus endanger the freedoms that no one else will cherish if we don't. When we allow our choice of studies to be governed by government subsidy, we have committed ourselves to the ends of the subsidizers. When pure curiosity guides us, we tacitly assert that the satisfaction of curiosity is more important than any other purpose that our research might serve. Along both roads we are likely to meet the amoral intellectual, whether for hire or self-employed. The prime contention of this indirect

review is that the biloquialist, by his acquiescence in the abuse of standard English as a weapon, forfeits some part of the respect which otherwise would be inspired by achievements which are sometimes brilliant, like Labov's. For despite the politician's scholar who says that scholarship is politicized when scholars question his privy politics, scholars *are* teachers, and scholar-teachers citizens.

Notes

1. Roger W. Shuy, *Discovering American Dialects.* Champaign, Illinois: National Council of Teachers of English, 1967.

2. To list the cited works more formally:

Alfred C. Aarons, Barbara Y. Gordon, and William A. Stewart, eds., *Linguistic-Cultural Differences and American Education.* Special anthology issue of *The Florida FL Reporter,* Vol. 7, No. 1 (Spring/Summer, 1969).

James E. Alatis, ed., *Linguistics and the Teaching of Standard English to Speakers of Other Languages or Dialects.* Report of the Twentieth Annual Round Table Meeting on Linguistics and Language Studies. Washington, D.C.: Georgetown University Press, 1970.

Frederick Williams, ed., *Language and Poverty: Perspectives on a Theme.* Chicago: Markham Publishing Company, 1970.

Denis Lawton, *Social Class, Language and Education.* New York: Schocken Books, 1968.

William Labov, *The Study of Nonstandard English.* Champaign, Illinois: National Council of Teachers of English, 1970.

Thomas D. Horn, ed., *Reading for the Disadvantaged: Problems of Linguistically Different Learners.* New York: Harcourt, Brace & World, 1970.

Doris V. Gunderson, compiler, *Language & Reading: An Interdisciplinary Approach.* Washington, D.C.: Center for Applied Linguistics, 1970.

3. Labov has repeatedly said as much, most recently in "The Study of Language in its Social Context," *Studium Generale,* 23 (1970), p. 52: "We have not encountered any non-standard speakers who gained good control of a standard language, and still retained control of the non-standard vernacular." The goodness of the acquired control of the standard language will not easily be assumed by students of hypercorrection, readers of H. C. Wyld on "Modified Standard," or teachers of Freshman English in state universities.

4. Roger W. Shuy, "Bonnie and Clyde Tactics in English Teaching," in Aarons, Gordon, and Stewart, *Linguistic-Cultural Differences and American Education,* p. 83.

5. Readers may satisfy themselves of the truth of this proposition by examining the table of contents in Walter A. Wolfram's *Sociolinguistic Description of Detroit Negro Speech* (Washington, D.C.: Center for Applied Linguistics, 1969) or by reading Wolfram and Fasold, "Some Linguistic

Features of Negro Dialect," in Fasold and Shuy, *Teaching Standard English*, pp. 41ff. A much more extensive work is the *Study of the Non-Standard English of Negro and Puerto Rican Speakers in New York City* by Labov, Paul Cohen, Clarence Robins, and John Lewis (2 vols.; Columbia University, 1968); but Chapter III of their first volume, "Structural Differences between Non-Standard Negro English and Standard English," is very far from a "complete" grammar of either dialect.

6. William A. Stewart, "Urban Negro Speech: Sociolinguistic Factors Affecting English Teaching," in Aarons, Gordon, and Stewart, *Linguistic-Cultural Differences*, p. 53.

7. Dr. Rosenbaum's oration in the twentieth Round Table report deserves special attention, but lack of space forbids an attractive excursus. A couple of quotations will suggest the orientation of this already eminent "linguistic engineer." (1) "*Learning* means acquiring new or improved control over one's environment. *Teaching* means structuring or manipulating an environment so that a learner through experience in this environment can with facility acquire the desired control" (p. 112). Just how this statement applies to a class in *Beowulf* may be left to Dr. Rosenbaum to explain. (2) "In experimental computerized versions of such an environment being developed by IBM Research, the tutor is a computer itself, communicating with a student by means of a terminal station equipped with a typewriter, tape recorder, and image projector" (p. 116). It would be unkind to blame the tutor computer for Dr. Rosenbaum's prose, since it is well known that he received conventional humanistic instruction at MIT; but even acknowledged masters of inanity might envy the following sentence: "As is understood by all, some students are weaker than others" (p. 114). An antiquated antiquarian (perhaps unduly vexed by the "structuring or manipulating" of the now well-oiled Gulf beaches) must ask forgiveness for doubting that a man who can write like that is likely "to devise a new classroom regime capable of satisfying all major language learning environment criteria" (p. 117).

8. William Labov, *The Study of Nonstandard English*, p. 27; Flannery O'Connor, "A Good Man Is Hard to Find," in *Three by Flannery O'Connor* (New York: New American Library, n.d.), pp. 133, 139, 142, 143.

9. See Labov's "Logic of Nonstandard English," reprinted by Williams in *Language and Poverty* from the twentieth Round Table report.

10. Basil Bernstein, "A Sociolinguistic Approach to Socialization: With Some Reference to Educability," in *Language and Poverty*, p. 57.

11. Siegfried Engelmann, "How to Construct Effective Language Programs for the Poverty Child," in *Language and Poverty*, p. 118.

12. "A Teaching Problem in Nonstandard Negro English," *English Journal*, 56.1312–1314, quoted by Wolfram, *A Sociolinguistic Description of Detroit Negro Speech*, p. 13.

13. "Toward a History of American Negro Dialect," in Williams, *Language and Poverty*, p. 351.

14. "Sociopolitical Issues in the Linguistic Treatment of Negro Dialect," in Alatis, *Linguistics and the Teaching of Standard English*, p. 215.

15. For example, Muriel R. Saville, "Language and the Disadvantaged," in Horn, *Reading for the Disadvantaged,* p. 124.

16. Raven I. McDavid, Jr., "Language Characteristics of Specific Groups: Native Whites," in *Reading for the Disadvantaged,* p. 136.

17. Labov, *et al., A Study of the Non-Standard English of Negro and Puerto Rican Speakers in New York City,* II, 339, 343.

18. Richard L. Venezky, *et al.,* Harry Levin, and William D. Sheldon, in Gunderson, *Language & Reading,* pp. 37, 123, 266, 271.

19. William Labov and Clarence Robins, "A Note on the Relation of Reading Failure to Peer-Group Status in Urban Ghettos," in *Language & Reading,* p. 214.

20. "Some Language and Cultural Differences in a Theory of Reading," *Language & Reading,* p. 80.

21. "Reading: A Psycholinguistic Guessing Game," *Language & Reading,* pp. 107–119.

22. *Reading for the Disadvantaged,* p. 2. Observe the opening for the educationist to decide who gets the works in school because he's disadvantaged without knowing it.

23. See Wayne O'Neil, "The Politics of Bi-dialecticalism" forthcoming, from which I have borrowed the ingenious idea that educational failure might still be political success for the backers of doublespeak.

24. William A. Stewart, "Urban Negro Speech," in Aarons, Gordon, and Stewart, *Linguistic-Cultural Differences,* p. 51.

25. Irwin Feigenbaum, "The Use of Non-standard English in Teaching Standard," in Fasold and Shuy, *Teaching Standard English,* p. 89.

26. Virginia F. Allen, "A Second Dialect Is Not a Foreign Language," in Alatis, *Linguistics and the Teaching of Standard English,* p. 194.

27. John C. Maxwell in "Riposte," *English Journal,* 59 (November, 1970), p. 1159.

28. *Loc. cit.* But I bet you guessed.

29. Fasold and Wolfram, "Some Linguistic Features of Negro Dialect," in Fasold and Shuy, *Teaching Standard English,* p. 80.

30. Robert J. Havighurst, "Social Backgrounds: Their Impact on School-children," in Horn, *Reading for the Disadvantaged,* p. 12.

31. William Labov, "The Non-Standard Vernacular of the Negro Community: Some Practical Suggestions," ED 016 947, p. 10.

32. Robert M. Maynard, "Children Controlled by Drugs," dispatch from Omaha to *The Washington Post,* in *The Austin American,* June 29, 1970, p. 1. Yet they jail the kids for smoking pot.

33. Labov, "The Logic of Nonstandard English," in Alatis, *Linguistics and the Teaching of Standard English,* pp. 28–29. Labov, who here as usual is much above his fellow biloquialists, is criticizing Bettye M. Caldwell's article "What Is the Optimal Learning Environment for the Young Child?" in

the *American Journal of Orthopsychiatry,* 37 (1967), pp. 8–21. *Ortho-* is a bit optimistic when the proposal is to disrupt the families of mothers whom Bettye M. Caldwell has judged inadequate.

34. Kenneth B. Clark, quoted by George H. Henry in reviewing Alvin C. Eurich's *High School 1980* in the *English Journal,* 59 (1970), p. 1165. Henry's review is a splendid denunciation of manipulators inside and outside the NCTE.

35. Edmund J. Farrell, "Industry and the Schools," NCTE *Council-Grams,* 31 (Special Issue for November, 1970), pp. 1–3. Farrell takes a strong stand against the takeover by industry—with the natural consequence that Robert F. Hogan, Executive Secretary of the Council, warns readers to "keep in mind that the point of view is Mr. Farrell's, not a reflection of Council policy or position." When George Henry called it likely that "English will find itself taken over by the USO—Foundation—Big Business—Pentagon Axis," he also said that the appeasing executives of the Council complain only mildly of such barbarian invasions, "because by virtue of being high in the Council one is eligible for a place in the Axis" (Henry, *op. cit.,* pp. 1168–69). But unlike RCA, Henry is not an objective evaluator.

36. Right again: John C. Maxwell, *EJ,* 59 (1970), p. 1159.

37. For such suggestions I have been told both that I believe that English teachers can change the world by political action, perhaps by revolution, and at the same time (because I oppose biloquialism) that I advocate "do-nothingness." Though I hope I have more awareness of human tragedy than to believe that the NCTE, or RCA, or even an Educational Laboratory can abolish pain, I would certainly not teach English if I did not believe that to some small extent English teachers indeed can change the world. If I did not believe that English teachers can act politically for good, by parity of reasoning I would not bother to attack the evil politics of doublespeak. On the subject of revolution, I wrote in the essay which has been criticized as perhaps inciting to revolt that "the only revolution we are likely to see is the continued subversion, by the dominant white businessman, of the political and religious principles on which the nation was founded" (*EJ,* 58, p. 1312). I leave it to the objecting and objectionable biloquialist to reconcile the conflicting charges of do-nothingism and political activism, but I do resent the suggestion that I consider English teachers brave enough to start a revolution. I have never entertained such a false and subversive idea in my life.

38. This suggestion has nothing to do with the self-seeking proposal by foolish linguists that the English language should be made the center of the English curriculum. I would indeed teach prospective teachers of English in the schools a good deal more about their language than they are usually taught now; but only a biloquialist would believe—or pretend to believe—that to suggest a college curriculum in English for prospective English teachers is to suggest the same curriculum for every schoolchild. A "language-centered curriculum" for the schools would be a disaster.

English for Survival
(1975)

In this essay Sledd takes a swing at almost everyone. It may well be his most purely nihilistic writing; yet his simple affirmation that "nobody can teach anybody else to write, but some people can help others learn if both parties have the urge" seems so obvious that it ought to be an axiom of all teaching rather than a point of contention.

As I wrote this lecture,[1] I had on the desk before me *The Chronicle of Higher Education* for September 23, 1974, and its front page took me back a good ten years. There once again was a picture of the Modern Language Association's Executive Secretary, looking as gloomy as if the Ford Foundation had just refused his favorite project; and beneath his gloomy picture was the familiar headline, "Crisis in English Writing." The Secretary had made page 1 by telling the country what every composition teacher knows: "On a national level we have failed to meet the challenge of illiteracy among college-level students." When I got past the headlines, I discovered that he had been even more contrite. He had not only said that "we have failed." "We have failed," he had said; and he had added, parenthetically, that we "have continued to fail."

I had the depressing feeling that I was reliving a past which I had not enjoyed the first time it went by. It was just ten years ago, in the report of the Commission on the Humanities, that spokesmen for the MLA made the same complaint about *their* students' writing. "A majority of college students," our public orators then complained, "do not speak, write, or read their own language well. Graduate instructors who direct master's essays and doctoral dissertations are shocked at the extent to which they must become teachers of 'hospital' English. Yet we are aware that many of these candidates for higher degrees are already" teaching freshmen. "If they cannot recognize and correct their own egregious errors, what is happening to the end-products of their teaching?" Concluding their lament, the Association's representatives confessed that like the rest of us, they had "no panacea to offer." They were certain only that the colleges must not be expected to dirty their hands with elementary composition. "Whatever the causes," they intoned, "correction must come at the lower levels, since by the time students enter college, any bad habits in speaking, writing, and reading have become so fixed and ingrained that colleges can do little more than stress 'remedial' work." In other words, professors of English did not see how they could teach the mass of their students to read and write and did not know why, after twelve or fifteen years of schooling, they still needed to be taught.

The past decade has brought no solution for our problem. On the contrary, the problem has grown worse. Complaints about the "crisis in writing," about our failure, and about the high schools' failure are more widespread now than ever. Roused from the fat dreams of the '60s by the foofaraw, professors who haven't taught comp for twenty years are scuttling noisily from one all-curing nostrum to another while pontificating with accustomed vigor; but as usual a substantial part of the oratory is devoted to the denial of responsibility. In *Time* magazine for November 11, "Maxine Hairston, director of freshman English at the University of Texas at Austin, blames the shortcomings on the fact that high school students do not read as much as their predecessors," and "Robert Hosman, chairman of the University of Miami's English department," announces once again that "the fundamentals are not being taught properly in secondary schools." For exhausted schoolteachers, it would no doubt be amusing to ask Professors Hairston and Hosman what fundamentals are and how much effective teaching of them goes on in their own courses.

It would be amusing, but it really isn't necessary. Teachers already know the answer, and even apathetic students are beginning to catch on. Pressures from those among them who want more and more practical training in writing, the *Chronicle* continues, "are forcing some English departments to re-examine their basic approach to the study of English. The predominant emphasis on literary studies is being challenged." If that is true, as the *Chronicle*'s evidence suggests, then English departments at all levels, from high school on, must have their worries about their future; for many of their patrons want two of the three R's, while many of their faculty manage to believe that their preference for literatizing is in fact a sacred duty. No doubt the colleges will continue to blame the high schools, and the high schools will blame somebody else, perhaps the state departments of public instruction; but buck-passing will get harder as more and more of us are driven to admit that we have not cared much and still know little about teaching young people how to write. The Executive Secretary emeritus of the MLA has phrased his successor's problem neatly. "We have," he says, "a new clientele that doesn't want English the way it has been, and we have a profession that won't have it any other way." Perhaps the perennial crisis in writing has finally gotten out of hand.

It certainly has if students in any numbers are actively seeking the discipline of practical composition, for the profession has not done much to encourage such practicality. The very idea of discipline—even the word itself—has come to be rejected, almost as an obscenity, by many English teachers. English, such teachers tell us, should not be looked on as a subject. Instead, it is an experience, a growth, an unfolding of the personality—or, in more fashionable jargon, an unstructured, experimental, student-centered process of self-discovery. Students themselves should decide what they want to learn and how they want to learn it, and the idea that a teacher ought to teach is only an etymological fallacy. Our real duties are to abet the wordy exploration of souls where there is nothing to be found and to encourage young barbarians to impose on literature whatever meanings help them to best deal with their neuroses. That is creative reading, and writing in a personal voice.

The strongest taste for irony would be satisfied if we should be rescued from such lunacy by our students' insistence that we must teach them something useful; but whether or not we can expect that fortunate humiliation, we can be sure that a country which does not love literature will not support us if we offer only parasitical lit crit or soulful socializing to students who should be learning how clear sentences hang together or how to read a history book or how to write a letter to their congressman. Irresponsible self-indulgence has landed us in a crisis which is not confined to writing. All three legs of the old familiar English tripod are so shaky now that together they will scarcely bear the weight of another year's periodicals from the NCTE.

In the teaching of language in the schools, the two undertakings which have concerned me most in the past thirty years have been the attempt to popularize a series of "new grammars" and the sociolinguistic effort to make minority youngsters "bidialectal." Schoolteachers began to talk about the new grammars in the '40s, when structural linguists joined forces with the educationists who had discovered, at least a century late, that the formal teaching of *traditional* grammars had little or no demonstrable effect on students' speech and writing. The linguists argued that although school grammarians had failed, structural grammarians would succeed; and so for ten or fifteen years schoolchildren and their teachers forgot about nouns and verbs and diagramming and talked instead about Class 1 words and Class 2 words and immediate constituents. Traditional grammar remained the only grammar that most teachers really knew, but they grew ashamed of knowing it.

In the middle and late '50s, the structuralists got their own comeuppance, when Chomsky routed their syntacticians and joined forces with Morris Halle to overwhelm their phonemicists. Instantly the popularizers set to work again. Recycling Chinese boxes into branching trees, conscientious teachers learned a third grammatical system and taught its elements to their charges. The less conscientious took an easier way out. They had been assured that the old grammar was good for nothing; they couldn't or wouldn't learn a new one every ten years or so; and by the middle '60s they were allowing thousands of students to escape effective grammatical instruction altogether.

The Dartmouth Conference and generative semantics finished the job which the educationists had begun. All zeal for linguistics among English teachers cooled notably after Dartmouth; and when the making of generative grammars proved harder than the naively optimistic had expected, and dissension broke out among the generativists themselves, schoolteachers were baffled. Should they try to understand what seemed like a crisis in generative circles? Should they dive into dialects and sociolinguistics? Or should they give up linguistic panaceas and try something else? Whatever their decision, one thing is plain to observant teachers now: after thirty years of confusing innovations, no grammatical tradition of any kind is alive and well in either schools or colleges today. The linguists didn't succeed in establishing the *new* grammars. They did come close to wiping out the old.

Teachers who kept any interest in linguistics in the late '60s and early '70s were likely to be devotees of dialectology, and linguistic entrepreneurs worked vigorously then to revive their industry. "Black English" was the principal object of investigation. Because black youngsters in northern cities weren't doing very well in school, and because some people thought that their language was a principal handicap, the conversation of teen-age gangs was minutely recorded, and the label *Black English* was attached to it, as if Roy Wilkins talked like the warlord of Chicago's Blackstone Rangers. Simultaneously, educationists devised the policy which

they labeled *bidialectalism*—a device for making black folks talk
like white folks so that they could join the whites in promoting
inflation, depletion, pollution, and the exploitation of the undeveloped countries by more subtle forms of slavery. White linguists and
white educators had a field-day, though it is not recorded that black
pupils profited equally.

The debates, therefore, about biloquialism (the new name
which was invented when *dialect* became a dirty word) have not
been debates about linguistics; they have been debates about competing values. Biloquialism rests on the belief that in America the
free, persons who cannot use the language approved by the dominant whites will be forever denied economic opportunity and social
acceptance. They cannot take part, therefore, in the great American
game of getting ahead. Getting ahead is what they want and must
want if they are to be upwardly mobile in the mainstream culture,
with its continuously rising standard of living; and so the duty of
the schools is to teach black youngsters to talk white on all occasions which the white powers consider it worth their while to regulate. Young ladies who drop the final /r/ when they playfully
charge their boyfriends with maternal incest will not get jobs as
telephone girls.

It should be obvious that opposition to such an exploitative
policy is not opposition to the teaching of standard English or to
equal opportunity for blacks. So far as I know, nobody has ever
opposed the teaching of a standard dialect to pupils who want to
learn it; and it is the bidialectalists, and not their critics, who insist
that equal opportunity is reserved for people who talk white. For
my part, I see no point in further argument, since brute fact has
already made a jest of bidialectalism. The insanities of brutalizing
Western materialists are at last destroying the affluent society; the
centuries of world rule by white Europeans lie behind us; and in
the unimaginable chaos of the future our schools can no more make
all young Americans talk white and right than our bombs can make
us loved in southeast Asia. Two hundred years of teaching in a
comparatively peaceful world have left the majority of *white* Americans still using nonstandard English, as the outcry about the crisis
in writing must remind us. In the world we live in now, bidialectalism is sheer hubris.

To turn from the linguistic leg of our tripod to composition is to
turn from general confusion to utter chaos, from neurosis to demen-
tia. The applicators of linguistics have at least been active, and their
activity has stirred up the profession; but in composition there has
been no such general interest. It is true that the MLA, now that it
has been frightened by falling enrollments, is trying to save its hide

by saving freshman English; but when students were plentiful ten or fifteen years ago, the Association did its best to make the teaching of composition another burden for the high schools. Unfortunately, the college professors had taught the high-school teachers, so they in turn knew better how to evade the job than how to do it. They wanted to teach literature, which was all they had been taught themselves. Neither teachers nor professors could even agree in identifying good, bad, and middling themes; and our professional irresponsibility was quietly symbolized when essay questions were dropped from the English Composition Test of the College Board.

They were replaced by an examination in proof-reading and detailed revision—precisely those aspects of writing which matter least but delight testers because they demand the least intelligence and so can be graded easily; and composition bums rejoiced to see their emphasis on niggling vindicated. The bums are the oldest and most numerous of the three schools which have dominated the teaching of composition in my lifetime. They are the virtuous souls who never give and whose own writing is as stiff and splintery as a pine board. In high schools, they tell pupils to write themes with an introduction, a conclusion, and three intervening paragraphs containing possibly three ideas. In colleges, they lower grades by one letter for each misspelled word, assign an *F* for a comma splice, and preside over computerized instruction in writing laboratories where nobody writes. The fundamentalists of the composition trade, they resemble the bidialectalists in their insistence that superficialities are basic; but whereas the bidialectalist offers upward mobility as the carrot to make the donkeys run, the composition bum stands firm for righteous case-forms and pure concords. He spends his whole life in doing badly what ought to be done well after the big jobs have been finished.

The mortal enemy of the fundamentalist is the liberated teacher who tells fools to look in their hearts and write and who gives all *A*'s if he gives any grades at all. I personally prefer the fundamentalists of my own undergraduate days to the libertarians of the '60s and '70s, for the libertarian has never learned that nobody ever found himself by looking. Making anything worth making, out of words or anything else, is always plain hard work, and the best way to find a personal voice is to do the work as it ought to be done. The man who taught me most of what little I know began his teaching with the quiet remark, "Young man, you write abominably." He was correct.

When I got my own first full-time job as a composition teacher some ten years later, the movement to bring classical rhetoric back into English classes was just beginning. It seems to have lost momentum now, but it had the great virtues of providing a rational content for our composition-teaching and of distributing emphasis rationally among the parts of that content. To essentially linguistic denominations like the fundamentalists, the rhetoricians offered the saving knowledge that reading and writing are not language arts but arts of which language is the medium, as the old three-fold division of rhetoric should remind us. But that division, invention and disposition come before expression—finding something worth saying, and organizing it, before wrapping words around it. To the libertarians, the rhetoricians offered both specific means of looking inward and the reminder that communication is directed outward. That is to say, the topics of invention tell us how to tap our own knowledge and experience, how to find what can persuasively be said on a given subject; and the emphasis on persuasion reminds the writer that his act of writing is incomplete until it has prompted the appropriate act of reading. *Time's* November story about "bonehead English" includes an anecdote of a Harvard student who "ran through the streets of Cambridge weeping" because his instructor was unmoved when the student tried to write what he was "really feeling." He was probably not feeling anything much and communicating rather less.

If we look for reasons why so promising a movement as the revival of classical rhetoric has lost its zing, I suppose as good a guess as any other is that teachers can't teach what they haven't learned, and English education has been mainly literary education without the trivium as a foundation. Most people my age began their English studies with a quite a-theoretical history of our literature. We read a great deal, if we were lucky, from *Beowulf* to the twentieth century, and we read commentaries which somehow strung authors and texts together in chronological order through conventionally labeled periods which were all quite correctly classified as ages of transition; but most of us never heard of historiography, and literary criticism was something which W. W. Skeat had preferred not to indulge in. We were either angry or frightened, in the '30s, when we finally heard about the New Critics.

Being moderately young dogs then, we managed a few new tricks; and our next stage is typified, for me, by a remark which I recall from a staff meeting in the '50s. The staff was making up an examination for a course called "Introduction to Literature," and on a dull afternoon nobody could think of anything to ask. "Let's analyze another poem," somebody finally said; and so we did. Some of us were Yalies; some of us had hearkened to the Neo-Aristotelians at Chicago; some of us talked about myths and archetypes; some of us looked for themes—like "Life is a mystery calling to a mystery"—while others thought themes like that were silly as hell; but we all could agree to "analyze another poem" in one way or another, as if the best thing about poems was that they made analyses possible. We had aped the self-importance of our betters.

For all our pedantic conceit, we still had something which we liked to call "respect for literature." Most of us liked to read, and to read the poem which the poet had written—not just to use it as a point of departure for our own fantasies or an ointment for whatever ailed us. I remember my shock, in the middle '60s, when I first began to get students who cared nothing for analysis because, they said, no reading is any better than any other, and the reader is free to choose or invent the interpretation that makes him happiest. I thought—and think—those students were mad and bad, and the only thing worse that I can imagine is what is happening now among my colleagues. In our panic, we have surrendered to anarchism; and to fill our classrooms and protect our jobs, we are offering students whatever courses they will sign up for—except composition. At UT Austin next semester, we will have more students in a course in Vonnegut than in our sophomore survey, five times as many in a course in Tolkien's yarns as in a course in Chaucer; and courses in something called "pop culture" are being invented at every level. With fewer and fewer students in our higher classes, few jobs—or none—for our new Ph.D.'s, no sense of a responsibility to teach ordinary reading and writing to the great mass of ordinary students, and no clear concept of skill or knowledge which all English teachers ought to share, we are peddling intellectual anarchy just because it can be peddled. If we do survive, we don't deserve to.

Amid the encircling gloom, I can draw toward a conclusion, now, by turning my kindly light toward an unkind future. I would be stupidly optimistic to predict that things are going to get better, and arrogant beyond all tolerance to pretend that I know how to make them so. I can only suggest how I think we might meet some real needs in our three fields of language, composition, and literature; and because even those limited suggestions will take me on to uncertain ground, I will make them rather casually, with more concern for brevity than formality. You can then have your turn to tell me how wrong I've been.

I will begin by repeating my earlier statement that nobody, so far as I know, has ever opposed the teaching of standard English to pupils who want to learn it. English is today the world's most popular language—the language of a great literature, the most widely used medium of international communication, and the most accessible storehouse of man's accumulated knowledge, especially the

technological and scientific knowledge that the new nations foolishly think will make them happier. It is a further advantage that
just about all our standard spoken dialects are intelligible among
the educated everywhere, and that edited written English is virtu-
ally uniform throughout the world. For all its advantages, however,
standard English is also an instrument of oppression and exploitation. Like the other standard languages of western Europe, it began
as a clique language, the language of the people who ran the show;
and whatever else it has become after centuries of cultivation by
artists and scholars who served the powerful, it is still essentially
the language of the decision-makers. Forgetting mutability, they
demand its use by everybody who aspires to make decisions; and
they have developed a special variety of their standard, called gob-
bledygook or doublespeak, by which executives and bureaucrats
cheat and baffle honest men. Doublespeak is the greatest possible
abuse of language—an infinitely graver offense than inelegant grammar. It breaks the social contract which links words to their meanings, so that words must be interpreted not as symbols but as symp-
toms. Man's most essential activity, his speech, is thus rendered no
more significant than the barking of a dog.

It is not enough, then, to say that we will teach a standard dialect to pupils who want to learn it. We must teach those styles and
uses of the standard *which serve good purposes,* and we must teach
even them in full awareness of the limits of our power. Students
who need and want to learn a standard dialect *will* learn it, at least
to some extent; and we can help them. Students who do not need
or want to learn such a dialect will *not* learn it, and we can't make
them. To say then that the non-learners will be forever denied economic opportunity and social acceptance is just as stupid as it
would be to say that nobody can vote in Albany if his grandmother
was a Methodist.

Should a regent of the University of Texas improbably ask me,
therefore, how I can justify the expenditure of the tax-paying Texan's
money in the teaching of the English language, I would reply in
general that educated men should learn something serious about the
nature of language and its place in human life. In our particular time
and country, good approaches to those central questions are the
study of the nature, history, and social functions of standard languages and the particular history of the rise of English to its present
but temporary status as the most popular language in the world. I am
sure my regent would agree with me that not even a fairly entertaining dialect, like that of the Texas hills, should bar a man from our
nation's highest office. I am sure I would not tell him—and I need not
tell you—that no approach to the study of language will be successful

if it weakly avoids the technicalities of grammatical theory. Though popularizers have indeed destroyed our only live grammatical tradition, the level of theoretical discussion among the competent is far higher today than it was thirty years ago. We ancients can have the pleasure, if we are strong enough, of learning from our juniors.

About the teaching of writing, my chief conviction is very much like my conviction about teaching a standard dialect: nobody can *teach* anybody else to write but some people can help others *learn* if both parties have the urge. We will have our best chance of success if we rouse some student interest by teaching the kinds of writing—if any—that students really have to do in other courses and when they get their jobs. For those students who do need and want to learn, extensive directed practice in addressing a responsive but critical audience of peers and teachers may be illuminated by direct rhetorical instruction; and I myself, in talking about rhetoric, would make a good deal of the concept of controlled or directed inference. You will understand what I mean if you ask yourself what a well-turned literary allusion used to do, or how a sardonic wisecrack can destroy both its object and its suicidal maker, or what you know of Auden and his view of Housman when he says that Housman "kept tears like dirty postcards in a drawer." A writer is trying to tell somebody something, but because he can tell only a little bit of what he wants to tell, he must so choose and arrange and utter that one bit that this reader will tell himself the rest. The writer's work is getting the reader to work with him.

A grammar may also be helpful in teaching composition, because without one, nobody can talk to a student about the linguistic surface of his writing; but ideally the composition teacher would be able to assume a grammar, which he would then proceed to use, not teach. Grammatical nit-picking, of the kind which the Educational Testing Service has most recently encouraged with its new test of "Standard Written English," is not the use of a grammar but its perversion. The new test, you'll remember, consists of fifty items like the following bad sentence, in which the students are bidden to determine whether or not an error is lurking and if one *is* present, where it is:

> The Secretary of State, as well as the other members of the cabinet, were summoned suddenly to the bedside of the ailing President.

Now I myself, if I were asked to judge that sentence, would say that the whole thing is an error. In fact, I probably would say that it is worse than an error. It is a botch. The phrases are prefabricated *(summoned to the bedside; the ailing President);* the phonetic echo in *summoned suddenly* is offensive; and the parenthesis between subject and verb is entirely artificial, put there for the sole purpose of sneaking in the iniquity which the students must sniff out. Two hundred years of teaching have apparently not taught the CEEB and the ETS that students don't learn to write by finding errors which silly people have hidden in silly sentences. Men use language to learn, to teach, to help one another, for innocent play. We *mis*use it to deceive ourselves, to mislead others, to hinder them in their work, to give them pain. And however we use or misuse language, we do not use it without a social context. What we do communicates, as well as what we say. Asking stupid questions on national examinations teaches *pupils* that stupidity is intelligence and invites teachers to cultivate stupidity.

With that outburst I arrive at literature; and in speaking on this last subject, because I've already let myself go on the ETS, I will do the flatly unforgivable and will express some feelings (they are too wishy-washy to be called ideas) which flow from my own life, are quite possibly phony even so, and almost certainly will provoke an embarrassed silence.

However:

As I have said, for five hundred years white Europeans have exploited the other races of the earth. Our craving for more and more *things*—for upward mobility, that continuously rising standard of living, a grosser national product—that lunatic craving compels us to rob and bully and enslave less powerful nations; and yet our craving is itself a form of slavery, an addiction, because it can never be satisfied. The crowds of people who hustle back and forth on New York's freeways, like their counterparts in Texas, detest their way of life but are afraid to change it; and their children, our students, are more and more disoriented and despairing. Nobody who *has* children has missed seeing that despair. Anyone with the guts to look can see it among students wherever he goes—young people who know how crazy the world is, who feel themselves driven to conform to its craziness, yet who want desperately to find that good universe next door where they can believe in what they are and what they do.

It would be preposterous, of course, to suggest that literature can cure these ills, just as it would be grotesque to pretend that a teacher's life-forces are inexhaustible; yet my own needs, if nothing else, drive me to look for ways to keep my balance, for purposes that will make me get up in the morning now that the blind urgency of life has weakened, for some antidote against the poison of preferring death. At the risk of gross absurdity, I suggest that maybe, for some few students and few teachers, good books—and particularly good fiction and good poetry—can be part of a survival kit. Instead of adding bars to their prison by changing their language to make them upwardly mobile, we might give some of our students a hacksaw and a file. We might teach them to read.

I'm not suggesting that we shirk our more prosaic tasks. I put them first tonight, deliberately. And I'm not suggesting the soulful oratory of teachers who like to be called "exciting" as they babble about books. Just as I think a man finds his voice-in-writing, not by looking for it, but by doing the job which brings him to his typewriter, so I think a man can draw strength from his reading only if he learns how to read well. That means hard work, close analysis, and every other practice—sometimes critical theorizing—which promotes understanding without murdering pleasure. Teachers will still have to teach, not vaporize, if they see literature as one means to survival.

I *am* suggesting, to quote myself, that without "parasitical lit crit or soulful socializing," and without neglecting "how clear sentences hang together or how to read a history book or how to write a letter to a congressman," we can and should join some of our students in learning something more. As I have said, we old dogs were lucky because our teachers made us read a lot and read respectfully. I still remember the English textbooks we used in a little Georgia high school in the closing '20s. They were called *Literature and Life;* and just forty-five years after entering Miss Mary Lou Culver's freshman class, I shame myself by suggesting (I think I am following Matthew Arnold) that a better title would change *and* to *for.* Almost none of my adolescent convictions has survived. Like most of my classmates, I suppose, I chiefly regret my cowardice and docility: we didn't do enough of the things that we were told were wrong. Yet somehow we depression babies, the infants of World War I and the adults of World War II, were slow to learn the *distaste* for life, for living, which is everywhere under the deceptive surface of our children's days. Maybe if we English teachers of all ages would live more ourselves, quit worrying so much about conformity, respond more generously to the rowdy, randy folks whose books we too often neuter and embalm in our courses in literature, maybe then our courses would help an occasional lost soul to abhor the deadly sin of loving what is deadly. Worse than a pratfall—may I say it?—is never getting off your ass.

Notes

1. At the invitation of my friend Morris Finder, "English for Survival" was read to a kindly audience at SUNY, Albany, at Thanksgiving in 1974. It's not the kind of thing that deserves solemn revision or a panoply of footnotes.

Or Get Off the Pot

Notes Toward the Restoration of Moderate Honesty Even in English Departments

(1977)

What follows is a savage attack on English departments as bureaucracies for assuming the corrupt values of the larger society while following the primary rule of all bureaucracies: survive and expand at any cost. English departments follow their golden rule, Serve Thyself ("The Profession serves the Profession"), while refusing to take the teaching of composition seriously because doing so would interfere with that rule. Sledd shoots at the Big Barn and hits many of the larger animals.

This paper has three parts and nothing to do with the assigned topic. It has three parts because it tells why, how, and with what results I most recently milked a billygoat. It has nothing to do with the topic because the questions set for review are trivial.[1] Only one of those questions makes even preliminary sense: "Who do we really serve?" For the Profession at large the answer is clear: the Profession serves the Profession. Given that understanding, we can ask what we propose to do about the situation and what our chances of success may be, but it is contradictory to ask both how we can keep our bureaucracy going and, in the same breath, what we know and what and how we can teach. Nobody can plant salt and harvest watermelons.

Part I: Why?

I went to the goat-yard because I already knew the essential facts of life in English departments, to which most of us belong. By their refusal to accept even minimal social responsibility, English departments are destroying themselves as fast as their worst enemies could wish. For years they have stubbornly refused their basic duty—to teach the mass of the college population to read and write no more ineffectively than the custom of the country dictates. Instead they fill the unread pages of *PMLA* and offer their bemused classes high truths of the imagination—for example, the assertion that *Rip Van Winkle* is a homosexual fantasy in which little men at bowls are in fact little boys at their balls.

And English departments are not alone in their self-serving. The few dozen big universities which set the pattern for higher education in the United States have ceased to be universities and have become research institutes for government, business, industry, the military. Their faculties, even in the humanities, hope to establish positions as the indispensable brains of our interlocking bureaucracies, and, since elementary teaching does not serve that purpose, most professors confine their teaching, if they can, to the higher levels. In fact, they dream of escaping teaching altogether and of devoting themselves to the amoral research and often barren publication which they have defined as their proper duty and the essential means to professional advancement.

By the majority of such entrepreneurs, teachers who actively concern themselves with literacy are considered freaks, either too incompetent to scramble upward in the usual ways or deluded by the real acceptance of ideals which the prudent loudly invoke while they quietly subvert them. In a moment of rare honesty, a much respected junior colleague once put the majority view succinctly when he said that he and other assistant professors wouldn't teach freshmen or sophomores if they could help it because teaching freshmen and sophomores doesn't earn raises or promotions. He had his facts as right as he had his values wrong. Academia's money, such as it is, is mainly in and for research, and (as an emperor once said of his revenue from an unsavory tax) the careerist can bear the stink if he hears the chink. We composition bums are as stupid as such people say we are if we expect them to reform themselves, and cowardly if we don't fight back when they frustrate our best efforts.

Our present hope—I almost said our last hope—is to generate public pressure for forced change against the obstructive will of careerists, bureaucrats, and the professional societies they dominate. Most of what English departments do today might just as well be left undone. Our haphazardly trained majors are commonly unemployable, unless they escape the welfare rolls temporarily as our graduate students and teaching assistants, and our graduate programs are reproductive only. Designed for self-perpetuation, they do nothing to increase the Gross National Product, to terrify those who threaten its annual growth, or—despite our soulful claims—to preserve the wisdom of the race by maintaining the continuity of the great traditions. The public is unlikely to support us in our inutility much longer, just as it is unlikely to provide professorships, when we are gone, for the mob of graduate students whom we have taught to want them; but a technological society does need literate upper underlings, and knows it needs them. English faculties can therefore save their jobs and—with the least knack for subversion—the best of their ideals by becoming *teaching* faculties, primarily teachers of freshmen and sophomores.

No one imagines that so drastic a change will be easily accomplished. But if the departmental bureaucracies, despite all we can do, still frustrate such reforms, the remedy is clear, though it would instantly reduce departments of English to vestigial status. The job of teaching freshmen and sophomores to read and write should be taken away from English departments and assigned to some other entity, perhaps a new one, which will not make it a mere excuse for recruiting an army of teaching assistants to fill the professor's seminar. Meanwhile, on the larger scene, we should press for decentralization, for the transfer of public support from the big universities to the colleges and junior colleges where teaching is still a respected activity. The function of research in colleges and universities, as distinct from research institutes, should be reevaluated, and the businessmen who most profit from research should be made to pay most for it.

Briefly, since the organized professional academic and the professional academic bureaucrat have proved themselves irredeemable enemies of education, we should make the case for reform before our fellow citizens and our elected representatives. If that effort also fails, it would be *sauve qui peut* for Anglicists of moderate honesty.

Part II: How?

Though the causes which set me to billygoat-milking operate at most of our big universities, one milks a goat where one finds it. I happened to find mine at the University of Texas at Austin; but the *cabron* is no more plentiful there than on most campuses, and my remarks will be totally misunderstood if they are taken as an attack on the university which pays my generous salary. There would be no point in making an argument from the one example I know best if I did not also make the secure assumption that in its neglect of composition, the University of Texas is typical of our big state unmental institutions.

I first tried hard to counter that neglect in the spring of 1969, when a new chairman rashly asked me to direct our freshman English program. Since then there have been two more chairmen, two more directors, and innumerable battles among rival ladies; but the situation in freshman English remains basically the same. The ranked English faculty at UT-Austin talks piously about the importance of composition and joins in the great hullabaloo about a "crisis in writing," but complaining that students can't write and helping them to learn are two very different activities. Our ranked faculty enjoys the first and scorns the second. Teaching assistants— 157 of them the last time I counted—teach almost all our freshmen and most of our sophomores.

Many of those TA's are unprepared to teach. Some hold only bachelor's degrees. Many have never taught before they enter our salt mines. And since most of them get their teaching assignments on the weekend before classes start, they are commonly just a few jumps ahead of their students. Paid for a twenty-hour week, they must often work thirty hours or more. In addition to their teaching, they are required to register for a minimum full load as graduate students, since the more graduate registrations we can show, the more money we get from the legislature for faculty salaries. Bad morale is not improved by the refusal of ranked faculty to accept TA's as genuine colleagues, by the knowledge that jobs are scarce for new M.A.'s and Ph.D.'s in English, by the obvious willingness of regents and administrators to keep admitting more freshmen than there is money to educate, and by the general bland denials that anything is wrong.

Such denials are as automatic as sneezing in bright sunlight, and after six years of exposing their falsehood in every possible campus forum, I finally decided, in the fall of 1975, that the argument for keeping university problems within the university family is in fact an argument for doing nothing to solve them. Only a slow learner would have tried so long to reason with irrationals. In the preceding spring, I had organized a survey to determine what kinds and amounts of writing UT's students in different fields and at different levels really have to do, and what kinds and amounts of help they get in doing it. The results had been shocking. About the same time, the English

department had once more proclaimed its devotion to composition—
but had refused to require each of its members to teach a writing
course so much as once every three semesters; and, as the new academic year began, a new president of the university had defended its
indefensible abuse of teaching assistants. I made one last speech in
a faculty meeting, got no support (as usual), and set out to publicize
the results of my survey and their underlying causes.[2]

Lots of writing courses, the survey showed, were being offered
on the Austin campus. There were over a dozen in the English
department alone, and a good many others elsewhere, especially in
the expanding School of Communication. As one has to expect in
an outsized university, however, the left hand was not allowed to
know what the right was up to. Even within English, it was hard to
find anybody who really knew what went on in the department's
various writing programs, and disagreement over values, aims, and
methods was so intense that the very notion of English as a
definable subject looked ridiculous.

The efforts of the writing teachers, it turned out, had not produced much satisfaction with the quality of student writing.
Though faculty and students agreed that the ability to write is
important to success at the university and afterwards, 709 of 1,365
faculty respondents said that undergraduates generally write rather
poorly; 164 voted for "quite," not "rather"; and only 52 called
undergraduate writing "good" or "very good." The remaining 440
took the Laodicean way and plumped for "adequately."

The lukewarm or indifferent respondent was clearly in the
minority on a faculty which knows that writing should be taught,
though it may not want to teach it. Over 450 faculty respondents—
about one in three of those who answered the questionnaire—took
time not just to put marks in the appropriate blanks, but to add
some connected comment. Personal letters prompted over 125 addi-
tional replies, some of them as long as three or four typed pages.
The characteristic adjective for student writing was "appalling."
One professor spoke for many in the brief complaint, "Students can
neither write nor speak their native language well." A colleague
who asked to see the comments said that reading them was like
sharing a nightmare.[3]

But the respondents' strong feelings did not mark them as soft-
headed. On the contrary, although somewhere between a fourth and
a third of the faculty at UT-Austin don't ask their students to write
at all, those who do ask ask mainly for workaday intellectual prose.
The most common writing assignments are essay questions on examinations (1,029), followed by term papers (729), research papers or
proposals (723), themes or short essays (only 644, although over 10

percent of the respondents were from English), laboratory reports (393), technical reports (348), and case studies (290). The respondents' identification of defects in student writing showed a similar practicality. A whacking 1,274 complained of poor organization, 1,122 of mistakes in grammar and diction, 1,117 of assertion unsupported by evidence or argument, 1,046 of bad spelling and punctuation, 995 of failures in logic, 844 of lack of significant content. Only a few were troubled by more narrowly rhetorical failings—551 by insensitivity to audience, 354 and 283 respectively by inappropriate projection of personality and inappropriate suppression of it.

These commonsensical attitudes probably account for some of the dissatisfaction with the English department's uncoordinated and sometimes unrealistic offerings in composition, especially at the lower levels, where Wonder Warthog provides material for one of the freshman courses and students can get good grades despite sustained assaults on English sentence structure and the English writing system. In any event, when students were asked how helpful freshman English at UT had been, their responses were as follows: very helpful, 206; moderately helpful, 447; slightly helpful, 483; not at all helpful, 394. Of all the students from freshman through graduate, only the freshmen gave the university's basic writing course a favorable majority: very helpful, 65; moderately helpful, 132; slightly helpful, 116; not at all helpful, 52. The more advanced the class, the more dissatisfaction there was, and most students would apparently agree with the professor who said, "More English courses of the type offered now won't help." Some students would accept as their spokesman the disgruntled senior major in psychology, who exploded, "This university doesn't do shit as far as educating people is concerned."

But criticism of the English department was not merely destructive, and judgment of the department not altogether critical. Over three-fourths of the faculty respondents approved of a suggestion that one of the required lower-division courses in English composition should be replaced, at the student's option, with an upper-division course adapted to the student's major.[4] Several respondents commented nobly that the entire faculty, not just the English department, should concern itself with student writing. The comment would be unnecessary if preachers practiced more consistently.

One cannot, therefore, put the entire blame on English for poor writing throughout the university, any more than one can say that English alone abuses the TA system. Of 500 TA's from over 40 departments who responded to a question about their duties, 326 said that they had complete charge of the classes which they taught. In at least one department (accounting), TA's teach over seventy-

five percent of the students—more than TA's teach in English. The
university deliberately phrases its *Handbook of Operating Proce-
dures* so that experienced TA's can teach juniors and seniors as
well as freshmen and sophomores, but conceals the amount of
teaching that TA's do by defining the teacher of a class as whoever
signs the grade sheet. The campus newspaper was thus quite right
when it said that TA's are in fact "the core element" of the university as it presently exists. Without them, the faculty entrepreneurs'
research machine would break down overnight.

Part III: Maybe Next Time I'll Try a Duck

As I turn from the how of my billygoat-milking to the results of the
enterprise, the statement bears repeating that what is true in detail
of UT-Austin is generally true of most big American universities.
My argument would collapse without the recognition that English
among the Austin departments, and Texas among the big universities, are less exceptional than typical. Professorial emphasis on
research is a response to overwhelming pressure from our businessmen, and from their bureaucrats in government, who need research
to exploit the world's resources and the appetites of its people. Our
"crisis in writing" results from the corruption of a whole society.
English departments are blameworthy only because they have not
done the little that they could to resist the rot. I trust I have also
made it obvious, from the fact that I am writing for an audience of
English teachers, that the abuses I am bitching about are institutional, not personal. The presence within the system of better people than the critic who is caught in it too should not protect the
system or obscure the duty to be offended by bureaucracy and to
give offense to willing bureaucrats.

Neither those excellent sentiments nor the admirable tradition
of free speech on the Austin campus turned away all the wrath from
the upper regions when my publicity campaign got underway, but
the most characteristic response was the straight-faced and no
doubt sincere assertion that what is, is not, and what is not, is.
Carefully providing my academic superiors with all the information
that I intended to make public, and routing my communications
through the prescribed academic channels, I was constantly reminded that in guerrilla warfare against the bureaucracy, the bureaucracy has all the advantages—and uses them fully in its great
work of self-preservation. The first blast of my popgun was received
with a loud silence. Documents showing the inability of our undergraduates to write, the refusal of the ranked faculty in English to

teach them, the university-wide abuse of the TA system, and the grand bureaucratic indifference to the whole subject went to the president of the university, one regent, one state representative from the university area, and three newspapers, two local and one in Dallas. The president, the representative, and the three newspapers said nothing; the regent politely acknowledged the communication —and said nothing thereafter. In accordance with the First Law of Bureaucratic Inertia, I was, if possible, to be ignored, like a little boy picking his nose in public.

The silence within the university's sphere of strongest influence contrasted sharply with the responses to two personal letters, one to a liberal state senator from another district, one to the conservative Speaker of the Texas House of Representatives. Both replied promptly and with interest, the Speaker asking for documentation of my charges. He shortly gave me an appointment for an hour's conference, and I then began some hundred hours of work to assemble the evidence I had and to determine the location of evidence the university denied me.

I did not, of course, give up my needling when the systemites ignored me. Though the president and the regent remained and remain silent on their peaks, the newspapers eventually responded to prodding, some of it more than a little impolite, and ran moderately extensive stories; a speech at a professional meeting in San Antonio got some more or less inaccurate coverage on TV there; and the editors of the university's alumni magazine agreed to run an essay, which has since appeared. My noisy persistence finally prompted a series of counter-statements by university administrators.

To detail the charges and counter-charges would most likely provoke the judgment that there is no truth in Texas. Maybe so. If noisiness can draw attention to an educational scandal, I am perfectly willing to be accounted a flaming liar, but my present purpose requires only selected illustrations of bureaucratic tactics for the instruction of others who may still prefer the milking of billy-goats to silent acquiescence in abuses. The great lesson which such babes in the goat-yard must learn is that Kafka's world is Everyman's. For example:

1. By a colleague, one of whose two faces smiles in my direction, I was warned in advance that the English department's defense would be to deny that my survey (which the department had joined in sponsoring) had any significance. Even a flaming liar was amusingly surprised by the nature of the denial. An Austin newspaper had published my statistics showing faculty discontent with undergraduate writing. The answer by the depart-

ment's official spokesman was that the figures were "skewed" because "teachers are naturally critical of students' writing." From that premise it would follow that composition should not be taught since it cannot be taught fairly, but presumably the argument was meant to prove that the English department's composition programs are above criticism, since criticism of their results is unfair by definition. In other words, the bureaucracy can do no wrong.

2. To my charge that TA's are often not qualified for the teaching they are asked to do, a Higher Power replied in part (in the same newspaper story) that "in English, only TA's with master's degrees are hired." The statement was proved false by statistics from the office of the same H. P., but as usual the H. P. showed no embarrassment when the falsehood was called to his attention. He simply shifted his ground and said that *most* assistants in English have their M.A.'s. In short, the premiere university of the Southwest *almost* conforms to the standards of the Southern Association of Colleges and Schools, which has said that all college-level teachers in the humanities "*must* have master's degrees" (emphasis added). (Over the entrance to the Main Building at UT-Austin there is the inscription, "Ye shall know the truth, and the truth shall make you free." The president of the student body proposed a change to "Money talks.")

3. An even greater Great Mogul responded to my statement, made on the authority of the director of our Center for Teaching Effectiveness, that TA's teach over sixty percent of all undergraduate contact hours at UT. The response was that "this fall . . . TA's taught 15.9 percent of the undergraduate credit hours." The reply seems devastating—until one asks the difference between credit hours and contact hours. When I made precisely that inquiry, I discovered that the University defines "to teach," in the Mogul's defensive statement, as "to sign the grade sheet." It would thus be possible, by the simple device of having a ranked faculty member sign the grade sheet for a TA's class, to assert that the TA who had done all the teaching had done none, while the faculty member who had done none had done it all.

So the argument has gone on the UT campus. I have still had no forthright response from colleagues or superiors. Not the least attempt has been made to silence me, but within the university I have met resistance far more effective than censorship: my charges have either been ignored or contradicted with small regard for fact. The experience has been like diving head first into a smothering mass of eiderdown.

The state's elected officials have continued to react quite differently. The Speaker of the House of Representatives has initiated a
study of the TA system at UT-Austin and at other state-supported
universities. The initially silent representative, when I got the
chance to discuss my argument in personal conversation, agreed to
support the study and has so informed the Speaker. None of the
legislators has either affirmed or denied that my charges are just,
but they have taken a serious protest seriously and have set out to
learn for themselves what the facts may be.

I think it is deeply significant that elected office-holders have
been so concerned for the truth which scholars' lives are supposedly dedicated to searching for. Whatever the ultimate verdict in
the case I have made, I have found legislators more accessible and
openminded than university authorities.

Point of Arrival

The Profession serves the Profession. Of that, as a third-generation
academic, I am now quite sure; and the comical story of one aged
child's crusade renews my conviction that the big state universities
have become enemies of any education which I value, and that the
only way to change them is to bring outside pressure so powerful that
they can't resist it. Such pressure will not come from big business
and its entrenched officialdom, which have been the principal agents
in turning the universities into research institutes, or from the professional societies, whose solemn troops can be counted on to defend
the educational establishment. We are left with the appeal to undergraduates and their parents, who pay high prices for a shoddy education; to the taxpayers at large, who want accountability; and to
their tax-levying representatives (*not* government bureaucrats), who
will act if the electorate demands it. We must look to the common
people whom our mandarins despise.

The basis of the appeal, for us in English, must be service—
service to the still widespread ideal of literacy, though humanists
may value literacy for one reason and the Middle American for quite
another. That means that we must no longer listen to the soulful,
whose self-indulgent "commitment to literature" has done nothing
much for literature and substantially less for literacy, or to the mandarins (the Brains of the Machine), who laugh at the ordinary tax-
payer and his representative as a couple of rednecks and insist that
universities must be autonomous, resolving their own problems in
their own independent way. We will do nothing for literature, literacy, or our own secure employment if we refuse to say, with the

Prince of Wales, "Ich dien." Either we serve, as public servants should, or we will soon be as vestigial as he is. Our hope, as I have said, is in precisely the social and political pressure which we have been taught to fear.[5]

Notes

1. The paper was written for a panel on "Composition as a Basic Academic Discipline" at the 4C's meeting in Philadelphia, 25–27 Mar. 1976. As it turned out at the last minute, nobody would pay for my airline ticket, but I sent the paper to the chairman of the panel anyway. The questions for review were these: "What do we *really* know? What should we *really* teach? How should we *really* teach? Who do we *really* serve? How should we *really* manage our programs?" The last of those questions was interpreted as dealing with "workshops and panels on teacher training, unionism, part-time teachers, graduate programs, in-service training, restricted budgets, legal challenges, extramural teaching, enrollments, professional rewards, hiring techniques, and our relations with other departments." I interpret the interpretation: How can we keep our bureaucracy going?

2. My amateur standing as a pollster is unchallenged. Recognizing from the beginning the undefined discrepancy between what academics *say* they do and what they do in fact, I still set out to learn, in the first instance, what academics at the University of Texas at Austin, both students and teachers, say they do about teaching and learning to write; I did not have the means to study direct evidence of actual practice, but I hoped to draw some plausible conclusions by inference both from thirty-five years of varied personal experience and from the expression as well as the content of informants' answers.

Course descriptions, syllabi, and textbooks were easily gathered from members of the English department, where I myself had taught at every level for a dozen years, including two as the director of the freshman courses. Other departments in the College of Humanities were also moderately familiar ground; but when I tried to imagine the very different worlds of scientists (real and behavioral), of accountants, nurses, social workers, pharmacists, architects, engineers, educationists, mathematicians, and all the other tribes which compose the academic non-community, I realized freshly that bureaucracy is nearly invincible because the multiversity is wholly incomprehensible. I wrote letters of inquiry to deans, chairmen, directors, and other personages; to unofficed friends and acquaintances whose duties and experience seemed likely to have given them special knowledge; to teachers of courses whose titles in schedules and catalogues suggested some special concern with writing; and to teachers in charge of multi-sectioned courses whose large enrollments might or might not allow much writing or much similarity in procedure from section to section.

The scores of generous responses brought a great deal of information, and a small number of personal conferences added their bit, too; but I got the feeling that the people who answered most freely and fully were those like myself. I was seeing only that part of the whole picture which I least needed to see, and I was getting almost no statistics. One questionnaire addressed to the whole faculty, and another to a sampling of students, came to seem necessary if the results of the survey were to be really useful. Accordingly, I framed two questionnaires, which Susan M. Hereford, Associate Director of our Measurement and Evaluation Center, translated into such form that the collected data could be coded and keypunched and subjected to computer analysis. Ms. Hereford reports that "completed questionnaires were returned by 1,454 members of the teaching faculty, reflecting a response rate of approximately 48 percent." Student responses numbered 2,484—a response rate of almost 50 percent. All statistical work was done and reported by Ms. Hereford and by Bernard Yancey, also of Measurement and Evaluation, so that the results would not be affected by any bias of my own.

The survey was approved by the president of the university, and sponsored and funded by the College of Humanities and the English department. Officials of the English department, however, made light of the results (without seeing the most telling of them) when they turned out to be damnifying.

Full statistics and copies of both questionnaires are now available in a report by Ms. Hereford (Measurement and Evaluation Center, 2616 Wichita, The University of Texas at Austin, Austin, Texas 78705).

3. Of the following comments by faculty members on undergraduate writing, no two are from the same department. Over forty departments are represented. And there are a lot more comments where these came from.

Dean: "It seems to me that the quality of writing being done in the university is declining."

Professor: "Students can neither write nor speak their native language well. We need more emphasis on undergraduate education in this university. Too often, we graduate a near-illiterate technician."

Associate professor: "Most of my students write poorly."

Assistant professor: "Most students can apparently neither read nor write."

Instructor: "A university is supposed to educate students. A person who cannot spell, write correctly connected sentences, or translate his thoughts onto paper cannot really be considered educated. The bulk of my lower-level students suffer from one or more of these inabilities. I consider this a major shortcoming of our 'educational' system."

Teaching assistant: "Undergraduates in my field generally write horribly."

Associate professor: "We cannot expect graduate students to do what we do *not* train undergraduates to do."

Associate professor: "'Graduating' students at UT cannot write."

Professor: "Lucid and organized expression is mainly lacking in most students—graduate and undergraduate."

Associate professor: "In fact, we need refresher help for faculty."

Professor: "More English courses of the type offered now won't help."

Associate professor: "I am appalled to find that even doctoral dissertations in English (written by T.A.'s who are teaching our students) are full of errors in grammar, syntax, punctuation, and organization."

Assistant professor: "After passing twelve units of English at UT, many students are still *totally* incapable of organizing and writing meaningful essays, reports, etc."

Teaching assistant: "I am most concerned about students' poor writing because many of our students plan to teach. Not only have these students been poorly prepared for composition, they will perpetuate a deemphasis on writing skills when loosed upon the school system."

Professor: "Courses are needed which heavily emphasize writing and composition. Somewhere a student must be taught to write clearly, logically, and grammatically."

Professor: "Prospective employers I have talked to have been unanimous in their assessment of the situation. Students have a very poor ability to express themselves either orally or in writing. They would be much more valuable to the employer if they had the ability to communicate effectively."

Associate professor: "They will need to be able to address themselves to a nontechnical reader on practical matters in a clear, concise, and well-reasoned way. Our students get little practice in this kind of writing."

Assistant professor: "A holder of a B.A. who cannot express himself in a clear and forceful way in his own language has been swindled."

Lecturer: "My graduate students come from a variety of backgrounds. When the research is done and it is time to write the thesis or dissertation, there are always problems. The students can't express themselves clearly, concisely, accurately."

Teaching assistant: "My students are all in elementary education and I am amazed at their lack of command of the language."

Professor: "Student ability in basic grammar and spelling is absolutely essential in my field, but that ability is at a lower level each year."

Associate professor: "I think there has been a steady degeneration of writing skills in the last several years, especially among undergraduates."

Assistant professor: "UT students seem to have more trouble with the English language than the students I have taught elsewhere."

Professor: "Many (most) law students write quite poorly."

Associate professor: "The chief problem in my work is that many students lack precision in what they write and say, and are unaware of the precision intended in statements made to them in class and in the textbooks."

Assistant professor: "My upper division students have *never* had an essay exam, nor have they ever written a research term paper, nor do they know how to use the libraries. They do not know English grammar or how to organize their arguments in a logical, concise presentation. It is appalling."

Assistant professor: "Many of my students have very poor communication skills (verbal and nonverbal)—yet they want to become teachers."

Assistant instructor: "I am aghast at the poor writing I see in my sophomore courses."

Teaching assistant: "Few of my students use what I consider to be college-level, literate English."

Professor: "The principal remedy in my field would be having classes small enough so that written assignments would be feasible. At the present time, I cannot do a responsible job of criticizing the writing of undergraduate students."

Teaching assistant: "More important than lack of writing ability is lack of *reading* ability. Who's going to do something about that?"

Professor: "They simply can't write a decent sentence."

Associate professor: "I have repeatedly been appalled at the low standards in spelling, formatting, sentence structure, logic of overall development, and mere neatness of papers submitted to me."

Assistant professor: "The large majority of students cannot write effectively."

Assistant professor: "The inability of students to express themselves (in either written or oral form) is simply staggering."

Assistant professor: "No one seems to be able to write *interesting* papers."

Teaching assistant: "Most of my students cannot write."

Teaching assistant: "I find my students unable to write clear, *one-sentence* answers."

Teaching assistant: "Students can't seem to communicate at all on the written level."

Teaching assistant: "They cannot think, cannot write, cannot read."

Assistant professor: "If a student cannot write clearly, intelligently and grammatically, then his thinking is unclear, disordered, and immature."

4. The committee of the English department to which this suggestion was referred rejected it, on the grounds that upper-division courses would be less pleasant to teach if they were required.

5. There may as well be a sting in the tail. Statements similar to those in note 3 above have been made for years—and consistently ignored. Thus: Beginning in 1967, the English department set out to reduce the university requirement in composition, which the department doesn't like to teach. At one point in the ensuing debate, *over sixty members* of the humanities faculty *voluntarily signed a public protest* of the department's action. Of the proposed reduction in the composition requirement, the sixty-odd protesters wrote: "The average knowledge of the English language possessed by our entering freshmen is already so woefully inadequate as to suggest that any reduction in the present requirement would be grievous."

And the public protest was by no means the first warning the department had received. When the department was planning its reduction in the composition requirement, it solicited opinions from deans and departmental chairmen. It ignored these, too, but here are some of the opinions that it got:

"I am often shocked to find out that students have not done *any* writing of papers before taking a philosophy course."

"I would like to see an English proficiency standard set, both for grammatical and technical matters as well as in composition and expository writing. Too many of our students get a smattering of education in this area, with no real achievement standards having been met."

"The English courses would be doing us all a service if they could teach students how to write decent prose. But that may be an impossibility."

"Many of the students are fearfully inadequate. Spelling, sentence structure, vocabulary—the bare elements are often lacking."

"Grammar and composition are the main defects—more work needed here, even among juniors and seniors."

"I have felt for years that our students need desperately as much more work in *composition* as can possibly be arranged. Very few can communicate intelligibly on exams or in papers."

"Our greatest concern is with the basic fundamentals of composition. We find that more and more of our students come to us with no understanding of these fundamentals and, even more unfortunately, complete their work and receive their degrees without having gained that understanding."

"In general, science students appear to me to be deficient in grammar, composition, and general understanding of word origins and meanings."

"The principal defect in the present lower-division courses in English lies in the fact that many are taught by TA's."

The total irresponsibility of departments of English—and Texas, remember, is only an example, not the object of special criticism—appears from the fact that they brushed aside all warnings until enrollments began to fall as the sixties ended. Until then, such Eminences as the Commission on the Humanities and the leadership of the MLA had baptized their masses of semi-literate students in crocodile tears while assigning the duty of teaching them to the overburdened high schools. But by the unjoyous Yuletide of 1972, when the MLA had realized that "many institutions of higher education are facing severe financial difficulties," its Delegate Assembly was invited to resolve that the MLA was concerned "at the trend in the U.S. toward abolition of basic requirements in English composition." As Mr. Edgar W. Hirshberg informed our departmental chairmen in the *ADE Bulletin* of December 1972, "In view of the drastic decline in upper division enrollments . . . , freshman English is becoming the chief reason for the continued existence of English departments at their present size in many institutions." (p. 35)

And for the continued existence of departments whose members announce that "composition stinks," *there is no reason.*

And They Write Innumerable Books[1]
(1982)

In this essay Sledd asks the age-old question: Why do we teach writing? He also asks us to consider why we think our students should learn to write, and suggests that the old-fashioned goal of helping students discover a "felt need" is the only truly legitimate purpose. Sledd chastises those who insist on maintaining a system of part-time "slaveys"—graduate students who can only look forward to teaching composition for their entire careers. He suggests that those not genuinely committed to teaching writing would be wise to leave the profession. Those wanting to stay should find their own ways of motivating students and should not rely on formulaic methods such as the writing process—"a vulgarization of Aristotle's topics."

A good deal more than thirty years ago, when I emerged from graduate school with a wife, two sons, and a new Ph.D., universities were just beginning three times as many fat years as the fat cows promised Pharaoh. Meanwhile those two sons have become English teachers in their turn, but the world they work in is grimly different from the world that was when for a second time all wars had just been ended and democracy made safe and when Americans hardly knew the name of the little country which theirs would devastate after only twenty years of the affluent society. When I look at my sons' academic world with the moderate detachment of one whose detachment from it will soon be total, what do I see?

I see first the majority of students whose life has given them no sense of any need to write the kinds of prose that we in English departments want them to. My present freshman class of two Mexican-Americans, three Blacks, and twenty-two Anglos is fairly typical of middle-class Texas. The average annual income of their families is $32,000; most of their parents went to college, and many to graduate or professional schools; and both the parents and the children read for pleasure, though probably not as much as they watch TV. A questionnaire turned up just none of the commonly given reasons for inability to write; but neither did any of those twenty-seven students, all of them of average or superior intelligence, score as much as 550 on the College Board's English Composition Test, and not one reported so much as a single occasion when poor writing had caused him or her any serious difficulty. They are taking composition only because they have to. Like the banker who told me that bad grades in Freshman English had not kept him from becoming a vice-president, my students are convinced that English teachers are a little odd. Some of them report that their other teachers, who require no great amount of writing, are of the same opinion.

Wider experience might of course have changed my students' judgment. Whatever executive types may really do in what they think is the real world, they're fond of saying that communication's the name of their game, and at least some segments of our society do value and sometimes demand the ability to write workaday academic-professional prose. In particular, there are colleges which demand such prose of freshmen and use the failure to write it as reason to punish and reject. They make the freshman composition course a filter to strain out the oppressed, whose world has given them no chance to learn what they are punished for not knowing. Open admissions then become a trap. Minority students are admitted, even recruited; but when they cannot do what no one thinks they can, they serve their time in bonehead English, flunk out, and get sent home marked "Failure."

One group of academics sets its hopes considerably higher than the ability to write bread-and-butter prose. Some of our most intelligent and cultivated colleagues (the word *cultivated* dates its user) talk about writing not just as a way of knowing but a way of being, and exhort their pupils, in all earnestness, to find, create, announce themselves, in weekly themes. I cannot call those exhortations nonsense. I still remember a theme I wrote, in 1932, about a river I had fished in northwest Florida; and thirty years later my second son, as a senior in high school, wrote a paper that I wish that I had written, about a soon-to-be-desecrated valley in California's High Sierras. Loves strong enough to link the generations can be shaped and

spoken in a classroom exercise. Only this year, when an inept syl-
labus demanded an inductive essay, a lanky, awkward, hill-country
Texan wrote me ten pages to tell how as a boy he had learned to
trap a fox. He will remember what induction is, long after his
trapping-grounds have become a subdivision.

But my examples are nostalgic. If there really is such a thing as
a literacy crisis, my generation of literary academics helped to cause
it; and my sons' generation, whom we prepared to teach nothing but
literature (or indeed to teach nothing if they could escape the classroom altogether), must set up shop today as composition specialists
or technical writers. Even if they manage to justify their claims to
those once scorned and rejected titles, they will find no gold-brick
roads to the land of their dreams. Their seniors will continue to
despise composition-teachers, and for some years those seniors
will still dominate a professional structure which systematically
penalizes the teaching of undergraduates, especially the teaching of
freshman composition. The big pattern-setting state universities are
not really universities any more. Instead they have made themselves research institutes for government, business, industry, and
the military; and the professors' goal is to be the brains of the great
interlocking national bureaucracies—and to be rewarded with an
appropriate share of The System's goodies. In an advanced technological society, the scientists may well be able to pull that cupidi-
nous trick.

The young humanists' chances for privileged affluence are by
no means good. Even if my generation's leaders had been wise, they
could not have played Canute to the flood-tide of brutal materialism, could not have checked inflation or the decline in the quality
of our lives which profit-seeking guarantees; and in fact our incredible self-indulgence and sullen refusal to meet legitimate social
needs or to adapt to changing circumstances have brought on the
crisis which the young now must suffer. Multiplying mediocre
graduate programs, we devoted ourselves for a full decade to over-
production. We needed graduate students as cannon-fodder for our
seminars and as slaveys to keep us from having to teach freshmen,
and when the graduate students finally caught on and left us, we
found new slaveys among faculty wives and the army of unemployed Ph.D.'s and ABD's. So we created the wage-section or
resource pool, the company of unranked unfortunates who teach
four classes a semester for a thousand dollars a class; and by so
doing we destroyed any plausible argument we might once have
had for our cherished tenure-system, for we cannot claim tenure is
essential to the protection of academic freedom if we choose to have
half our classes taught by people who have no chance for tenure.

We ourselves are reasonably well protected in our ancientry. Instead of firing us, our boards of regents will probably think it less bothersome to let us die on the vine; but new Ph.D.'s will have to play dog-eat-dog. Even if the outcry about a crisis in writing makes administrations generous, assistant professors now in office will resist the appointment of enough tenure-track competitors to replace the wage-section; and since the professoriat has selfishly argued for years that untrained people can teach freshman composition well enough, the most generous administration is likely to encourage defenestration or maybe operate a revolving door.

The logical consequent choice for the young humanist is to get out of English now unless he or she has a real vocation and the patience to endure. By *a real vocation* I do not mean only the urge to read, the love of good books. I also mean the urge to write as well as one can, and a zeal for literacy (whatever may motivate that zeal) which will survive years of elementary teaching. For as much of the future as it makes any sense to predict, most English teaching in most colleges will be the teaching of freshmen and sophomores, and those who hope to live by such teaching while their hearts are somewhere else will quickly be exhausted and embittered. Unless the country abandons universal education altogether and settles for technocratic rule by one-hundredth of one per cent of the citizenry, the young English teacher's foreseeable future is less likely to be *graduate* studies than *Basic* studies.

That pedagogic territory is uncharted—almost a great blank, like the interior of Africa on old maps; and the teacher who enters it fresh from graduate school will quickly discover that many elephants now trumpeting in the composition-jungle are there just because research in composition is the coming racket, the label *composition specialist* the passport to scarce jobs. I am superior to most of my generation in that I have at least kept trying to teach composition for forty years; I am typical in that I have never learned how to do it.

That is the first bit of practical wisdom that I've gathered—the knowledge that I do not know. I will risk obscurantism by saying that I doubt that anyone knows much (despite much silly chatter about a "new paradigm"), for learning and teaching to write are mysteries, like learning or teaching a native or foreign language. After all, we probably can't *teach* anyone to write, certainly not unless the student wants to learn. If the student lacks that desire, we can do nothing. If the student has it, he or she will not so much be taught as helped in learning.

That help can be of as many kinds as there are students and teachers; for there are no fast, hard rules for people helping people, and if there were, the truly helpful would soon learn how to break them. But the mechanical operators of the Research Machine will see an opportunity in the fact itself that there *are* no universal answers and very little simply formulable knowledge. Research and publication bring promotion; and research and publication, if they cannot give us answers, will provide an endless series of always changing fads, so that one year we will talk about pre-writing and *the* writing process (as if there were just one), and the next year we will clamor for certified assessors of writing quality or shout "One lobe good, two lobes better!" like the sheep on Animal Farm.

The process people are the most tiresome now. They talk about "intervening in the writing process" as if they had made some glorious new discovery, but until they define the indefinable or at least set some chronological limits on it, their catch-phrase is inane. It would make sense to say, for people who really learn to write, that a whole semester is one long writing process, or even a whole career; and a college teacher's best chance to intervene successfully in the production of her students' papers has usually been lost before the students get to college. Even if one arbitrarily limits the writing process to the time between the assignment and the final submission of a single paper, at some point every teacher has always intervened, even if only to require correction and rewriting before assigning a final grade. The real questions have always been when to intervene, and how; and since I am not aware that those questions have been authoritatively answered, I take the process talk as mainly another salespitch. I would never buy an automobile from a manufacturer who told me he was interested in the process, not the product.

Besides the scarcity of knowledge and abundance of fads, most of the researchers in composition and many of its teachers, forgetting that example teaches at least as well as precept, will suffer the further handicap that they themselves don't write—and maybe can't. There is no better suggestion in the "literature" than the old one that teachers should write together with their students; and I would add that students can teach together with their teachers. When both parties want to write, each learns from each and from the other. The old familiar is a good trick for a good class: to keep photocopies of the week's papers in a quiet, accessible workplace, so that students if they wish can add their comments to the teacher's —and to the teacher's writing.

Such public criticism is a good antidote for the kind of pompous self-righteousness I suffer from. To cite an instance: because all of us, however we try to protect our individuality, are subject to the pressures of the encompassing society, we are tempted to evade our moral responsibilities by such devices as linguistic relativism or the proclamation of "upward mobility in the mainstream culture" as a proper motive for learning and teaching. I have made great fun of relativists and the anxious climbers, and I will continue to make fun of them; but it has been good for me to have students ask why then do I resist the imposition of a standard language or how then do I differ from the classic Southern reactionary.

Though I still have no patience with relativism, good linguists have taught me much of what little I know. They can help us think about the nature, history, and social functions of standard languages —essentially instruments of dominance, potentially means to liberation; they can illuminate the problem of the colonial writer or— more generally—of any provincial as he tries to take what he needs from the dominant, perhaps superior culture and its linguistic traditions without betraying himself or his native speech; and they can protect us against fashionable absurdities like the claim that written English—the imperial grapholect—has not significantly changed since Johnson wrote his *Dictionary.*

Of other, more direct applications of linguistic knowledge and method I am often sceptical. For example, though the teacher of composition must have a grammatical vocabulary to talk about the linguistic surface of his students' papers, a grammar should be learned outside the composition class, and learned mainly for its own sake. Without universalizing, one can agree that in present circumstances formal grammatical instruction in the composition class is at best a forced diversion from writing and at worst an actual impediment to it, and I am inclined to pass the same hard judgment on transformational sentence-combining, which strikes me as usually the making of aimless big sentences out of aimless little ones. Neither long sentences nor short ones, Flesch's sentences nor Francis Christensen's, are either good or bad in themselves; and my fogyism is better content with the popular title if not with the popular book: *Writing with a Purpose.*

"*What* purpose?" is of course the great question which we must not dodge by talking about relative readability or the impossibility of agreement in the judgment of semantic intentions; and in a way my objection to E. D. Hirsch is the same as my objection to an equally influential writer whom I deeply respect despite the objection, Mina Shaughnessy. Repeated readings of her book have left me with the unhappy feeling that aside from her hardly original attempt to describe some causes of error, she offered us only some more elaborate ways to teach traditional grammar, no hard evidence that her methods were genuinely successful, and no serious examination of the purposes of the whole undertaking. Hirsch's deep purpose is sufficiently clear: he is the ideologist of bureaucratized assent. So far as I can tell, Shaughnessy asked no questions about the aims of education but instead accepted whatever purposes bring students and teachers together in composition classes and proceeded to devise techniques for reducing the number of conventionally defined errors to a level which middle-class academics might be expected to tolerate. But the CEEB should have taught us long ago that the unexamined examination is not worth giving.

Indeed, if I were addicted to prayer, I suppose my daily petition would be, "Lord, I am tempted to believe; help thou my unbelief." In our world of television and Jimmy Carter [Eheu!— author] and professional societies and advertising, one is driven to the primitive retreat of believing only what one's own experience confirms, and my experience tells me that students may parse like demons and get all their verb-forms right like prosperous white folks yet still be incompetent to write a decent paragraph. For the same reason, I remain sceptical of the presently voguish talk about heuristics. I had the privilege, long ago, of taking a fine seminar with Kenneth Burke, but I've never used his pentad to explore a subject. Such writing as I've done, as a run-of-the-mill academic, has in one way or another been done to order, so that circumstances forcefully hinted at what I should say; and on the occasions when my writing has been to any extent successful, it has been so because my whole mind was involved. When one's mind is fully involved, one wakes up in the middle of the night to write down ideas which have come from God knows where. A fully active mind doesn't need a vulgarization of Aristotle's topics or of Jakobson's analysis of the communication situation, complete with distracting geometric figures.

How does a teacher strike the spark of full involvement? In as many ways as there are teachers and students, as I've said. But experience always brings me back to the matter of felt need. The dentist's son who has written me a dozen adequate, dull papers is a fifth-generation resident of the little town of Marble Falls, twenty miles away from my cottage on the banks of LBJ's Pedernales River. Mr. N wants to be Dr. N, like his father, and he knows that his father fills teeth skillfully but almost never writes. In a university where writing is of no importance in at least one-quarter of the courses, sensible Mr. N will remain content with marginal adequacy. Perhaps his work would be better in a university where at least a whole faculty and its administrators had dramatized their conviction that the ability to write is genuinely important. In such a university

(Michigan once seemed likely to be the first), students might come to share that same conviction and might want to learn to write themselves.

To write? To write *themselves*? That one small difference hints a huge complexity, which we begin to uncover when the making of assignment compels us to ask *what*. Maybe we have the best chance for success if we guide our assignments by our students' likely needs—needs both as students and afterwards, in their careers. Such writing as most of them may do will be that workaday writing, bread-and-butter writing, writing of useful but special kinds which we English teachers often aren't highly competent to teach. Once more, experience points us to the trite but true conclusion that whole faculties must teach composition if it is successfully to be taught. (I grant that Kenneth Burke would need all *ten* fingers to find arguments which might *persuade* whole faculties to that honorable work.)

Of the innumerable ways of helping student writers, the ways that English teachers favor will work best with students like themselves. For some students, the way of self-discovery, finding a voice, is more than a good wallow in egotism, an exercise in navel-watching. They need instruction less than they need a listening ear and grunts of friendly attention. For others among our special audience, the best way may be writing about literature, especially if the literature provides appropriate models. Without lots of practice, there can be no good writing of any kind; and there can be no useful practice without some formed and forming intention, some inner or outer model which the practice looks to.

But *All roads lead to Rome* is a better motto for composition teachers than *Strait is the gate*. Good writing is something made—made by a living human being, who most clearly calls his own number (as Burke says) when he himself doesn't know what his number is. Learning to write is learning to use all one's mind in making. Our enterprise therefore remains as various, as strange, as vexing, as absorbing, as people are; and we will be wrong past all recovery if ever we persuade ourselves that only we are wise. The final importance of our work, if we can keep from freezing in the snowstorm of student papers, is that in our petty way we cannot help dramatizing the essentiality of the free maker.

So I cannot see my sons' academic world as the generally comfortable place my undeserving generation lived in. I would no more blame them if they left it than I would be surprised to see English departments go the way of departments of Latin and Greek. But years spent in teaching composition have not all been wasted [in

1982 I am less self-congratulatory], and I would like to believe that
the best rewards remain though the fat jobs are gone.

Notes

1. This platitudination is a lightly revised version of a paper which I read
to Bernie van't Hul's TAs in Ann Arbor on December 8, 1978. I remembered
it when Elspeth Stuckey asked me for something about basic writing. No
doubt it was unkind to send her a stone when she asked for bread, but
pontificators on the universal evils of universities have at least the rhetorical advantage of being their own best arguments from example.

In Defense of the
Students' Right[1]
(1983)

This is James Sledd at his best, arguing for what should but will not come to pass: respect by The Profession and the professoriate for what Wordsworth called "the real language of men" and what English teachers and linguists call "non-standard English." The "radical" 1974 NCTE statement that insisted teachers respect the language used by their students was never taken seriously by many teachers, but it did cause a furor.

Once again, during our 1993 conversation in Austin, I asked Sledd about the contemporary relevance of this issue that he had raised twenty years earlier:

FREED: This is written in 1983 and that document passed in 1974, I think. Why do you think in '81 or '82 or '83 they were trying to dismantle a document that basically had never been taken seriously?

SLEDD: They thought it had displeased powerful people. You've seen the little green book that the College Board put out on what entering freshmen should know?

FREED: No.

SLEDD: Well, they make the most absurd demands on entering freshmen. All entering freshmen, when they enter, must be masters of spoken and written standard English. Now, these people wanted to be in line with the powerful, who were saying we want a work force which will increase our profits, and in the information age that means people who can speak and write standard English.

FREED: Same old story?

SLEDD: Same old story.

FREED: It's still very strange that they would bother to attack something that had never really had any impact whatsoever.

SLEDD: They would have done much better to ignore it.

FREED: Right. Although, even now—this came out in '83—do you think anybody talks now about students' right to their own language?

SLEDD: Geneva Smitherman probably does.

FREED: Well, I still keep passing the "Rights" statement out to my students to get them to talk about it. I ask students, what does this mean, and they look at me like I'm crazy. "I don't know!" they answer.

SLEDD: Well that's one of the penalties of being sane. The insane have taken over and have locked up the keepers.

Living in the uncomfortable meantime between (on the one hand) the death of world-domination by white Europeans of the capitalistic breed and (on the other) the advent of whatever rough beast eventually manages to get birthed in Beirut or Bethlehem, not-yet-bankrupt teachers of English in the U.S. of A. are constantly tempted to believe, as beneficiaries of evil, that by proper incantations they or their masters can make the dead arise and walk. We are tempted all the more severely because, in the evil old world which for us was not so uncomfortable after all, one socially approved function of the academic humanist was to divert attention from the facts of dominance and exploitation, to provide a veneer of pretty fictions to hide the ugly realities. Telling the truth about English education has always been dangerous in departments of English. Seduced or intimidated, we hold tight to a dead identity because we haven't the sense or courage to let go, to struggle for some possible new being in a world which struggle has not yet created. The reduction of the middle class to poverty may at last beat the nonsense out of some of us, but our conversion would be less shameful if it were willed and willing.

A small step in that direction was that somewhat confused and much berated document of the '70s, the *Students' Right to Their Own Language,* and in the present general retreat from fact to fantasy, it is only natural that the *Students' Right* should be attacked by the very organization which produced it. In a letter of September 30, 1981, William Irmscher of the University of Washington proposed a new statement on "the language problem"—for a "new decade" a "more informed" statement which would reflect "both an idealistic and a realistic assessment of the language situation in this country." . . .

The present essay is an attempt to open the topic to public discussion and to challenge the postulates of linguistic reaction, so that a handful of professors and bureaucrats, frightened by today's predictable response to any defense of freedom for either students or teachers, will not fasten a destructive policy on the tomorrows of a whole profession. If no one harbors such intentions, a public disavowal will be a modest assurance of continuing virtue.

A good beginning is the characterization of standard English which a former president of the National Council published in a Council volume over forty years ago. In the first chapter of his *American English Grammar* (New York: Appleton-Century, 1940), Charles C. Fries defined "the 'standard' English of the United States" as "that set of language habits in which the most important affairs of our country are carried on, the dialect of the socially acceptable in most of our communities" (p. 15); and though Fries could play the already familiar tricks with the word "acceptable," still he acknowledged that as the language of those who claim to decide what the world should accept and what it should reject, our standard English "has become a social or class dialect" (p. 13). In fact, it had been the bosses' language from the beginning. As Einar Haugen has said in *The Ecology of Language* (Stanford, Cal.: Stanford University Press, 1972), the standardized national and international languages have "nearly always been clique languages, either grown up in or regulated by the ruling network of a country" (p. 259). Deliberately unified and cultivated, "they are everywhere the result of a concentration of political power, which establishes dominion over an area in which it is convenient for that power to have a single language for communicating with its subjects" (p. 258). The convenience of those "subjects" (subjects in that sense are treated as objects) is another matter. Centralized administrative power is reflected in the very name—Chancery Standard—for the standardized written English which became common first in official documents during the decades immediately after 1430; and when the critic Puttenham in the sixteenth century characterized the more recently enjoined standard speech, he found it confined to the privileged and powerful in and around the capital city of London, within a radius of no more than sixty miles.

The belief that the linguistic behavior of the bosses is and should be normative was part of the oppressive baggage which the colonists brought with them as they tried to find freedom in a change of longitude. Although linguistic classmarkers have never become so firmly established in the United States as they remain in Britain, where it is estimated that no more than three per cent of the population use the "Received Pronunciation" of the "socially acceptable" (Arthur Hughes and Peter Trudgill, *English Accents and Dialects* [Baltimore: University Park Press, 1978], p. 3), there is nonetheless no question that standard American English also is by its origin and nature a class dialect, essentially an instrument of domination. One must insist that over the years a standard language becomes much more than that; but dominance is still its essence: a class dialect, an instrument of domination. The correlation of linguistic variation with socioeconomic status is a commonplace of sociolinguistics in both Britain and America, despite unsubstantiated mumblings in English departments about an imaginary and unchanging grapholect. . . .

Defenders of established brutalities habitually claim, in contrast, that protest against those brutalities is useless because the brutalities are built into the unchangeable scheme of things. "Inevitable" and "inevitably" are favorite words among such apologists, and the levying of penalties for saying "ain't" is treated, pompously, as an instance of a sociolinguistic universal. Alternatively, the apologists escape the responsibility for choice and action by pretending that the unjust distribution of political and economic power is not the work of cruel and greedy people but results from the accidents of history and geography. Nothing of the kind is true of the establishment, development, use, and abuse of standard languages. Standard languages don't just happen, don't just emerge of themselves and grow like toadstools on a soggy lawn. Haugen is right in saying that they are the result of "deliberate unification and cultivation" (p. 258) by and for the established powers. It follows that standard languages are subject to human control, and the apologists who shout "Inevitable!" when privilege is threatened are in fact language-planners, intent on changing the language of the dominated for the sake of the dominant. The eminent language-planner Charles A. Ferguson made it all quite plain some twenty years ago, in another volume from the NCTE (*Social Dialects and Language Learning* [Urbana, Ill.: NCTE, 1964]). Talking about American ghetto blacks, Ferguson observed that he and his fellow planners had "to face a rather difficult decision as to whether we want to make these people bidialectal . . . or whether we want . . . to impose some kind of standard English on these people and to eradicate the kind of substandard English they speak" (p. 116). He was right at least in that *somebody* had to *do* something. There is nothing inevitable about educational policies toward nonstandard forms of speech and writing or toward the people who use them. Instead, there are human choices to be made—including the choice of who shall decide about whose language.

On one choice, so far as I know, all or nearly all the actual and aspiring decision-makers are in agreement: to the best of my knowledge, there is nobody who would not teach standard English, spoken

or written, to students who want to learn it (just as there is nobody
who *can* teach it to students who *don't* want to learn). The point is
important because spokesmen for the NCTE and the Center for Applied Linguistics have tried to confuse real issues by maintaining that
criticism of their policies is an attempt to deny access to standard
English to some or all users of nonstandard varieties. My own experience is an instance so significant that I will risk the charge of vanity
by rehearsing it here for the benefit of those who cannot acknowledge
that nice people can do un-nice things.

In the *English Journal* in 1969, I published a piece which I entitled "Bi-Dialectalism: The Linguistics of White Supremacy" (58
[1969], 1307–15). To frustrate the expected *tu quoque,* I repeatedly
attached an adjective to the noun "bi-dialectalism"—"compulsory,"
"mandatory," "imposed," "coercive," "enforced," "obligatory,"
"regimented," and maybe one or two others. Such tedious iteration
should have made it plain that I was raising the question of motives
and methods, and in *College English* in early 1972 I added the ex-
plicit statement that "there is not, moreover, and there never has
been, a serious proposal that standard English should not be taught
at all, if for no other reason than because its teaching is inevitable"
(33 [1972], 455). Again, in a speech at the NCTE convention in November of that year (published in an NCTE cassette and in the *English
Journal* in May of 1973), I warned that there are "plenty of good
reasons why many blacks do value the mastery of an appropriate
form of standard English and why the schools should do what they
can to cultivate such mastery" ("After Bidialectalism, What?" *EJ,* 62
[1973], 770). Despite those public statements, and despite my personal, written protest in advance, Karen Hess and John C. Maxwell
announced, in a big "kit" which the NCTE published in 1974 under
the title *Dialects and Language Learning,* that "James Sledd is OP-
POSED TO giving students who speak nonstandard dialects an opportunity to acqure [sic] skill in speaking the dialect standard in their
region" (*Leader's Manual,* p. 65).

Truth is not greatly valued by politicians in Texas or in education. In yet another article, in *College English* in 1976, I printed the
facts which I am presently reciting and repeated that "bureaucratic
pretenses to the contrary notwithstanding, nobody has in fact
opposed, or in reason could oppose, the teaching of standard
English, for good ends and by good means, to students of any age
who want to learn it" (38 [1976], p. 236). None of my protests had
the slightest effect. The NCTE continued to promote the Hess-
Maxwell kit, English educationists repeated its accusation without
bothering to read what I had written, noisy creolists added their
wild embroidery to the pattern, and in 1979 Donna Christian of the

Center for Applied Linguistics joined the representatives of the National Council in the old familiar falsehood: "Whereas many of the other treatments mentioned above advocate various degrees of use of standard English in the schools, Sledd argues that any such policy has a racist motivation" (*Language Arts and Dialect Differences* [Arlington, Virginia: Center for Applied Linguistics, 1979], p. 12). Christian's pamphlet is in a series called *Dialects and Educational Equity.* Readers conditioned to see no evil should ask why the bureaucracy multiplies such fabrications.

Since everybody agrees, then, that standard languages should indeed be taught to people who want to learn them, informed debate must concern the motives for that teaching, its methods, and the treatment of students who have either no desire to learn a standard dialect or no real chance to learn it and who consequently leave us, as they came, speaking and writing nonstandard English (if they write at all). At this point another canard is sure to fly up quacking. Repeatedly, when someone states the simple truth that some students have no real chance to learn a certain skill or a certain body of knowledge, the reply is made that the statement either is unjust in calling the students incapable or is irresponsible in denying the teacher's duty to teach against all odds. The reply ignores our daily experience. It is a simple fact that many students, regardless of their intelligence, cannot learn what the school asks them to—cannot learn because of hunger, fear, grief, disease, or other circumstances beyond their own control. The obverse of that truth is that circumstances beyond control by teachers often make it impossible to *teach* the prescribed subjects: teachers cannot do what an unjust society at once requires and forbids them to. It is the denial of these facts, not the recognition of them, which is unjust to both teachers and students, and that same denial diverts attention from the deep social causes which are the roots of the trouble and which ought to be dug up and removed.

One consequence of this kind of destructively false optimism is the accusation that because teachers can always teach if they only try, teachers have uniquely failed if street blacks from a South Side high school in Chicago can't write standard English as well as pampered white youngsters from Evanston or Winnetka . . . (deletion of 575 words).

The first issue of motives and methods, therefore, is the still unfaced issue of teaching the compulsory, mandatory, imposed, coerced, enforced, obligatory, regimented use of standard English simply to flatter the prejudices of the powers that be, and it does no good to argue that by coercing students now, we give them "freedom to choose later." However it may be concealed, the chief purpose of present coercion is to condition students to comply with later coercion, and two coercions do not make one freedom. Some students will already want instruction in standard speech and writing; they should get it. Others can be rationally persuaded of the advantages of learning the prestige dialect, despite the obvious dangers; they too should be prudently assisted. It is futile, however, to demand the standard of students who see no need and have no desire to learn it, and it is damaging to them and us to drive them to drop out or to tell them that they must content themselves with menial jobs and can never hope for social acceptance. The pedagogy of the oppressed doesn't work that way.

Any wider analysis of the commonly accepted motives for teaching standard English in the schools will confirm the conclusion that in the United States the motives of the learners are not primary. The learners just get told. Many of those who tell them are themselves naive conformists, doing unto others what was done to them, on the unquestioned assumption that Good English with a capital G is good for what ails you. Other conformist decision-makers, such as E. D. Hirsch, are by no means naive or unquestioning but have evolved or accepted an ideology of bureaucratized assent, imposing the dubious values of undefined "correctness" and relative readability (by an audience halfway between the *Reader's Digest* and the *Washington Post*), and dreaming of a happy day when only "certified assessors" of those values will be allowed to teach composition in that nonexistent "classless and unchanging grapholect." Relativistic linguists must also be classified among the conformists, despite their claims of emancipation from the bonds of a particular culture. Calling themselves not just linguistic relativists but cultural relativists as well (the more inclusive term), these popularizers destroy all rational motives for the imposition of a standard dialect by maintaining that all languages and all dialects are equal in value and in complexity. But having thus erased the possibility of rational choice, the relativists proceed to do what the denial of rational choice makes easiest: they try to impose the dialect of established power. The wits among them sometimes misquote Orwell, saying that among equal languages some are more equal than others.

Coercion, imposition, is of course the last thing that teachers in the land of the free will willingly confess. More commonly, we cite the good of the student in one form or another. A favorite goody in justifications of the teaching of standard English is "upward mobility in the mainstream culture." As a disarmingly frank teacher in the public schools of Austin, Texas, put it several years ago, "I've made it to steak, I'm headed for lobster, and I want to take my students with me." But upward mobility, on the American scale of size and value, means the continually accelerated conspicuous waste of the biosphere's irreplaceable resources, the continued exploitation, by the United States, of the nations which we are pleased to call undeveloped or developing; and the very notion of upward mobility presupposes a society whose classes are ranked in terms of wealth and waste, a society where putting the nose of one's neighbor out of joint is the end of life. Those who cite as their motive for teaching standard English the assistance of their students to upward mobility assume in fact that the unlucky who don't move up move down and that there must always be the defeated at the bottom of the heap, rejected and condemned by the voracious consumers of things which the hucksters at the top have made all classes want. Briefly, upward mobility would be an evil goal even if it were a possible goal, and it isn't possible. The United States can no longer be the domineering thief of the world, and English teachers (of all people) should know that *down-ward* mobility is a more likely fate for the majority of Americans than moving up. That isn't necessarily a cause for grief. One dreams of a world where everyone might hope for food, clothing, shelter, medical care, work that isn't soul-destroying, some leisure; but the material paraphernalia of many middle-class lives could be much reduced without real loss. There is no students' right to their own lobster.

Less groveling justifications for teaching standard English have sometimes been adduced, such as the notion of participation in the society's institutional life. Undeniably, that notion has some validity. As Fries said, the linguistic vehicle of public affairs in the United States is the American version of standard English, and the lack of productive mastery of that dialect (even when no obstacle to communication is created) will be used as an excuse to *deny* participation to unwanted participants. But the catch-phrase "participation in the society's institutional life" is vague, offensive in its suggestion of devices like literacy tests for voters, and easily abused in a society where productive mastery of standard English is neither a necessary nor a sufficient condition for voting, holding office, or high socioeconomic status. The whole idea of rights can be destroyed by reducing them to false promises, and no sane human being would want to participate in our institutional life today without the hope of changing it. But professional societies, as part of the apparatus of state-supported education, must always be expected to support the state while pretending to do otherwise. The *Students' Right,* for all its weaknesses, was a brave attempt to break that depressing pattern.

I hope it will be acknowledged, by those who choose to continue that attempt, that nothing will be accomplished by moving from indifference to the motives of learners to subservience to them. Like upward mobility in the mainstream culture, some motives of some learners are indefensible, and there will always be some differences between the motives of learners and the motives of teachers, partly for the simple reason that official teachers are adults and many learners aren't (reversal of roles must happily be allowed for). When such differences exist, we rationalizing teachers must make sure that our real goal is some real good of students which students have not yet realized but which we in our greater wisdom can lead them to . . . (deletion of 100 words).

It remains true that no matter how firmly grounded in the students' good the teachers' motives are, teaching cannot succeed unless the students' motives are also engaged. . . . I am driven to ask what motives for learning standard English may make sense to the children of poverty and rejection. They have much greater concerns than the details of usage, the study of socially graded synonyms. They want first of all to survive, to get some immediate control over their own lives so that they will see tomorrow's sun come up; and the world in which their innate curiosity operates is not the protected world of middle-class English teachers, while their desire for self-expression finds its outlets elsewhere than in the English classroom, to them an alien territory. There is always the possibility that our traditional demands for standard English (especially the demands of cloistered, cushioned English profs) are irrelevant and damaging in a world which our students know but we do not.

I respect the *Students' Right* because its framers tried to deal with just such realities and possibilities. They were not inimical to the teaching of standard English. They did not "condone ill-organized, imprecise, undefined, inappropriate writing in any dialect" (p. 8); they recognized "the need for a written dialect to serve the larger, public community" (p. 5); they wanted their students "to grow more competent to handle a fuller range of the language" (p. 13); they insisted on the necessity of informing "those students who are preparing themselves for occupations that demand formal writing that they will be expected to write E[dited] A[merican] E[nglish]" (p. 15); and they were quite ready to help those students toward their chosen goal "by making them feel confident that their writing, in whatever dialect, makes sense and is important" (p. 15). Given those statements and others like them, the really savage attacks on the *Students' Right* are to me incomprehensible.

To the more judicious critics, I would suggest that the framers of the *Students' Right*, whatever mistakes they made, gave public recognition to certain essential truths. For one thing, they recognized that not all students are alike—that a student who feels no need and has no wish to write in standard English cannot be made to learn, and that such students can still be taught to read and can thus be educated, not dismissed, because "reading . . . involves the acquisition of meanings, not the ability to reproduce meanings in any given surface forms" (p. 7). We as receivers of our students' English are abusing the language by frustrating its main function of communication when we join or even tolerate the linguistic bully-boys who shout "Standard English, and the hell with anything else!"

A second essential recognition by the framers of the abused document is that a head-on attack on the students' language is self-defeating. Even the successful teaching of the details of English usage (those socially graded synonyms) takes up time that might be given to teaching something else, like how oppression operates and how it can be resisted; and the expense of spirit in teaching is utterly wasted if immediate and sustained assaults on "error" drive students to their last, impenetrable refuge of hostile silence. It is equally hopeless to resolve, in a fit of high-emptymindedness, that all students "have a right . . . to a standard spoken dialect," by which presumably is meant a prestigious accent, like Received Pronunciation in Britain or High Cronkitian (Network Standard) in the U.S. of A. A remarkable detachment from reality is required for even a resolute resolver to believe that a teacher in Washington, Georgia, or Brownsville, Texas, or Watts, or Harlem, can in 250 minutes weekly for nine months yearly prompt thirty students to change the constantly reinforced pronunciation habits of a decade or more. The framers of the *Students' Right* were wiser. "Teachers who understand phonology," they wrote, "will not try to impose their own sound systems upon their students," and "it is unreasonable for teachers to insist that students make phonemic shifts which we as adults have difficulty in making" (p. 16), particularly when the reward for thus abandoning a deep part of one's being (p. 6) is distant and improbable (p. 14).

By background and training English teachers are too often simply cut off from the lives and language of the poor. We take for granted the desire for education, and by education we mean the kind of education that we were given, with lots of guff about the roots of our culture (a highly exploitative one of many) and the wisdom of the race (which stands poised to self-destruct). We find it hard to believe that people in worlds next door to ours may be not just indifferent but actively hostile to that preparation for a kind of life which they know they will never live. Hence we get back to the need for social change—for altering, not perpetuating, the country's institutional arrangements. After over fifty years as student and teacher in the English departments of major universities at home and abroad, I have concluded that English teachers should oppose the educational bureaucracy, including their own professional societies, because the bureaucracy will never oppose the corruptions of our corrupt society. I am driven to ask, by long experience, whether English-teaching in the United States is a fit occupation for persons with a social conscience. Certainly the socially conscious and conscientious, if they do choose English-teaching, must be prepared for a life of constant opposition to the bosses, and the risks of living such a life are high. Among English teachers, if determined rebels against ancient and still powerful oppression don't begin as freaks, they are likely to end in freakiness, for they must live by the occasional successes of individual efforts, or as members of tenuous networks of like-minded people, whom news-letters and little magazines less often tell of successes than of failures. Radical teachers and progressive caucuses no doubt do what they can to keep the vision and the hope alive, but if working within the System to right the System's wrongs ends constantly in failure, why should one not at last say "Smash it all!"

The abrogation of the *Students' Right* is quintessentially foolish precisely because it compels to alienation. In a world of incomprehensible changes and unimaginable dangers, the reactionary advocates of its abrogation pay no honor to all the humane and decent things it stood for. They forget that a time comes, for the oppressed, when resistance costs less than submission, and if it should be answered that such a warning is melodramatic proof of freakiness, the givers of that answer should first tour the slums of Detroit and should then re-read James Baldwin in the *New York Times* for Sunday, July 29, 1979. "A child cannot be taught," wrote Baldwin, "by anyone who despises him, and a child cannot afford to be fooled. A child cannot be taught by anyone whose demand, essentially, is that the child repudiate his experience, and all that gives him sustenance." Maybe, Baldwin concluded, the white Powers, because they cannot learn, have nothing now to teach.

If the repudiation of the experience and the identity of those outside the polluted mainstream is not the demand which the attack on the *Students' Right* is making, the attackers should explain how they can simultaneously a) demand a standard dialect, both spoken and written, for all occasions which the dominant consider serious enough to be worth regulation, b) deny that by that demand they are condemning the dialects of the dominated (not to be used on serious occasions) or are asking them to abandon the values which support their identity, yet c) acknowledge that the linguistic forms which they demand from all their students are arbitrary, idiosyncratic, and intrinsically insignificant.

One freaky old privileged Southern white professor says he's still listening for the still ungiven answer.

Notes

1. The history of this essay illustrates one of its main theses, that English teachers should oppose their professional bureaucracy.

On January 28, 1983, my friend and one-time colleague Louie Crew wrote me that he had been appointed "to a CCCC Committee charged to report whether CCCC needs to revise 'The Students' Right to Their Own Language.'" He enclosed a report on the committee's work, made by its chairman. One document was a statement which had been prepared for the NCTE some time before and which had been described, in the committee, as especially valuable. That statement concluded that the "'Students' Right to Their Own Language' should be set aside as representing the position of the National Council of Teachers of English." It will be remembered, of course, that the *Students' Right* did not come from the NCTE but from CCCC, which adopted it, at the 1974 business meeting, by a margin of about four to one.

Believing that the basic policies of a professional organization should be set by its membership after full and free public discussion, I set to work to alert a number of my friends, and by February 7 I had finished and typed up an essay which I submitted to Richard L. Larson, editor of the CCCC journal, *College Composition and Communication*. Acknowledging receipt of the essay, he replied, on February 22, that he needed the advice of readers but that he hoped to "get back" to me "within two months." I heard no more, and on May 25 I wrote Larson a) to say that my paper, if it was to affect the current proceedings of the bureaucracies of CCCC and NCTE, must be promptly available to the CCCC membership and b) to ask, accordingly, what decision he had made. On May 28, Larson replied that he was inclined against publication but that he was still waiting for a report from a fourth reader "before making a final decision." On July 18 he wrote to reject the article because, he said, it added nothing new to an old debate.

The present version consists of such portions of the original essay as the editor of *College English*, Donald J. Gray, was willing to print. When Larson's two months had grown to three and a half, I concluded that his rejection was a foregone conclusion and on June 3 tentatively submitted the paper to Gray, saying that I assumed rejection by Larson, that I had been invited to submit a shorter version elsewhere, but that I would like to know if he as editor of *College English* might be interested. Unless the in-group's actions, I wrote, could be opened to public discussion by autumn at the latest, defense of the *Students' Right* would be very difficult.

Gray's reply (dated July 15) was that he would publish the essay provided I removed "all references" to "matter not already published." In effect, that meant that an attack on the *Students' Right,* a CCCC document, could be prepared for the NCTE and officially circulated, with words of praise, to the members of an officially appointed CCCC committee, yet that members of CCCC and NCTE could not refer to that attack in an NCTE journal. Gray specified the deletions which footnotes and ellipses now mark.

Because it was crucial that even a fragmentary version should appear by the November meeting of the NCTE (where, oddly, the first action on the CCCC document is to be taken). I withdrew the essay from Larson's protracted consideration and proposed to Gray that *College English* should print it with the ellipses and with this note. I will be happy to provide a photocopy of the original typescript, with full documentation (five cents a page plus postage), to readers who may wish to consider the difficulties of bringing the unpublicized but consequential actions of bureaucracies to public light. Allow a functionary to define and apply the distinction between private and public, classified and unclassified, and that person will at once become *rhetor irrefragabilis,* the Great Communicator, first cousin to the Grand Inquisitor. That is the lesson of all "covert operations." The outcome of the whole unnecessarily tangled business remains uncertain, though apparently some good has been accomplished by making it obvious to the CCCC committee that the *Students' Right* still has defenders. My latest document from Crew, dated July 15, indicates that one suggestion of mine is apparently to be embodied, without acknowledgement, in the committee's report— namely, the offering of a resolution that the CCCC reaffirm its commitment to the *Students' Right.* Such a resolution, if it passed, would make open abrogation difficult, but what actually gets done will be much more important than what is said. Ronald Reagan calls the MX missile the Peacekeeper.

Permanence and Change in Standard American English
The Making of "Literacy Crises"
(1986)

Claims that there is a decline in public literacy, reaching emergency proportions, date back to at least the ninth century. This issue gained credence in the eighteenth and nineteenth centuries and especially wide acceptance in the twentieth—due in large part to the complex impact of modern communications media. Sledd has argued with precise logic that the terms literacy *and* crisis *have to be defined very carefully before meaningful discussion can take place. Throughout the years, Sledd has criticized those who use the vaguely defined idea of a "literacy crisis" for personal gain and professional self-promotion. In 1993 he had this to say:*

FREED: In looking over the supposed "literacy crisis" that you have analyzed for years, I wonder if anything ever changes?

SLEDD: No. I read an essay in *The Atlantic,* on the literacy crisis of the '90s.

FREED: Tell me about those recurring "crises."

SLEDD: Well, what's meant by a literacy crisis? The fact is, the general population has never been as literate as ideally it should be, so there's a perpetual literacy crisis. In another sense, there's a perpetual literacy crisis, because each new generation has to be made literate. But literacy crisis as you see it in the newspapers, never has anything really to do with the state of literacy; it has something to do with changing demands by the people who run the show. You make a literacy crisis by making demands on the schools which they've never been asked, before, to meet. And then you blame them for not doing what nobody had ever asked them to do before.

Actually the schools did pretty well what they were asked to do in the
'70s. But in the '80s and '90s, people asked for different things, and said,
"look here, you aren't doing what you should do." So you can create a literacy crisis anytime you want to just by getting the powerful to agree that
graduates don't have the skills and qualities which allow the powerful to
get richer. And that's what a literacy crisis is. "The richest has the plea-
sures, the poorest takes the blame. They're crying the whole world over.
Ain't it all a bleedin' shame." You know that song?

FREED: No, what is it?

SLEDD: It's a British song. "It's the rich as has the pleasure . . ."

In the United States, profit-seeking employers can create a "literacy
crisis" by demanding kinds and degrees of literacy which they have
not asked before. By blaming the schools for what they themselves
have done, the employers then tighten their control of an already
subservient educational system. Such processes can be illustrated
by recent developments at the richest of the state universities, the
University of Texas at Austin, which is proud to promote the unity
of national, state, and local governments, state-supported education, and the predatory corporations that govern the governments.
One result will be the enlargement of the permanent underclass of
the minimally employable, to whom the standard English imposed
by the dominant is partly unknown, wholly irrelevant. Thus, ever-
changing standard English nonetheless continues to exist in the
U.S.A., and, as a class dialect, continues through all changes to perform its ancient function of mobilizing and controlling the people
in the service of the ruling class. Sociolinguists and other confused
academics respond to this situation either by briskly ignoring it or
by debating the nature and very existence of the changing dialect of
dominance, whose unchanged functioning is obvious to all who are
not paid for blindness.

To question the existence of a standard American English is
silly: so long as the American class-structure survives, the standard
will remain, changing constantly even if superficially to meet the
changing demands of the powerful. At the moment, though no one
accent can be regarded as a national norm (devotees of network
papcasters to the contrary notwithstanding), the phonological differences among educated varieties are relatively minor, and all the
regional standards are easily intelligible to educated listeners anywhere in the world. In its written form, the American standard is
not only national but global: serious printed English prose is much
the same on every continent, with just enough variation in grammar

and especially lexicon to provide employment for patriotic lexico-graphers and material for jingoistic debates in the popular press.

Like the other versions of standard English in other nations, the American standard is a class dialect, as it has been from the beginning. Questions have of course been raised, on various grounds and with various intentions. Ideologists of bureaucratized assent, like E. D. Hirsch, have imagined a "grapholect" which, they assert, is classless and unchanging;[1] but Hirsch's arguments rest on a profound ignorance of linguistics and considerable misrepresentation of familiar writings by Jespersen and Henry Bradley. For quite different reasons, some black writers and academics have questioned the existence of a single linguistic norm for all ethnic groups:[2] because they rightly resent the dominance of the white power that sets the norm, they wrongly deny the existence of the norm itself.

But both the arguments for a single, classless grapholect and the arguments for different standards for different ethnic groups are political resolutions, not factual assertions, though they must masquerade as statements if they are to be effective as resolves; and the facts are sufficiently plain from the numerous sociolinguistic investigations which have shown neat correlations between linguistic variation and socioeconomic class.[3] Commonsensical observers had arrived at the same conclusion long before the sociolinguists took the trouble to provide statistical proof of what needed no proving; for every adult American has had the experience of socially judging and being socially judged by choices made and noted among socially graded variables.

A typical instance may be found in a pamphlet entitled *Mother Got Tired of Taking Care of My Baby,* a study of high-school drop-outs by the Austin (Texas) Independent School District (1983). From interviews with about a hundred of the hapless, the investigators constructed five imaginary case studies, "composite descriptions based on the interview responses of several students." In all five cases, the first-person narrators of the encounters use English which would be accepted as standard anywhere, but the dropouts are represented as using stereotyped nonstandard forms: "The people who seen it wouldn't say the truth," "I never got in no trouble," "My parents, they ran off and deserted me," "Them teachers are prejudice," "I still can't read or write very good." Such forms can be heard in London or Sydney or Chicago as well as Austin, and everywhere their interpretation would be the same: people who talk like that proclaim and confirm their membership in the classes which our society considers lower and drives lower still.

Why then, if these things are so, should there be confused debate about the nature and very existence of a standard American

English? One reason is as plain as the existence of that American standard. The standard languages of western Europe and its present and former dependencies are indeed the creations and instruments of dominant social classes. They are the languages of established power, and it follows that when the nature of social power changes, uncertainty about the nature of the linguistic norm must follow.

Recent developments at the University of Texas at Austin, the richest of the American state universities and the intellectual center of the Sunbelt,[4] are significant in this connection, and significant linguistically, though their significance may not be instantly apparent. Numbered paragraphs may conduce to clarity and brevity in the following account, which is not only a catalogue of titillating Texiana.

1. *How to avoid teaching the arts of literacy.* In 1982 the University of Texas raised its standards for admission, formerly low enough to accommodate even some football players, who of course get special treatment. For example, the same performance on a standardized test which barely saved a freshman at the University of California in Berkeley from remedial incarceration in bonehead English (Subject A) exempted a freshman at UT from the first composition course, though dissatisfaction with the quality of student writing on the UT campus was a favorite topic of bilious comment. Efforts were even made, a dozen years ago, to lower that low exemption score, so that the "burden" of teaching average freshmen would be lightened. Raised admissions standards are a different road to the same destination.

2. *From "culturally biased" to "culturally oriented."* Whatever its level, a principal barrier to the admission of doubtful candidates has been and remains the Scholastic Aptitude Test (SAT) of the Educational Testing Service and the College Board. When a report to the University Council by a University committee in 1982–83 described the SAT as "culturally biased," Dean Elspeth Rostow, wife of Walt Whitman Rostow of Viet Nam fame (the best and the brightest), successfully moved the amendment of *culturally biased* to *culturally oriented.* Ironically, the idle children of affluent Anglos in Dallas are now complaining that the demand for higher SAT scores excludes them also from UT, to which Blacks and Mexican-Americans have traditionally been admitted only in numbers far below their proportions in the state's total population.

3. *Them as has, gits.* Despite the general dissatisfaction with student writing, the University has just abolished the second of its

two semesters of freshman composition, replacing it with a course in the junior or senior year, when students have chosen their major subjects and can be instructed in the kinds of writing which professionals in their fields demand. The unanimous opposition of the student members of the University Council was impatiently dismissed. The result will be that despite their acknowledged ineptitude, the great majority of entering freshmen will not get all the help they need when they most need it, but the University and its faculty will have to teach only half as much freshman composition as they had to teach before. Besides, before the junior year the weaker students drop out in large numbers. The best education is to be reserved for those who come with the best education.

4. *It's the rich as has the pleasure.* What might have seemed, a few months ago, only the normal indifference, at the people's University, to the needs of average children of average people, has come to look more sinister in May, 1983, when it has found its place in a more ambitious pattern. The Microelectronics and Computer Technology Corporation (MCC) is a "research consortium" of twelve computer and semiconductor companies, with a projected budget of perhaps 100 million dollars but at present just one employee—namely, its head, the retired admiral Bobby Ray Inman, former chief of the National Security Agency and deputy director of the CIA.[5] As sites for its operations, the newly organized MCC considered some 57 cities in 27 states, but by the spring of '83 it had narrowed its list of eager bidders to just four: Atlanta, Austin, North Carolina's Research Triangle, and San Diego. In March, the government of Texas and the millionaires who govern the government got rolling. Governor Mark White, the Chancellor of the University of Texas System (E. Don Walker), reactionary computer plutocrat H. Ross Perot of Dallas, and an overload of similar moneybags offered astonishing inducements; and by May 18 Austin's small-town newspaper began Texas-sized bragging that California, Georgia, and North Carolina had been spurned for the open arms of Austin. *The* University and its cooperative rustic rival, the Texas Agricultural and Mechanical University, had provided "the juiciest bait," and seducing MCC was "sweeter than a football championship or a new Nobel laureate on the faculty"—ambitions of equal importance in the eyes of Texas.

In fact, despite the rejoicing in Austin, MCC had given little and taken much, with incalculable but ominous consequences for the education of plain Texans. Only a relatively small number of employees will be recruited locally, and those for the lower ranks, while most holders of the two or three hundred top research jobs will be newcomers; and the companies in the consortium have committed their money for just three years in the first instance—the same short period for which Inman as honcho is committed. In return, he demanded—and got—everything but the state capitol (rendered less than normally attractive by a recent fire). From the U.S. Justice Department and prominent United States senators (including millionaire Lloyd Bentsen of Texas), MCC got assurances that antitrust laws would give the consortium no difficulties; and from local individuals and institutions it got up to 2 million dollars for temporary office and laboratory space, use of 20 acres of land for a permanent site, 20 million dollars for the construction of the permanent plant, free use of one or more Lear jets with a two-member crew for two years of recruiting, 20 million in home loans at special rates for the recruits, bridge loans for down payments by recruits until they can sell their houses elsewhere, special assistance for the recruits in finding new houses for their families and new jobs for their spouses, discounts on rental cars, and a relocation subsidy of up to half a million for the corporation itself. In addition, the University promised to enrich the intellectual environment with a 15-million-dollar endowment for faculty in electrical engineering and computer science, 30 new faculty positions over three years in computer science and microelectronics, three-quarters of a million yearly for new graduate fellowships, 1 million annually in research support, and 5 million in the next two years for laboratory equipment—all that from an institution which has only just granted telephones to its English faculty and whose Mississippi Dean of Liberal Arts has publicly stated, within the year, that the institution will never provide the money to hire a full staff of the tenured or tenurable to teach its composition courses. Yet still the jet-set superspy asked for more. Inman proceeded to tell the state and local governments that MCC would expect an attractive "business climate" and a high quality of life, with no "ticky-tacky growth," and that it must have a good education from kindergarten through university for the children of its much-pampered researchers, whose salaries are predicted to range upward from 50 thousand annually. With all that, the moguls of city, state, and university were delighted.

5. *It's the poor as takes the blame.* Meanwhile, life for the ordinary mortal, in Austin and elsewhere, remained the usual struggle. Over one-fourth of all children in the United States were living close to poverty. Perhaps 40% of minority youth were classified

as functionally illiterate. President Reagan had proposed a federal budget which would provide unprecedented sums for deadly weapons but would cut food stamps, meal subsidies for children, and benefits for the aged, blind, and disabled. It was reported that the cost of education had increased by 12.40% in 1982. When the National Commission on Excellence in Education called on the federal government to spend more for schooling, Reagan replied that more money would do no good but that voluntary prayer in schools and the abolition of the Education Department might help; complaining that too many teachers were mediocre or incompetent, he recommended tax credits for parents pecunious enough to send their children to private schools. On May 21, over 2,000 impecunious teachers (one placard read "High Tech—Low Check") marched on the capitol in Austin to demand the raise which Governor White had promised them during his campaign but which the Legislature had refused to fund. In April, unemployment for teen-aged Blacks in Texas stood at 53% and probably more. Federal job-training programs were soon to become the responsibility of Austin businessmen, but nothing much had been done about them. About 1,000 students a year continued to drop out from Austin's high schools, with Hispanics dropping out at roughly twice the rate for Anglos. Many dropouts were unemployed, and the lucky ones who had jobs worked usually for minimum wages. Nationwide, jobs were scarce even for college graduates if their degrees were in the humanities. To make room for its own expansion, the University of Texas, which could provide 20 acres of valuable land in Northwest Austin for MCC, used its right of eminent domain to evict poor families from their homes in poverty-ridden East Austin. Appearing at UT Austin's Graduate School of Business as the first speaker on the Inter First Bank Dallas Endowed Centennial Lectureship, newly Republican Congressman Phil Gramm proclaimed that the recession was over. The gross national product, he said, was rising. So, too, was the human scrapheap, the most toxic of all wastes. . . .

What emerges from this tragicomedy in five paragraphs is that Texas and its University are on the cutting edge of reactionary politics in the United States. In the euphoric era after World War II, when goodies were abundant in the land of the free, it was the American way to keep the underlings quiet by allowing them a modest share in "the good life" (defined for vulgarians among the hills and lakes of central Texas as booze, boats and broads); but now that goodies are growing scarcer, America's Powers have decided to cut the rations of the have-nots so that the haves can have still more. The weakest will just be junked, in university classes as well as on the job market, for the Powers are creating a permanently submerged underclass of the minimally employable. The U.S.A. is becoming more and more like the oppressive nations of Latin America, where the Giant of the North supports merciless exploitation.

The *linguistic* relevance of the Texas story and of similar events and developments elsewhere is equally obvious. With the enlargement of the lowest class, to which the linguistic norms of the privileged are unknown or irrelevant, linguistic stratification in the U. S. A. will grow sharper, and that sharp stratification will increase the difficulty of "moving up" for those at the bottom of the ladder. Already in the '50s and '60s, when black students were at last admitted to the educational system, middle-class teachers found themselves confronted with kinds of speech and writing which they had never known before; in the '70s, that experience was agonizingly repeated when open admissions brought a flood of lower-class students into the city colleges of New York; and in affluent Austin now, the papers of many students in the city's junior college are in stark contrast to even the modestly literate performances of their contemporaries at the University. Yet the students in Austin Community College are among those who still have hope. They have not dropped out because them teachers are prejudice.

Toward the other end of the social scale, changes in language and language-attitudes have also ensued. In the United States, the divorce of power from traditional linguistic and literary cultivation has been (one might say) finalized, and the demands on the users of English which the computerized culture of high technology is making are new demands, demands which academic humanists are by training and (one wishes) by conviction ill-equipped to meet. Hence the complaints by scholars like Douglas Bush and sciolists like John Simon[6] that our language has been polluted and our paradigms are lost; and one must admit, though English is now closest of all languages to the old dream of universality, that some of its cherished continuities have been irreparably shattered in the U.S.A. American linguists themselves are notorious for their bad prose (the Center for Applied Linguistics has provided priceless specimens); and (for another example) the American public can tolerate a "most unique and saleable" condensed version of the Bible, put out by *Reader's Digest,* whose editors boasted that they had reduced the volume of God's Word by forty per cent through the elimination of His "repetition, rhetoric, and reduced relevance." The same issue of UT's prize-winning student newspaper, *The Daily Texan,* which reported this accomplishment (September 27, 1982), carried an account of the defeat of the University of Missouri Tigers by the University of Texas Longhorns (also known as Steers): "In short, whatever Missouri's balanced offense offered, the Texas defense managed to taketh away. And destroyeth." That is wit in the Cambridge of the Southwest. Leavis shouldeth be living at this hour.

But it is as silly to lament the death of the world's most flourishing language or the linguistic discomfiture of professional mossbacks as it is to deny the existence of a standard American English. Much more important are those new demands for uses and varieties of English which will serve the interests of the multinational corporations as they manage a nation which has lost its brief empire and its technological supremacy over both friends and enemies. Degrees in arts from the world's best universities do not equip their holders to make salespitches, to recruit whiz-kids for Bobby Ray Inman, or to talk to or about the computers of H. Ross Perot; and though corporate recruiters conventionally complain that even the resumés of candidates for recruitment are weak in spelling, grammar, and punctuation, they are not interested in traditional elegance or in the qualities of language which befit free citizens. Their purposes are so set by the greed which guides their system that a candidate who asked "What for?" (with Leavis) would destroy his chances. They want their trainees, with no thought for any purpose but upward mobility in the corporate world, "to generate polished work products or to make impressive sales or other presentations."[7] In that one phrase, any humanist worth his pipe and tweed would object to the jargon of *to generate* and to the pattern of modification in *sales or other presentations.*

It is the impossibility that overworked and underpaid teachers should prepare candidates to meet these new demands by the corporate bosses which accounts for the present outcries against the schools by such profundities as *Newsweek,* President Reagan, the Twentieth Century Fund, the National Commission on Excellence in Education, the National Task Force on Education for Economic Growth, and the Business–Higher Education Forum. Somewhere in their self-righteous prating there is always the inadvertent confession. Says *Newsweek,* reporting on the report of the Commission on Excellence, "The gains inspired by the challenge of sputnik a quarter of a century ago have been squandered, leaving a generation of young people ill prepared for the new era of technology and global competition."[8] "The United States must strengthen its position in the world market," say the seventy-eight executives in the Business–Higher Education Forum, by adopting educational policies that will "elevate the competitive challenge to the top of the national agenda."[9] In a world where millions of teen-agers don't know enough arithmetic to count money in a fastfood restaurant, the College Board declares that high school graduates should know algebra, plane and solid geometry, statistics and probability, and should have "the ability to use computers for self-instruction and problem-solving, as well as to understand the social, economic, and ethical implications of computers."[10] A wiser demand would be for students who could understand the social, economic, and ethical implications of the present outcries.

For the "literacy crisis" currently alleged in the United States is, in fact, the creation of the corporate bosses who now cry out against it. Twenty-five years ago, sputnik provoked a clamor similar to the clamor which the loss of empire and of technological supremacy provokes today. The complaints represent no adequate assessment of national educational progress; for corporate progress is human retrogression, and the tools for adequate assessment are simply lacking. In fact, for the past quarter-century the schools have done much of what was expected of them: they have domesticated the young, discouraged their critical consciousness, kept them off the street and off the labor market; and the anti-intellectual values of teen-agers have reflected their accurate perception that conventional academic accomplishment was less likely to provide access to "the good life" than inherited privilege and the conventional chicanery of executive types. The Powers blame the schools for losing a game whose rules the Powers change to suit their own needs and interests. In this situation, as youngsters quickly learn, the only constant is *sauve qui peut,* the law of jungle greed. At the University of Texas in April, 1983, the marketing senior whom *Newsweek* in a supplement chose to honor as a student entrepreneur explained himself like this: "The money is pretty important, but I enjoy the game. In high school I always found a friend in the class, and I always tried to beat that friend in a grade. In business you want to beat your competition." The self-styled stereotypical young businessman went on, "I get mad when I see other people doing real well."[11]

Thus, between the launching of sputnik and the launching of astronomical deficits by the president who promised a balanced budget, American education has moved from alleged crisis to alleged crisis, and educators have responded with predictable docility, as indeed they must if they too entertain hopes for "upward mobility in the mainstream culture." A primary characteristic of their efforts has been indifference to the felt needs of students. Holding out false promises of that same mobility in the mainstream, the bidialectalists tried to alienate black youth in urban ghettos from peers and parents by teaching them to talk and write like the middle-class whites whom they disliked and feared.[12] The genuinely heroic Mina Shaughnessy, in her famous *Errors and Expectations*,[13] unquestioningly took as her norm for "basic writers" the linguistic prejudices of middle-class academics and employed a Rube Goldberg version of traditional grammar in an unsuccessful though benevolent effort to impose those prejudices on students whom open admissions gave brief access to New York's colleges.

E. D. Hirsch (deserving of a paragraph unto himself) invented a preposterous scheme for regimenting the teaching of composition nation-wide according to the standards of undefined "correctness" and "relative readability" by an audience half-way between the *Reader's Digest* and the *Washington Post*. Having abandoned that "linguistics of literacy," with its notions of a classless and unchanging grapholect, Hirsch now proposes a new form of cultural imperialism, "*the* ideology of literacy" [emphasis added], which "implies specific contents as well as formal skills."[14] His argument, such as it is, is oddly perverse, and indifferent to questionings of purpose. Because it is hard, as he informs us, to read and write on subjects which we don't know much about, one might conclude that the schools should cultivate openness to new ideas, wide reading, and general intellectual curiosity, and that they should provide constant practice in the reading of texts which rest on alien presuppositions—briefly, that the educational system should do all it can to promote the rational acceptance and indeed the positive evaluation of diversity. Citizens of the three superpowers and their house-boy states find it hard to keep even the awareness of the brainwashing, subtle or blatant, to which they are subjected daily. But Hirsch draws a different conclusion. "A certain extent of shared, canonical knowledge is inherently necessary," he says, "to a literate democracy"; and from there he goes on to define "the minimal aim of schooling" as "acculturation into a national literate culture," the learning of "what the 'common reader' of a newspaper in a literate culture could be expected to know." The whole of Hirsch's new argument (which ignores the question where one finds a literate democracy) reduces to the assertion that because we should all be able to write easily what we all should easily understand, a national authority should define some body of "canonical knowledge" and require instruction in it. Maybe, Hirsch concludes, the Educational Testing Service should be praised as "our hidden National Board of Education."

"What for? what for? whatever for?" as Leavis cried in Cambridge. If Hirsch is contrasted with Paulo Freire and his "education for critical consciousness," one is tempted to compare the real powers that govern American education to the repressive Brazilians who drove Freire into exile because he taught too many of the oppressed how to read and think and act as free makers of a truly human world. Language intervention in the United States has always worked from the top down, in the interests of the interveners and their corporate bosses, and that is another reason why, after twenty-five years of interventions, American education has only moved from the proclamation of one crisis to the proclamation of another.

But amidst all uncertainties, one thing is regrettably certain: state-supported education in the U.S.A. will continue to support the state. One example must stand for the possible multitude. The Conference on College Composition and Communication is the country's professional society of composition-teachers. The planner of the program for the 1984 CCCC convention (a Texan) has chosen as her program-theme "Making Language the Cornerstone of an Education for Freedom," but her definition of freedom may be guessed at from her admonition to the profession: "In 1984, teachers cannot live in a walled city, shut off from politics and the profit motive. If we want to influence our society and make language work for the causes of freedom and individual growth in that society, we must, in the words of Mina Shaughnessy, dive into the mainstream." It is idle to guess at the proportions of self-deception, spiritual blindness, and conscious hypocrisy in that statement. The metaphor of the mainstream, as the black novelist Ralph Ellison once remarked, reflects a society where dissenters and other minorities are consigned to the swamps and backwaters; yet if the profit motive is the inclination which makes the mainstream run, a billabong is a healthier habitation.

At last to summarize what perceptive readers have not perceived as a political manifesto remote from language-planning or applied linguistics:

    a. Teaching is a political act. Language-planning is people-planning. Language-planners and appliers of linguistics in the U.S.A. must choose whether to resist or to surrender to the ongoing revolution by the radical right, the false conservatives who for their own profit seek to change the very form and texture of our lives by high technology, creating by their changes a Lumpenproletariat, a despised and rejected, ever-growing human scrap-heap.

    b. The only rational prediction concerning the inescapable choice is that American academics will choose to go along to get along, ignoring the needs and interests of reluctant students as they go. By that choice, upwardly mobile academics will eventually force upon their conscientious colleagues a further choice between the revolution from the right and—if spontaneous combustion eventually sets the human scrap-heap blazing—revolution from the left. But it is childish to believe that a nation half slave and half free cannot survive. The United States exists.

c. A standard language also continues to exist in the U.S.A., and, as a class dialect, continues through all changes to perform its ancient function of mobilizing and controlling the people in the service of the ruling class. As the gaps between classes widen, linguistic stratification can be expected to grow sharper.

d. The function of the standard in social control remains a constant; but changing demands by the rulers in the changing world of computers and high technology will force changes in the repertory of approved linguistic forms and kinds of discourse and accompanying changes in the educational system which, among other duties, imposes those forms and kinds on ambitious students and sends the incapable or unwilling to the scrap-heap. The Powers who rage about the current literacy crisis created it themselves.

e. Though long in dying (like King Charles), the liberal arts in the United States are moribund, except for purposes of display—comfortable Culture for the petulant wives of the big rich; and traditional academic humanists don't clearly know the arts of language which the bosses now demand. That is why today American colleges at least talk grandly about "writing across the curriculum"—instruction by professionals in the kinds of writing which are actually demanded in their fields. For one reason or the other, for survival in opposition or for mildly profitable acquiescence, traditional academics must learn the new demands and how to meet them.

f. As the nation sharpens its social and linguistic distinctions among classes and enlarges the permanent underclass which doesn't know the standard language and cannot do the only jobs which the big corporations make available, the problem must be faced of what to do with the present crop of affluent, insolent teen-agers who are also incapable of meeting the new demands.

g. Academic politicians—apologists for power—must deny Platitudes a–f by maintaining, politically, that scholarship must not be politicized. They must avoid hard questions of ultimate purpose, for the ultimate purpose of America's rulers is unspeakable: to satiate their own greed.[15]

Notes

1. E. D. Hirsch, Jr., *The Philosophy of Composition* (Chicago: Univ. of Chicago Press, 1977).

2. Geneva Smitherman, ed., *Black English and the Education of Black Children and Youth* (Detroit: Center for Black Studies, Wayne State University, 1981), pp. 306, 309, 390f.

3. Labov, Shuy, Wolfram, and others in the United States; notably Trudgill in England; etc.

4. The Sunbelt is the tier of Southern and Southwestern states, whose warm climate and cheap, docile legislatures and labor make them attractive to predatory corporations. European readers will better understand the discussion of high jinks at the Sunbelt's premier university if they recall some elementary facts about education in the U. S. of A. The College Board (CB) and its lengthening shadow, the Educational Testing Service (ETS), are the arrogant gatekeepers of American education, equally free from self-criticism and public control. The academic life-span of the American undergraduate is four years (freshman, sophomore, junior, senior). The first two years are largely occupied by partying and required elementary courses, among which one or two courses in the writing of tolerable prose have been prominent and unsuccessful for most of this century.

5. In this account, I follow the *Austin American-Statesman* for May 18–22, 1983.

6. Douglas Bush, "Polluting Our Language," *The American Scholar,* Spring 1972, pp. 238–247; John Simon, *Paradigms Lost* (New York: Clarkson N. Potter, n.d.), *passim* if you can stand it.

7. Pete Foster, senior vice-president of the American Bank in Austin, quoted in *The Daily Texan* for April 18, 1983.

8. *Newsweek,* May 9, 1983, p. 50.

9. Edward B. Fiske of the New York Times Service in the *Austin American-Statesman,* May 16, 1983.

10. *Academic Preparation for College,* quoted by William Raspberry, *Austin American-Statesman,* May 17, 1983.

11. *The Daily Texan*, April 29, 1983.

12. For a first account, see James Sledd, "Bi-Dialectalism: The Linguistics of White Supremacy," *English Journal*, December 1969, pp. 1307–1315, 1329.

13. Mina P. Shaughnessy, *Errors and Expectations* (New York: Oxford University Press, 1977).

14. *The Philosophy of Composition;* and now "Cultural Literacy," *The American Scholar*, Spring 1983, pp. 159–169.

15. A generous editor allows the addition of a final note, dated July 24, 1985. The teaching of writing at the University of Texas has been still more severely crippled. In the past spring term, the much advertised new writing program was butchered before it had been well inaugurated: the new junior-senior course was "suspended," and the one remaining freshman course was bitterly attacked by professors of literature who feared that their sacred domain was threatened by upstart "compositionists." In July, a state agency has proposed a "competency test" to determine which students shall be allowed to advance to their third year of study. To demand "competency" without providing the means to achieve it would be like tossing children into a lake without first giving them a chance to learn to swim; but academic terrorism is now much in vogue in Reaganite America.

References

Austin American-Statesman, 16–22 May 1983.

Bush, Douglas, "Polluting Our Language," *The American Scholar*, Spring 1972, pp. 238–247.

"Can the Schools Be Saved?" *Newsweek*, 9 May 1983, pp. 50–54, 56–58.

The Daily Texan, 27 Sept. 1982, 18 and 29 April 1983.

Hirsch, E. D., Jr., "Cultural Literacy," *The American Scholar*, Spring 1983, pp. 159–169.

Hirsch, E. D. *The Philosophy of Composition*. Chicago: Univ. of Chicago Press, 1977.

Labov, William, *Sociolinguistic Patterns*. Philadelphia: Univ. of Pennsylvania Press, 1972.

"Mother Got Tired of Taking Care of My Baby": A Study of Dropouts. Publications of the Austin Independent School District, No. 82.44. Austin, 1983.

Shaughnessy, Mina P., *Errors and Expectations*. New York: Oxford Univ. Press, 1977.

Simon, John, *Paradigms Lost*. New York: Clarkson N. Potter, n.d.

Sledd, James, "Bi-Dialectalism: The Linguistics of White Supremacy." *English Journal*, Dec. 1969, pp. 1307–1315, 1329.

Smitherman, Geneva, ed., *Black English and the Education of Black Children and Youth.* Detroit: Center for Black Studies, Wayne State Univ., 1981.

Trudgill, Peter, *The Social Differentiation of English in Norwich.* Cambridge: Cambridge Univ. Press, 1974.

Trudgill, Peter, ed., *Sociolinguistic Patterns in British English.* London: Edward Arnold, 1978.

Wolfram, Walter A., *A Sociolinguistic Description of Detroit Negro Speech.* Washington: Center for Applied Linguistics, 1969.

See and Say

(1987)[1]

Here again Sledd criticizes university professors who, for the most part, do nothing more than protect their own self-interest while refusing to face the political implications of being in a language classroom. The essay is radical in its condemnation and radical in its proposals: "Our ultimate aim," Sledd concludes, "should be social revolution."

When I asked Sledd about the impact of this essay, he said:

I think that's the paper that prompted the Wyoming Resolution. That was the paper I read at that Wyoming meeting. They had me there about 1976 or so. John Ciardi was a speaker at that time. And then, after ten years, they had me back, along with some other people, in a sort of retrospect. I think I was to be just sort of decorative—look at this funny old geezer—that sort of thing. I know Linda Flower read a paper before this, and they sort of hoped to get all the discussion on her paper, and my paper wouldn't even be read. But the chairperson frustrated that, and when I read the paper, it took over the meeting and changed the whole direction of the discussion. Some of the people there came up with the Wyoming Resolution; I guess we all learned a sad lesson when that effort came to nothing.

This paper is a skeptical view of the unfriendly neighborhood and divided house in which we teachers of English lead our professional lives.

To highlight my skepticism at once in all its starkness, let me offer a few quotations which I consider damaging in their unrealistic optimism. The first is from James Britton's opening address to the Third International Conference on the Teaching of English, in Sydney in 1980. Announcing "the decade of the teacher," Britton proclaimed "that what the teacher can't do in the classroom can't be achieved by any other means" (quoted from *English Journal,* March 1986, 27). Not long afterward, but in a very different context, Joseph Gibaldi of the MLA surmised that devotion to teaching might well be our professional salvation: "In a time that increasingly demands a rededication to undergraduate teaching of the humanities and to the idea of a liberal education, it may well be that our sometimes divided and fragmented profession will rediscover a sense of purpose, unity, and community in its concern for and commitment to teaching" (Bessinger & Yeager, 1984, p. ix).

Optimism like Gibaldi's has extended to fields of particular interest to teachers of freshmen and sophomores—teachers whom ambitious researchers quickly learn to scorn. In 1985, the National Academy of Education's Commission on Reading predicted that "America will become a nation of readers when verified practices of the best teachers in the best schools can be introduced throughout the country" (Commission on Reading, 1985, p. 120). In 1986, with Reagan still in the White House, George Hillocks was as enthusiastic about writing as the Commission was about reading. "The climate for improving the teaching of writing," Hillocks says as budgets for education shrink, "has never been better" (Hillocks, 1986, p. 17). The old warfare between compositionists and the literati, it has been suggested, is coming to an end. "Recent developments in critical theory and in the teaching of composition suggest," according to William Stull, "that a reconciliation is in the works" (Stull, 1984, p. 134).

James Kinneavy has gone even further. Properly prepared and unified, the English department, he has said, could become "the center of the entire university," on which the department's writing courses would impose "a common language" by "forcing all students of the college to speak about their specialties to the uninformed generalist" (Kinneavy, 1983, pp. 16, 20). Thus the *multiversity* would become once more the *university,* and my respected friend Jay Robinson's dream of a common public language for the entire society would come true: "A common language, a public discourse, must bridge not only from discipline to discipline, from the jargon of anthropology to the jargon of literary criticism, but from each equally to the discourse systems constructed for our students by their ways of being in the world, the discourse systems of self, family, and neighborhood. Community is made possible only when diversity and its expression are made equally possible" (Robinson, 1985, p. 495).

All of that strikes me as pie in the sky. It is at best the dreaming of academic humanists so insulated from the encompassing society that they cannot recognize the narrow limits of their own small power, at worst not even dreaming but the rationalization of academic empire-building. Teachers alone can never change the system of corporate control which pays them (rather badly) in the expectation that they will preserve, protect, and defend it. In fact, most academics accept the system's values. The primary concerns of academic humanists as a group (please note the qualification) are their own status and comfort, which research and publication, they hope, will guarantee. Their primary accomplishment is cloning and the over-production of lit crit. Like adolescents on Chicago's South Side streets, they protect their own turf, and the literati will no more tolerate the compositionists' threat to their departmental dominance than Jackie Presser will share control of the teamsters' union. Hence, for example, Kinneavy's own much-advertised writing program at the University of Texas (which thinks of itself as a flagship among state universities) was scuttled almost before it had been instituted. As a participant in that prototypical conflict, I can say with a document-hoarder's confidence that the literati at first had seen the Kinneavy program as (among other things) a means to lighten the "burden" of staffing and teaching many scores of sections of composition; but when the "burden" was not lightened (because the department and the administration botched the logistics) and when the untenurable lecturers who taught many of the composition sections began to demand the rights and privileges of "regular" faculty, the literati staged a palace coup. They defended their coup with public falsehood. And mere truth, as usual, made nobody free; for the powerful ignored it.

So much for the dream of an English department as the center of an intellectual community unified by a common public language. The real center of the prototypical state university is specialized research, especially research for the Department of [so-called] Defense, and if we leave the one example of the University of Texas and look more generally at other recent examples of language planning by members of English departments, we see the same paradox repeatedly: teachers of English in the U.S.A. are so much a minor part of the dominant economic system that they either cannot or will not recognize the functions and limitations which the decision-makers in the system impose upon them. (Obviously the qualification *as a group* will continue to apply in all I say; for if my judgment were universal, I would not waste your time and mine in hopeless argument.)

The selective account of our recent language planning which now follows may properly begin with Sputnik I; for as John Gerber said a few years ago in his history of the Association of Departments of English (Gerber, 1983), it was Sputnik which prompted not just the creation of the ADE but such undertakings as Project English and the summer institutes of the College Entrance Examination Board and the National Defense Education Act, and in those enterprises a certain amount of language planning was involved. I cannot imagine a better instance of the way in which academics are driven by the corporate system which they serve, for "the supposed crisis in education after Sputnik," like the supposed crisis in education in the '80s, was really an attempt to bring education still "more fully into the service of the military-industrial complex ... so that advanced technology would continue to assure American hegemony. Those who question the adjective *supposed* may be reminded that scores on the notorious Scholastic Aptitude Test (the main evidence for the most recent proclamations of educational disaster) were at their highest in 1955–6 and 1962–3"—dates which bracket the launching of Sputnik in 1957 (Sledd, 1987). I will return to the crisis-criers later.

Again like our present Toyota-and-technology crisis, the Sputnik crisis of the late fifties was used by academic empire-builders for their own advantage. The aged and aging will remember *The National Interest and the Teaching of English,* and some may remember Paul Roberts, H. A. Gleason, and even Harold Allen's *New Dimensions in English.* Just as Kinneavy would make rhetoric the heart of all the humanities, so Allen and his colleagues defined English as "the study of the English *language* and of its use as a medium of communication" (Allen, Newsome, Wetmore, Throckmorton, and Borgh, 1966–7, "Teacher's Guide," p. 2, emphasis added); but the pop linguists' challenge to the entrenched literati soon fizzled out. The linguists, indeed, gave the literati a weapon by foolishly maintaining that all languages and all dialects are equal in complexity and in value, and classroom teachers were further put off when they were asked to learn first one "new grammar" and then another. The linguistics which had been a panacea in 1960 had become the root of evil by 1980.

The compositionists, too, have remained well below the literati on the English department's totem pole. *Research* in composition has indeed become a monstrous industry, with its fully developed professional apparatus of conferences, grants, seminars, institutes, journals, and paradigmatic feuds; but the *teaching* of composition in the pattern-setting universities remains a slave-trade. The egregious humanist Richard Lanham exemplified the value-system of the literati when he wrote that teaching literature is "self-renewing" but that teaching composition turns minds "to oatmeal" (Lanham, 1983, p. 112).

Thus neither the old crisis nor the new has shaken the domination of English departments by the literati, who defend their turf with stubborn skill. Though they shun composition themselves and look down on those who teach it, the literati are still reluctant to let composition leave the English department, as "Speech" did long ago and as serious linguistics has more recently done. According to Lanham, "graduate student teaching assistants do 40 percent of the undergraduate teaching at UCLA" (154). They also fill the advanced courses in literature. As long as any demand for degrees in English is kept alive by the need of the corporate executives for at least a moderate supply of traditionally literate employees, the literati will keep the benefits of their odd subculture.

Ironically, then, departments of English, in which linguistics has been pretty well killed off, have been inescapably involved in the most ambitious language planning in the United States in the past quarter-century—namely, the attempt to impose the standard English of the privileged on students to whom society has denied its natural mastery. That attempt was most highly publicized and subsidized in the two decades after *Brown vs. Board of Education,* when middle-class white teachers in Northern cities discovered that lower-class black immigrants from the South didn't talk as *they* did; but space needn't be wasted here on familiar details of the profitable study of Black English by white linguists, of the failed movement called bidialectalism, of the 4Cs' brave statement of the *Students' Right to Their Own Language,* of the inconsequential Ann Arbor "Black English Case," or of the sneaky effort, by moguls of the 4Cs and the NCTE, to abrogate the *Students' Right* as the eighties began.

The essential facts of all that mad activity are distressfully clear. No argument was ever made out that specific features of standard English were superior, as instruments of communication, to the features of the Black English vernacular which they were intended to replace; and no analysis of specific occupations ever showed that gainful employment and productive work were impossible for speakers of nonstandard dialects. Instead, it was simply proclaimed that users of nonstandard English would be forever denied economic opportunity and social acceptance. The very motive which was urged upon the students—the achievement of "upward mobility in the mainstream culture"—involved a deep contradiction. Not only was the promise of upward mobility false for the vast majority. Upward mobility itself implies initiation into the insane consumerism on which the U. S. economy depended until the happy inauguration of the arms race. Victims of the consumerist society, that is to say, were tempted with the false promise that if they abandoned their language and all it symbolized, they might become diseased consumers too and from their new height might look down on their old comrades, who had to go down when others went up. Since the bearers of the White Man's Burden, in this foolish undertaking, had neither the detailed knowledge of dialects nor the sophisticated methods of teaching which their scheme would still have demanded under the best of social conditions, its failure was preordained. Luckily for the burden-bearers, the victims were available to be blamed.

The bidialectal debacle was another splendid example of the way in which academics ignore societal constraints even while they themselves are motivated by the society's sick values; yet similar endeavors have gone on, and continue to go on, outside of bidialectal circles. With no reason whatever to hope for success, Mina Shaughnessy, in genuine benevolence, attempted to impose the grammatical prejudices of her middle-class colleagues on her lower-class students by means of "error analysis" (long familiar among linguists) and of what she herself called "A Rube Goldberg grammar." E. D. Hirsch built *the* philosophy of composition on such notions as the supposedly classless and unchanging grapholect and a cock-eyed definition of "relative readability" by a middle-brow audience. John Fisher keeps talking about the unalterable grapholect (the "school English" to which he sees no alternative) after Hirsch himself has precipitately abandoned composition's sole philosophy for an equally quixotic program of banality-sharing to create a common culture. Other compositionists stress "bringing our students into the academy." They urge us to teach students "the language of academic discourse," to integrate them "as enfranchised members of the academic community," to immerse them "in academic discourse communities which will enable them to do the kinds of reading, writing and inquiry appropriate to such communities" (Robinson, 1985, p. 494; Kutz, 1986, p. 390; Nan Elsasser, personal communication, March 17, 1986; Richard M. Coe, Karen Burke-LeFevre, and James A. Reither, 1986). The apparent implication is that the academy is a benevolent and abiding institution which students want (or ought to want) to enter. Thomas Farrell adds a new twist with the announcement that black students can't think abstractly because they don't use standard English but mutilate the verb *to be* (Farrell, 1983), and the College Board goes him one better with the astonishing assertion that without mastery of standard English (both written and spoken), "knowledge of history, science, language, and all other subjects is unattainable" (College Board, 1983, pp. 7–9). It is all as though much-cited Paulo Freire had been read but had not been comprehended. The existing society is assumed as the inescapable given, and students are to be initiated into its practices and values, without regard to the quality of those practices and values or to the students' own desires.

The College Board's aberration is especially significant, for the Board and its Siamese twin the Educational Testing Service used the uninterpretable decline in SAT scores to stir up the recent hysteria about our schools and profitably to exacerbate the craze for standardized testing. There is, of course, no conclusive evidence that schools and teachers have so failed that education is in crisis and Ross Perot must save the life of the mind in Texas. The College Board's own "Advisory Panel" on the test score decline admitted as much, in its backhanded way, in its little weasel-worded report *On Further Examination.* "There are no reliable comprehensive measures yet," the panelists confessed, "of the comparative competence of today's youth with yesterday's" (College Board, 1977, p. 23). In 1983, the Assessment Development and Analysis Department of the NAEP made a similar confession (Mullis & Mead, 1983). In the National Assessment's data, the Department said, "there is little evidence" to "support the idea that there is a reading or writing crisis." Paul E. Peterson of the University of Chicago said much the same thing in a "Background Paper" for the Twentieth Century Fund's report *Making the Grade.* Supporting his judgment with an array of evidence unmatched in the usual proclamation of catastrophe, Peterson said flatly that "while areas of deficiency can be discerned, there is little evidence for concluding that the American system of education is in serious trouble, much less that it has failed" (Peterson, 1983, p. 35). He showed by reiteration that he meant what he had said. "The data . . . provide little support for the sense of decline and deterioration in education that many believe currently exists" (38). "The crisis in American education is greatly exaggerated" (157).

My own belief, after reading a good many of the recent reports of educational disaster, is accordingly that there is no conclusive evidence of a crisis in American education but that there is a deadly crisis in American society and American government; yet if that is so, one has to ask, suspiciously, what motivates the attack on education. Paul Peterson provides an initial answer. "Just as Sputnik inspired concern for the quality of American education in the 1950s," Peterson writes, "so Japanese technology and vigorous competition from other foreign countries have awakened public interest in education *as the means to enhance national productivity*" (161; emphasis added). I prefer to substitute the phrase *corporate interest* for *public interest.* The supposed educational crisis of the eighties results from the imposition, by the executives of the big corporations, of new demands on the educational system; and the attack on teachers for not doing what before they have not been asked to do is simple intimidation. For the sake of their own profits, the corporate executives intend to maintain, extend, and solidify their control of American education from kindergarten through graduate school. Two revealing themes run through reports like *America's Competitive Challenge, A Nation at Risk,* and *Action for Excellence.* One theme is the constant demand that business have a louder voice in educational governance and that governments enlarge the special privileges of the transnational corporations. The other is that the educational system must contribute to economic growth by preparing the "work force" which will enrich the executives and their shareholders. In particular, workers are warned that they must accept the inevitability of forced technological change. Workers must realize that for the sake of profit, their bosses will destroy existing jobs by technological innovation and that consequently the jobless must repeatedly retrain themselves as they move like rootless nomads from old jobs to new and from one section of the country to another. Just as English teachers assume that students must be initiated into the academy as it is, so corporate executives assume that workers must accept whatever work the executives offer in their quest for profit.

What is presented to a gullible public as an educational crisis is thus in fact a crisis in the encompassing society, a crisis whose causes are offered as its cures. Essentially, executives who care nothing for either literacy or illiteracy except as profit is involved, have set out to make most of us "settle for less" so that they themselves can have more. In the process they are dividing the population into a shrinking minority of richer haves and a growing majority of poorer have-nots. Already that division has sharpened noticeably, as one can see from such documents as the report by the Children's Defense Fund, *Black and White Children in America.* "Compared to five years ago," that report informs anyone who bothers to read it, "black children are more likely to be born into poverty, lack early prenatal care, have an adolescent or single mother, have an unemployed parent, be unemployed themselves as teenagers, not go to college after high school graduation" (Children's Defense Fund, 1985, p. vii).

Much the same ugly story must be told about Hispanics, the nation's fastest-growing minority. In Texas, which I mention again because I know its situation at first hand, the high school dropout rate is over 35 percent. It is higher still for Hispanics—twice as high as for blacks, three times as high as for Anglos. Among Hispanic dropouts, the unemployment rate is 36 percent, and the average wage of the dropouts who do have jobs is $3.21 an hour, less than $130 for a 40-hour week. Yet by 1990 Hispanics will make up 30 percent of the state's total population (statistics from *Austin American-Statesman,* June 11, 1986). The comparable uncertainty of even the Anglo workers' future was suggested by a story in the same issue of the Austin newspaper which discussed the Hispanic dropouts. Data General, the headline said, was closing its Austin plant in "a corporate expense-cutting move." The move would cost Austin 375 jobs.

It is in that situation that governments are cutting education budgets and the corporate reformers of education are urging more requirements, fewer electives, higher standards, and entrance and exit examinations. The performance of the College Board is typical. In its "Green Book" *Academic Preparation for College,* the Board demands, among other impossibles, that every entering college freshman be able to read standard English at a high level, to speak it clearly and effectively in public presentations, and to write and revise it in various styles, "with correct: sentence structure; verb forms; punctuation, capitalization, possessives, plural forms, and other matters of mechanics; word choice and spelling" (College Board, 1983, pp. 7–9). That is to ask that all entering freshmen be able to do what few graduating seniors can; yet at the same time "our structures of class and power, and the recent policies of our governments, are closing off the equal access to education which optimists hoped for in the sixties but which was never achieved" (Sledd, 1986, p. 28). In other words, the corporate executives who complain loudest about the failure of the schools to cultivate literacy are themselves the guilty parties, for they direct a social system which values literacy only as a means to corporate profit. We do not need a task force or commission to tell us that far too many Americans are illiterate or nearly so. That has always been true. But the "reforming" executives are now concerned because they would like to pick and choose among high-level literates as upper servants in their high-tech world. For the mass of American students, doomed either to unemployment or to ill-paid, unskilled labor, the executives care nothing at all.

I conclude that like the two-hundred-year-old effort which preceded it, the past quarter-century's attempt to impose the standard dialect on users of nonstandard varieties has foundered on its own contradictions. One cannot impose subservience in the name of freedom. Teachers of English as a group, however, seem quite unable to see beyond the narrow confines of their own departments into the wider world which simultaneously commands and forbids them to lead all their students to literacy. It is sadly characteristic that the one activity which the name itself of *English teacher* immediately suggests is the futile teaching of Latinate prescriptive grammar by constant correction and mindless drill. But traditional grammatical nit-picking survives precisely because its lack of function makes it functional. Having nothing to do with good-faith communication, it teaches concern for petty differences among "proper" and "improper" synonyms, contempt for speech and speakers branded as improper, and unquestioning obedience to even irrational commands. The grammar class is an academic bootcamp where absurd rituals performed under constant threat and bullying teach recruits that there is no upward road without submissive anguish. Pupils who take such teaching at face value may then go on to become English teachers and to criticize the language of the dominant for its "impurity."

Such is my account of our recent past. At a conference on "language in its social context," I say that we have been unable or unwilling to recognize the social context of our students' language or of our teaching. But I am bidden to speak not just of retrospect but of *prospect,* and though I cannot pretend to optimism or to any faith that our lives are in our own control, I will obey the terms of my invitation and will ask what, as teachers of English, we should do in our present situation.

Our ultimate aim, though it sounds grandiose to say it, should be social revolution, since unjust privilege in a destructive system will not be willingly surrendered; but social revolution from the Left (if it ever comes) is an adventure for younger generations than ours. In that social revolution, English teachers would anyhow have only a tiny part to play. We must make content with the unheroic efforts for which we may be suited—for example, with fomenting departmental revolution to break the departmental dominance of the literati. Academic claims for the study and teaching of literature by academics are exaggerated. Literature would survive the MLA.

Linguists and compositionists, however, should not try to replace the petty Empire of Literature with an equally petty Empire of Rhetoric or Empire of Linguistics. Great schemes for organizing the academic world are damaging. Academic departments are historical accidents, and none the worse for that. They should try to keep live concerns alive and open, not to impose some theoretical organization which commands no wide assent and which would stifle more useful activity than it would nourish.

In whatever academic structure, teachers of English should recognize that learning and teaching presuppose aims freely shared by teachers and students, aims which with luck might allow students to become active shapers of their own lives, not anonymous members of a subservient "work force." One such aim is literacy as a means to liberating action. For that reason, composition should have an honored place in English departments—and not just *research* in composition. Rationally, the *teachers* who cultivate literacy would be rewarded as their work deserves: the use of part-timers and the exploitation of graduate students are expedients which disprove the claims of the literati for the moral influence of their study of literature. Similar arguments justify a place in English departments for serious linguists, whose work is essential if the standard dialect is to be made generally accessible (accessibility being distinct from imposition).

Such a reshaping of our departments implies the abandonment of research and publication as the primary criteria for professional advancement—more generally, the abandonment of the cupidity on which our socioeconomic system is built. Paulo Freire talks of "making our Easter," of dying to "be born again with the beings who were not allowed to be" (Freire, 1985, pp. 121–142). Richard Ohmann (or somebody just as intelligent) talks openly of a sort of intellectual conversion. Rational teachers would not find such talk irrational, even in the scarcity of converts.

Whatever else is done or not done, we should practice the critical thinking that we talk so much about. We should *see and say*—see our work in its full social and educational context, speak out against the hypocrisies of our society and our profession even when whistle-blowers take a beating and our best efforts seem ludicrous and pretentious. Even for the timid, there's no sense at all in passivity, in accepting the vicious adage that education must not be politicized. Education is political by nature, and the politics of the a-political is the greatest obstacle to rational work by rational teachers.

Finally, political commitment must eventually lead to a search for allies outside the academy. By ourselves, we teachers of English can do very little. Great social changes may come if ordinary people ever decide that continued submission will cost more than resistance. Meanwhile, we should break the habit of aligning ourselves with the privileged. We are downwardly mobile, not upward, and our right allies are the oppressed, the struggling—ordinary people leading ordinary lives. To recognize that fact would make at least one breach in the wall which cuts us off from social reality.

Works Cited

Allen, H., Newsome, V., Wetmore, T., Throckmorton, H., & Borgh, E. (1966–7). *New dimensions in English.* Wichita, KS: McCormick-Mathers.

Bessinger, J., & Yeager, R. (Eds.). (1984). *Approaches to teaching Beowulf.* New York: Modern Language Association.

Children's Defense Fund. (1985). *Black and white children in America: key facts.* Washington, DC: Children's Defense Fund.

Coe, R., Burke-LeFevre, K., & Reither, J. (1986, May). *Teaching invention as a social process.* Workshop at the Fourth International Conference on the Teaching of English, Ottawa.

College Board. (1977). *On further examination: report of the advisory panel on the scholastic aptitude test score decline.* New York: CEEB.

College Board. (1983). *Academic preparation for college.* New York: CEEB.

Commission on Reading, National Academy of Education. (1985). *Becoming a nation of readers.* Washington, DC: National Institute of Education.

Farrell, T. (1983). IQ and standard English. *College Composition and Communication, 34,* 470–484.

Fisher, J. (1981). School English and public policy. *College English, 43,* 856–57.

Freire, Paulo. (1985). *The politics of education.* South Hadley, MA: Bergin & Garvey.

Gerber, J. (1983). ADE: then and now. *Profession, 83,* 7–12.

Hillocks, G., Jr. (1986). *Research on written composition.* Urbana, IL: National Conference on Research in English and ERIC Clearinghouse on Reading and Communication Skills.

Hirsch, E., Jr. (1977). *The philosophy of composition.* Chicago: University of Chicago Press.

Hirsch, E., Jr. (1983). Cultural literacy. *The American Scholar, 52,* 159–169.

Kinneavy, J. (1983). Writing across the curriculum. *Profession 83,* 13–20.

Kutz, E. (1986). Between students' language and academic discourse: interlanguage as middle ground. *College English, 48,* 385–396.

Lanham, R. (1983). *Literacy and the survival of humanism.* New Haven: Yale University Press.

Mullis, I., & Mead, N. (1983). *How well can students read and write?* (ECS Issuegram 9) Denver: Education Commission of the States.

Peterson, P. (1983). Is there a crisis in American education? In *Making the grade* (Report of the Twentieth Century Fund Task Force on Federal Elementary and Secondary Education Policy). New York: Twentieth Century Fund.

Robinson, J. (1985). Literacy in the department of English. *College English, 47,* 482–498.

Shaughnessy, M. (1977). *Errors and expectations: a guide for the teacher of basic writing.* New York: Oxford University Press.

Sledd, J. (1986). A basic incompetence in the defining of basic competencies. *English Journal, 75* (7), 26–28.

Sledd, J. (1987). Literacy crises and the survival of the inhumane. In R. Narveson (Ed.), *An olio of notions concerning the politics of writing instruction,* 18–34. Lincoln: Department of English, University of Nebraska.

Stull, W. (1984). Literature, literary theory, and the teaching of composition. In M. Moran & R. Lunsford (Eds.), *Research in composition and rhetoric,* 125–151. Westport, CT: Greenwood Press.

Notes

1. This paper was read at the Wyoming Conference (Summer, 1986), which focused on "language in its social context." I have chosen to keep an informal style of oral delivery, in the hope of breaking down the wall of academic detachment.

Product in Process
From Ambiguities of Standard English to Issues That Divide Us
(1988)

By 1988 James Sledd had become an emeritus professor, but his anger at the economic powers of the "external" world who exert tremendous control over university instruction, particularly in determining how professors attempt to teach standard English, had not—and has not—diminished.

I. Context[1]

In the United States today, the executives of the transnational corporations and their flunkies in the military-industrial-educational complex are working a technological revolution within a society as stratified in fact as it is egalitarian in theory. One obvious part of this military-industrial-educational strategy is a drive to maintain and extend corporate control of schooling and—more generally—corporate control of the accumulation, storage, and dissemination of knowledge. The rich and powerful (need one say it?) mean to profit at the expense of the poor and powerless while proclaiming their concern for the good of all.

We who teach the use of English can expect no honored place in the corporate executives' envisioned world of computerized high technology. The language of their Institutional Voice already differs observably from the Standard English which some of us have known and all of us have claimed to teach. To be sure, we have our own creaky modulations of the Institutional Voice. They are prescribed by the style manuals of our professional societies—societies which by and large accept the social assumptions of the dominant and cultivate modes of expression calculated to set upwardly mobile professionals apart and to reduce lay people to a lower level of mystified awe. Yet English teachers can hardly even pronounce and certainly can't understand the magic words of entrepreneurs and technologists like those who want to "make space a marketplace." At public expense, the necromancers spangle the firmament with satellites for military-industrial communication while they expand the lexicon with verbified nouns (like *to architect*), mysterious acronyms (like TRAC, the Texas Reconfigurable Array Computer, with its "banyan interconnection network"), and unutterable string compounds (like the infamous *liquid oxygen liquid hydrogen rocket powered single state to orbit reversible boost system*). In the high-tech world, English teachers are less "marketable" than computer programs that solve physics problems.

More ominously, we teachers of English seem equally unable (or unwilling?) to understand the significance of the innumerable reports which allege and lament a crisis in public education and loudly remind school-people that they must contribute to the national priorities of technology, productivity, and defense against Nicaragua's threat to Harlingen. We ought to be terrified, but aren't, at so familiar a spectacle as the University of Texas at Austin. A "flagship" among the state universities, UT not long ago abruptly terminated the employment of some fifty lecturers in English, especially in English composition, while about the same time it made vast commitments, which it proudly called unprecedented, to hasten the development of microelectronics and computer engineering. The corporate Canutes who rule the state and its universities are determined to repel the Toyota tide, no matter what the cost to traditional literacy and the liberal arts.

In these circumstances, I stubbornly commit the *faux pas* of an old-fashioned and provincial academic paper. Before the paper itself, I have attempted this three-paragraph account of our political situation. After the paper, I will ask what we might do, situated as we are, to resist those who think of education only as "education for economic growth." I say little about classroom practice, for the emphasis on how-to-do-it embodies the assumption that our present socio-economic system is beneficent and stable, so that we teachers know without thinking what we ought to teach and can concentrate on the best ways of teaching it. Maybe it is arrogant to

question such dominant assumptions. Certainly the questioning
will prompt some readers to replace the actual argument with a
favorite banality and then to reject the actual argument as banal.

II. Argument

Standard written English, we of the U.S.A. are assured by eminent
authorities, is a classless and unchanging grapholect, a public idiom
in worldwide use which is presently our unofficial official language
and which promises to remain almost unchanged, because "we"
want it to, as long as our civilization also remains. It is more useful,
however, and more accurate, to speak of standardization in the
interactive media of both speech and writing and to speak of Standard English not as changeless but as a product in constant process.
The constantly changing spoken and written language which the
dominant call standard is a creation and instrument of the dominant for purposes of domination, but an instrument in being whose
becoming creates the possibility of controlling the controllers or
escaping their control. The reference of the pronoun *we* must vary
as speakers identify themselves with either the dominant or the
dominated: minorities are now the majority in the schools of Austin, and in Brownsville (if not in Harlingen) one is in the colonial
periphery. In the U.S.A. today, no teacher of any subject can claim
exemption from social and political responsibility, and teachers of
English can no longer claim the status (if ever they could, rightly)
which Professor Douglas Bush assumed when he rebuked Mr. Secretary Connally for confusing *virulence* with *virility*.

The standardization of Standard English was conducted
through now familiar stages during the four centuries, roughly, from
Chaucerian to Johnsonian times. When Chaucer was born, no single
dialect of English was recognized as standard. When Johnson died,
a standard had been established for both speech and writing, its
approved structure and proper use had been described in authoritative grammars and dictionaries, and the language thus codified and
regulated had come to rival or replace both French and Latin in all
the functions which may be served by the fully elaborated varieties
of a great national and international language. The norm which had
been created for the official documents of the central bureaucracies
had been successfully imposed throughout England and to a large
extent in Scotland, Ireland, and Wales; the ruling class and its intellectual upper servants in the London area had also imposed their
judgment of their English speech as better than the speech of the
people, better even than the speech of the gentry in the North and

West; and as writers in English had created for the privileged a literature which stood comparison with the literatures of Greece and Rome and their derivatives, a language of administrative power had become a language of literary tradition and privileged social status. The exclusionary aspect of a doctrine of correctness had become increasingly evident.

The weakness of Johnson's plea for retarding change is that unless a language changes, it cannot meet the needs of a changing world. Johnson's death was approximately contemporary with England's "take-off" into self-sustaining economic growth, with successful revolution in the Thirteen Colonies (and in France), with maintenance of the Empire in Canada, and with its expansion into Asia, Africa, and the South Pacific. In such circumstances, even if (as literary students) we knew nothing of *Lyrical Ballads* or *The Adventures of Huckleberry Finn* (where the real language of persons in *very* low and rustic life was mimicked in ways that would have astonished Wordsworth), still we would predict coincident changes in the standard language as both political and cultural instrument and in people's thought about it.

The old "high" culture of Western Europe could not be transported to Europe's colonies intact. As English, then, became a world language, new linguistic standards had to be developed for new lives in different lands, among greatly differing linguistic and ethnic groups. The conditions of colonial life, and the imposed but widely accepted dogma of colonial inferiority, made the development of autonomous standards slow and difficult, completed only in this century in even the most powerful of the former colonies, the United States.

Despite all differences, however, familiar structures of social and linguistic domination were at least partly replicated throughout the now vanished Empire. One result is a world language of international intelligibility, varying somewhat in lexicon but little in syntax and—among the privileged—sufficiently uniform even in phonology to make communication relatively easy among those who wish to communicate. Ironically, the language by which the Empire had been governed was ultimately turned against imperial domination; and today, world English in many countries is essential in the pursuit of political, social, and personal liberation.

It also remains an instrument of domination by the privileged, not just by powerful aliens but by indigenous elites from India to the U.S. Virgin Islands. World English is still primarily the language of the dominant, too often inaccessible to the majority; and more diverse and less widely intelligible varieties range downward, as the dominant would judge, to pidgins and creoles. The condemnation of the nonstandard dialects of English and of the English-based pidgins and creoles, though often shared by their own speakers, ignores the fact that no language and no variety of any language would survive if it did not serve some purposes for some people better than any other language or variety serves them. It is an arrogant absurdity for the dominant minority to despise the languages and language-varieties of the majority, in which most of the world's work gets done.

From this history, irreconcilable differences and inescapable responsibilities arise for English-teachers. Every language-variety has both its praxis and its norm or norms, which testify (when a norm becomes conscious and is overtly stated) that praxis varies. The norm of a standard language, in general based ultimately on the praxis of the dominant, is *always* conscious, so that an elaborated and codified standard is never a mere emergence but in part a creation (not *ex nihilo*), the product-in-process of deliberate intervention in linguistic history for the purposes and profit of the intervenors. Standard languages as sociolinguists describe them are in no sense "natural" or universal but have been developed at distinctive stages of relatively recent social evolution and have been purposefully imposed, most typically by centralized national power.

It follows that what was deliberately created in one set of circumstances can be deliberately changed (as always, within limits) in another. It is simply false that there is no alternative to "school English," that the conservative power of an established grapholectic norm is irresistible. In learning, teaching, and using languages and dialects, real choices have really to be made. At least some divisive issues admit no responsible compromise.

The real issues cannot be dealt with until false issues have been set aside. For readers of academic journals printed in Standard English, there is no point in refuting the trendy assertion that Standard English does not exist. To be sure, there is conflict and variation within both norm and praxis (though less variation than in nonstandard varieties), and since that variation not only exists but is closely though not exclusively linked to distinctions of nation, region, sex, age, and social class or subclass, the ambiguities of the standard will increase in a changing, divided society where the masses distrust the dominant. The economic power of the risen redneck in a high-tech world makes the redneck's praxis more important to changes in the norm than either the norm or the praxis of the traditionally educated, and when the dominant close the doors of educational and economic opportunity to the majority, as current educational "reforms" in the U.S.A. are doing, the nature of the standard will be modified by the resultant sharpening of sociolinguistic stratification; but under all such changes, the standard continues to exist—and continues to exist as an instrument of domination, the primary means of social control. Standard English remains the accent and dialect of the Institutional Voice where the Institutional Voice is Anglophone.

A second false issue is the argument that although Standard English does exist, it is *not* an instrument created by the dominant for purposes of domination. The evidence to the contrary is so vast that in brief remarks it can hardly be mentioned and cannot be summarized: the origin of the "grapholect" in Chancery Standard; sixteenth-century descriptions of the then newly recognized standard speech; the collapse of standardized languages like Aelfric's Old English, the Middle English of *Ancrene Wisse* and related texts, and fifteenth-century Scots, because they either lost or never had the support of centralized national power; the imposition of Standard English as the "public language" of the Celtic periphery; the correlations between linguistic variation and social class which sociolinguists have demonstrated in both Britain and the United States; the similar correlations in the Third World as a result of policies like that formulated in Macaulay's "Minute"; the Third World's revolt against external standards after the break-up of the Empire; the similar refusal by many Blacks to accept white English any longer as standard for Black communities; and overt statements and actions, in the immediate past and in the present, by persons claiming authority in the United States. In the '60s, our proponents of bidialect(al)ism asserted that students who did not master Standard English would be denied economic opportunity and social acceptance. In the '80s, United States Senators Hayakawa and Huddleston have pushed for a constitutional amendment making English the one official language of the nation; some states, including California, have succumbed to fear of the Yellow-Brown peril, and others are tremescent; oil refineries in largely Spanish-speaking Corpus Christi (Texas) have imposed English-only job rules; and the College Entrance Examination Board has demanded that all college entrants must already control both the spoken and the written standard—all this at a time when even transitional bilingual programs are under attack and when the Reaganite social and educational policies make it quite impossible for the majority of young Americans to meet such demands as those of the College Board. The bi-dialectalists' assertion of the '60s is being officially verified twenty years later.

The last false issue which needs immediate dismissal is the spurious argument whether Standard English should be taught. The argument is spurious because absolute opposition to such teaching does not exist but has been invented in a deceitful ploy to discredit real opposition, not to the unqualified teaching of the standard, but to teaching it in wrong ways and for wrong reasons.

The genuine issues which have thus been industriously obscured are questions of motives and methods, of deepest purpose and the best means to accomplish it. In general they fall under the rubric of the Freirean opposition between domestication and liberation, between animal training and the emancipatory education of human beings. In the United States today, when the executives of the transnational corporations and their flunkies are strengthening and extending their control of the educational system at all levels, teachers of English cannot escape the conflict by crying "Peace! peace!" For there is no peace.

The most widespread of the politic evasions is the relativism which destroys the distinction between *Standard* English and *good* English and makes reasoned choices impossible by stripping the words *good* and *bad* of any meaningful application to languages and language-varieties. The long process of standardization, and continuing use as the linguistic vehicle of all activities which the dominant presume to regulate (including literature), have made Standard English the most useful all-purpose dialect we have. That assertion is neither a denial of the unique values of every dialect nor a commitment to foolish notions that literacy in an alphabetically written language works wonders for the cognitive faculties. The assertion is simply an acknowledgment that the slogan "Difference, not deficit!" is false to fact and guarantees that deficit will be perpetuated. If linguistic deprivation and cultural deprivation were not real, protests against injustice would be gratuitous trouble-making.

A second evasion does not deny meaning to the terms *good* and *bad* but defines them simplistically by equating *good* with *standard*, *bad* with *nonstandard* or *substandard*. Again the possibility of choosing is denied, on the assumption that since the bossed would like to become bosses, they must talk boss-talk so that they may be "upwardly mobile in the mainstream culture"—that is, so that they may encourage the sin of envy by conspicuously wasting more of the world's irreplaceable resources than other wasteful Americans waste, always on the further assumption that the inferior peoples of the Third World are rightfully to be exploited. In the United States, to teach for the goal of upward mobility is tacitly to assume that devotees of that strange abstraction the American nation should enjoy special privilege. One result, if such teaching should be successful, would be that world English would remain primarily a tool for world domination. Present bosses, however, would be pleased by the pedagogic treason because it would provide them with a docile, efficient "work force" while discouraging real change in the structures of power and class.

For teachers who refuse to equate the good and the standard, the most difficult choices all remain, for good English must be defined. Consensus in such matters of value is certainly impossible and probably undesirable, but that inconclusive conclusion at least suggests a strong judgment on a last real issue—last for lack of space, not of matter for argument. How much variation from whatever norm they choose should teachers of English accept without protest or should even encourage? How much change, as a *consequence* of variation, should they also accept or encourage? It is pointless to assume that change in either norm or praxis has been stopped, or can or should be; yet Johnson's argument for retarding at least some changes is only a generalized antecedent to specific opposition by contemporary pedagogues to abuses like doublespeak. As Leavis said, "Life is growth and growth change, and the condition of these is continuity"; but how does one treat the product of the past in the present process?

The difficulty of agreement in matters of value, and the fallibility of consensus even when it is achieved, suggest that puzzled teachers should generally accept or maybe encourage more diversity, not less, than they are inclined to. "Maximum diversity compatible with intelligibility" is a good slogan for world English because English will remain a world language only if its users everywhere can feel that in some sense English is their own, so that diversity and individual identity will be served as well as tradition and wide intelligibility. Attempts to impose a single narrowly regulated standard at the expense of pidgins, creoles, and nonstandard dialects are disastrous.

They are as disastrous at conferences and in classrooms as they are in wider arenas of "the real world." Speaking and writing may be considered as arts of controlled inference; for it takes two to converse, and unread writing is an abortion. We are using language, that is, when we read or listen as well as when we write or speak, and we frustrate both transactions if we assume a position of strength and attempt by strong demands on our interlocutors' language to impose our own ideas and values. That is one of many reasons why the absurd dream-world of the advocates of "cultural literacy" would be a nightmare. Banality-mongering and grammatical nit-picking are laughably inadequate to the creation, maintenance, or reconstruction of a culture.

III. Bodement

At least in the United States, our schools, colleges, and universities are not primarily devoted to education for freedom. Primarily, they serve the dominant—in the United States in 1988, the executives of the transnational corporations and their shareholders, whose morality has been abundantly exemplified by Ronald Reagan and his administration. To call the world of corporate executives and cowboy diplomats "the free world" is farcical: the free world is the indispensable dream which never will come true. In the corporate world and its appendages, the critical thinking which we talk about has no place except as it is devoted to the service of the dominant or conducted on the educational periphery by suspect teachers and their suspect students. The number of such students and such teachers isn't large. The great majority of students in the U.S.A. don't want a liberatory education: they want degrees as means to jobs that will offer them "the good life" of high status and conspicuous wastefulness. Teachers, though somewhat older, resemble their students and indeed the majority of the human species in this respect—that reasoned argument rarely overcomes immediate self-interest, narrowly conceived. The least critical thinkers of all are professorial types who imagine that they are quite exempt from these human frailties.

Until masses of people are convinced, then, by some unforeseeable catastrophe, that resistance will hurt less than continued submission, popular revolution will remain impossible in the United States; but vigorous revolution from the Right has been in progress for some years under self-styled conservatives of both parties, who mean to corrupt our minds and lives in order to satisfy their greed. In these circumstances, teachers who choose resistance must avoid self-dramatization and content themselves to be small voices in their own small wildernesses. Ambitious imperatives without power are damaging because they make those who issue them feel virtuous without doing anything. Awareness of our true situation and clear statement of it make a better beginning for the ultimately necessary search for allies.

Some truths about the usual arguments for the forceful imposition of Standard English will appear if we consider the standard language as an institution and apply Claire Lerman's description of the Institutional Voice. In "any institutional discourse," Lerman says, "the Underlying Topic is still the defence or retention of personal or political power," but for its "discourse of power" the Institutional Voice "uses the language of morality." "The primacy of the institution" (in the present application, Standard English) is assumed as "a basic tenet of institutional discourse" on matters linguistic. It becomes a point of "higher morality" to protect the standard language by arguments either pragmatic (without a standard, communication will break down) or theological ("the tongue that Shakespeare spake" must be kept "pure"). "Any threat to those transcendent values" constitutes a "crisis," in which defenders of the standard protect the nation's glorious linguistic heritage by playing on fears of "the external enemy" (the English of West Africa or South Asia, perhaps) or of "the radicals or dissidents within" (the Black English vernacular, or English Hispanicized). By "defining the issues of the other as a threat to national values," the Institutional Voice suppresses all topics but its own, which by their routine conventionality "preclude substantive discussion." In such rigged arguments, the enforced use of Standard English by the dominated as well as the dominant *enacts* institutional values. Nobody who *is* anybody listens to the suggestion that English-based Caribbean creole might be developed and standardized as an official national language or that "Black English" might be used and accepted "in the social domain." Nobody who is anybody answers the question of which "proper" modes of expression are really useful and which only bolster class-distinctions.

Lerman's insights may help to explain why more than a century of criticism has not checked the teaching of socially graded lexical and syntactic synonyms by drill and constant correction within the framework of Latinate tradition. The trick of such teaching is that relentless emphasis on the insignificant drives home the essential implicit lesson. The differences between synonyms like *convince to* and *convince that* or like *finalize* and *make final* are never significant for communication in good faith. In fact, the differences would not serve their deep purpose as class-markers if they did interfere with communication, because then everybody would learn them without instruction and the washed could no longer scorn the gamy. Traditional grammatical nit-picking survives because its lack of function makes it functional. It teaches respect for "proper" English and its users, contempt for speech and speakers branded as *improper,* and unquestioning obedience to even irrational commands.

Such absurdities will remain unless and until we teachers of English learn our real place in the world of the corporate executives. We are downwardly mobile, not upwardly, yet our boasted professionalism (in fact a humble tribute to our masters) is an attempt to distance ourselves from the powerless and to lay some feeble claim to status. We can't do much alone; at our conferences, we only talk, and talk only to each other; but we turn our backs on lowlier victims of our society and put our trust instead in organizations like the NCTE and the MLA, which in the last analysis support established power, no matter what its quality or action. The baffling question is how we might move beyond mere understanding of corporate behavior and of its consequences for our lives and work. Can we find allies whose interests we share and struggle together for power with, not power over—for institutions whose voices we could respect? Certainly we will never find the needed comrades if we keep looking in wrong places, and we will never be good teachers if we are teachers only. It's a bad joke to pretend that when we walk into our classrooms and close the doors behind us, we are really in charge.

Notes

1. An earlier version of this paper was read at the Fourth International Conference on the Teaching of English, in Ottawa, in May of 1986. When I submitted that version to *College English,* readers and editor rejected it except possibly as "an opinion piece." Publication under that obscure rubric is not (the editor assures me) a warning that the paper does not contain true knowledge or report profound research; but the label *opinion* does conveniently excuse me (since the length of "opinion pieces" is strictly limited) for omitting notes and documentation. The one essential reference is to Claire Lindegren Lerman, "Dominant Discourse: The Institutional Voice and Control of Topic," in *Language, Image, Media,* ed. Howard Davis and Paul Walton (New York: St. Martin's, 1983), 75–103. Only I am guilty of my (mis)treatment of Lerman's concept. Other benefactors who may recognize their ideas in my paper should not conclude that lack of footnotes means lack of gratitude.

How We Apples Swim
(1991)

Sledd is no less skeptical—or funny—in 1991 than he was in 1961. He is also no less clever, pointing out that English teachers still look in the mirror and smile, secure in the knowledge that they remain the fairest of them all. With this attitude, Sledd suggests, English teachers are not likely to bring about social revolution.

What are we really doing at this conference?

Our assigned theme is "The Right to Literacy." The organizers have defined literacy broadly, in ads and announcements for the conference, as "the ability to use language in order to become an active participant in all forms of public discourse." So defined, literacy is impossible in the United States, and there can be no right to the impossible.

The proof of those wounding propositions is easy. Competent public discourse requires a large supply of general and special information; for without information, "the ability to use language" is only the ability to babble aimlessly. The assigned definition therefore requires that literates shall have not just a productive and receptive command of many linguistic registers in both speech and writing but also free access to needed information and free access to the media by which information may be exchanged. Those huge requirements are nowhere met. In the United States, the people who control the educational system and the media do not even want such free, informed, and general participation in public affairs.

To exemplify, consider first the familiar situation of a composition teacher—a big state university's primary worker for literacy. At

159

the University of Texas at Austin, in many ways a representative institution, composition has been and still is mainly taught by underpaid but overworked graduate students and lecturers. They have only the smallest of voices in university governance, and administrators provide them only such information as the administrators choose. A few years ago, some fifty lecturers had to learn from the campus newspaper that their appointments would not be renewed for the following year. Too late for a hopeful job-hunt, they were simply set adrift. In the late spring of 1988, graduate students similarly learned from the campus newspaper what the administrators had known for weeks—namely, that the law would no longer allow the university to pay the students' insurance premiums. Without insurance, an already impecunious family could be ruined. Thus, by the definition established for this [1988 MLA "Right to Literacy"] conference—a definition which makes information essential to literacy—verbally gifted literacy workers at UT must be judged illiterate. They cannot participate actively even in discourse concerning their own work in a public university.

If literacy is confined to active participants in public discourse about university matters, then tenured and tenurable faculty at Texas are themselves by no means fully literate. In getting and giving information relevant to their employment, they have difficulties comparable to those of the graduate students and part-timers, though less severe. Within the university, information flows mainly downward—when it flows at all. Administrators, and especially the higher administrators, have their newsletters and other brag-sheets. They have their wide network of administrative communication, national as well as local, and they can easily make themselves seen and heard in the newspapers and on radio and TV. They are the university's public voice, with an Office of Institutional Studies to provide them with whatever statistics may best suit their purposes. Faculty, on the other hand, speak publicly as private citizens only. They are well advised to limit voluntary communication with their academic superiors to channels established by the administrative hierarchy, and crucial information may simply be denied them. Rash souls who ask to see their own personnel files may not even be aware that administrators may first edit those files severely, and questions addressed to administrators in such bodies as the University Council may be evaded with doubletalk.

By the definition of literacy which has been assigned to us, illiteracy is indeed the prevailing condition of *all* citizens in the Land of the Free. In the recent past, congressional investigators were by no means able, even if they were willing, to learn in detail how a corrupt shadow-government made war on Nicaragua, in defiance of the citizens and their elected representatives. The former President and Vice-President of the United States went so far as to imply publicly that, by the MLA's definition, they too were illiterate. They did not know, they said, what was going on. The general tenor of their behavior makes that claim most plausible.

Perhaps a reminder is in order that the preceding examples of illiteracy *are* based on the MLA's own definition. Conferees must assume that the definition was carefully framed with an eye to its implications and that it is not a mere cover for hidden purposes. That obligatory assumption combines with the given examples to enable us now to say at least what we are probably *not* doing at this conference. Despite the assigned theme and the assigned definition of literacy, we are hardly participating, with the Modern Language Association, in "the building of a national upheaval" (Kozol). It is most unlikely that the moguls of the MLA have acquired a sudden interest in helping to work the deep social, economic, and educational changes which would be necessary to make active participation "in all forms of public discourse" open to everyone. For whatever mysterious reason, we are not abiding by the definition's undeniable implications.

The most plausible *affirmative* answer to the question what are we doing is then disheartening. Unless we do abide by the letter and spirit of the assigned definition of literacy, we are only serving ourselves, in disregard of logic. We are polishing apples and egos, padding our resumes, proving that "the ability to use language" without logical content is rightly characterized as the ability to babble. Some of us are babbling the catchwords of "cultural literacy," the contradictory, unworkable, and therefore much praised scheme which E. D. Hirsch has based on misunderstanding and misrepresentation of inadequate linguistic authorities. And as we serve ourselves, we may very well be impeding rational action by giving the false impression that rational action is already being taken. The wordy wars of inveterate conference-goers usually bring nothing else about.

If by some freak the conference *should* have some real effect, the emphasis on language in its definition of literacy is likely to be narrowly confining. If we teach the formal competencies of reading and writing to students who cannot hope for free access to information and the media, we may simply provide our bosses with another instrument of domination. Our bosses want a citizenry which is open to dictation. They want a "work force" which has been brainwashed into docility but which has the technical abilities from which the bosses profit. A true concern for literacy must therefore also be a concern for social revolution. But the MLA is not in the revolution business, no matter *how* it defines literacy.

I turn now from the conference and its organizers' puzzling choice of a definition of the literacy to which they affirm a right, and accordingly the pronoun *we* now shifts to a more restricted reference.

Only a fool would expect professors of English to lead a revolution; but some few small things we *can* do (if improbably we will). We should begin at home, in a sustained attempt to break the prevailing system of exploitation in our own departments—the exploitation of graduate students and part-timers, the general dislike for teaching composition, the general injustice to composition teachers. In the exploited, our effort would have the crucial support of an articulate group motivated by a genuine grievance.

Sue Ellen Holbrook's paper, "Women's Work: The Feminizing of Composition," at the 1988 meeting of the 4C's was a most articulate documentation of that grievance. Here is one paragraph from her abstract:

> Pedagogic in focus, its place in the curriculum conceived as "service" and elementary, extensively using paraprofessionals, allied with education departments and school teaching, and saturated by women practitioners, composition has become women's work. And so it will remain as long as those conditions remain. The transformation of composition from women's work to a sexually integrated and well-esteemed profession can come only as a part of the larger complex processes of raising the status of teaching itself and the other service occupations in a capitalist society, breaking down the sexual division of labor, achieving social and economic equity between women and men, and re-valorizing socially produced differences between the masculine and feminine genders.

The attempt, of course, to make the teaching of composition in the universities as respected as it is respectable would face the entrenched self-interest of many of our colleagues, the established literati who dominate the MLA. Even more frighteningly, it would face our country's whole damned and damning economic system—by which, to cite an outrageous instance, the University of Texas refuses ever to pay a tenured or tenurable composition staff yet can find millions and millions for the consortium known as the Microelectronics and Computer Technology Corporation and for the greedy band of corporations called Sematech, which the great Democrat Michael Dukakis tried to lure to Massachusetts.

Bruising experience teaches that such taxing and spending adversaries, like hard-core Reaganites, are inaccessible to rational conversation. Talkative conferences won't overwhelm corporate communities of knowledgeably grasping peers. Besides, the corporate executives control the accumulation, storage, and dissemination of knowledge and the media by which it is or isn't disseminated. Concerted action to escape that control, at least on one small academic front, would have to come before sane talking could even be heard. But if the MLA's professors are genuinely concerned for literacy, they ought to support such radical acts as loud resignations by directors of exploited composition staffs, equally loud refusals to fill the vacated directorships, unionization, repeated teach-ins in lower-division courses, well publicized demonstrations by teachers of composition and their students and friends, even strikes, walkouts, and the peaceful occupation of the offices of deans and presidents.

If such action did make at least a narrow gap in the prevailing limits on the thinkable and the speakable, then proponents of humanely employed literacy might make a successful appeal to the people. Parents alarmed by talk of a "literacy crisis" might be even more alarmed if teachers could tell them, openly and strongly, how little the higher-education establishment really cares for general literacy among an informed and active majority. The MLA might be prodded into *acting* on the implications of its definition of literacy.

Those proposals are very limited. They touch only that small proportion of the total population, mainly white, which makes its way to the big universities. Even so, to make them as the world now stands is to invite ridicule as a foolish dreamer. It may still be answered that ridicule is not reserved for the ridiculous. A society cannot reasonably demand that all students master its standard language unless the society gives them all a real chance to learn and use it and real rewards for using it well, and it is not contemptible to set one's own house in order before sermonizing one's neighbors. University professors of English do dominate the MLA.

Dominant professional attitudes, it has been said, not only guarantee but will continue to guarantee that teachers of English cannot contribute to significant social change but help instead and will keep helping to maintain the present unjust system of dominance and submission. The challenge to this conference is to refute that uncomfortable accusation, at least in some small way.

If we do not refute it, we should be required every day to contemplate the old saying, "How we apples swim!" Tilley's *Dictionary of Proverbs* records Roger L'Estrange's exposition of it:

> Upon a fall of rain, the current carried away a huge heap of apples, together with a dunghill that lay in the watercourse. As they went thus, the horse-turds would be crying out still, "Alack a day! How we apples swim!"

Why the Wyoming Resolution Had to Be Emasculated

A History and a Quixotism
(1991)

It could be argued that this essay is one of Sledd's most important. Written by a man more than seventy-five years old, the essay argues against the institutionalized abuse of those who are just beginning their college teaching careers. It is fitting that this collection conclude with a cogent analysis of what is so terribly wrong with the profession that Sledd has officially left but cannot stop worrying about—especially as the practices of that profession harm those who are unable to protect or defend themselves. Sledd spent many years trying to promote the well-being of teaching assistants and adjunct faculty. He continues to be as scaldingly critical of the new generation of "boss compositionists" as he was of the old abusers of "slaveys." Here is the work of a vibrant mind, of a man whose voice needs to be heard today, possibly more than ever. If the profession has remained the same—that is, corrupt, unyielding, reactionary— so also has James Sledd remained consistently critical, angry and eloquent—and usually right on target.

This essay is a revision of a paper I read in Portland in the summer of 1990 at the annual conference of writing program administrators. Its aim, in antique terms, is less to persuade than to bear witness by answering two questions. First, in the five years after the once-so-promising Wyoming Resolution, why has so much talk produced so little action to check the exploitation of composition teachers? Second, what can be done, if anything, to right this wrong? To the first question, a long history answers that administrators, literati, and eminent compositionists have been led by misconceived self-interest to perpetuate old injustice. To the second question, a short quixotism answers that emancipation proclamations unsupported by determined power are in fact obstructive. In the foreseeable future, public opinion will not allow the abolition of the postsecondary teaching of writing, and intelligent self-interest forbids the maintenance of a permanent academic ghetto. But the exploited themselves must use the power of organized agitation if there is to be any real reform.

A History of Iniquity

I begin my history with old, unhappy, far-off things, iniquity long ago. "Poor Mr. Doe!" my unctuous professor said as we stepped out of the elevator which Mr. Doe's daughter was operating. "Poor Mr. Doe! If he had only lived till springtime, he would have learned that we had voted him a two-hundred-dollar raise."

That was the obituary of a composition bum, spoken in the 1930s by a member of his budget council, overflowing with putrid feeling. Mr. Doe had belonged to the academic underclass which O. J. Campbell described in 1939 when he called for the abolition of freshman English. Staffing the freshman course required the recruitment of crowds of young people who then languished, Campbell said, at the foot of the departmental totem pole. They were the perpetual instructors, happy if they were granted trifling raises, ecstatic if at last they made assistant professor; but too often, in Campbell's view from above, they became infected with contagious disappointment and rebelliousness. They were also prerequisite to the existence of a professoriate glorying in autotelic research and unread publication.

Laboring beside the composition bums, already in the 1930s, were teaching assistants—graduate students who were supported by their spouses, if they were lucky, or who supported themselves in their common task of hunting down comma faults and berating faulty diction. After World War II, when every crossroads college set out to become a graduate research institution of international repute, composition bums grew rarer while teaching assistants multiplied. In 1959, however, an authoritative bureaucratic manifesto,

"The Basic Issues in the Teaching of English," sadly reported that the state of the indispensable composition teacher was still not good. English departments, their spokespersons insisted, were the home of a "fundamental liberal discipline," to which literature was central; but devotees of the supposed discipline faced the general complaint "that students do not know how to read or write" (7, 5). The blind were leading the blind. "Our teaching-assistant graduate students and young Ph.D.'s," the report went on, "may expect ninety per cent of their first six years of teaching to be in freshman and sophomore composition. Yet the typical Ph.D. program is almost completely void of courses dealing primarily with language and rhetoric" (12). Nor did acquisition of the degree bring prompt emancipation, for "the teaching of composition [was] regarded as drudgery, [was] paid badly, and [offered] little opportunity for advancement in rank" (12).

Those who regarded composition-teaching as drudgery and paid it badly were of course the professorial literati themselves. At Allerton Park in 1962, in a conference on research, John Fisher of the MLA quite clearly stated their dilemma. "Belief in the value of literary study for all," Fisher said, "is the creed we live by," but "by continuing to staff freshman English courses we acknowledge that part of our task is to train students to read and write." How could those two undertakings be reconciled? For Fisher, it was unthinkable that English departments should turn themselves "into enormous service departments of composition and the language arts," yet abandoning the cultivation of literacy "would only leave a vacuum to be filled by someone else who [was] quite willing to be of service" (21). Though Fisher didn't say so, the abandonment of freshman English would also have left the literati without graduate students and their departments with much reduced budgets.

Since 1962, the history of big English departments, especially in the pattern-setting state universities, has been largely a history of varying attempts to solve the problem that Fisher saw: How can the literati maintain their dominance, avoid the teaching of composition, yet use the freshman English course to keep up their budgets and to guarantee enrollment for the seminars that profit from their research (and sometimes do it)?

An early attempt at a solution got little further than a plea that the schools should do what the universities wouldn't. The committee representing the MLA, in the 1964 *Report of the Commission on the Humanities,* joined the perennial lament of a literacy crisis yet coolly assigned the cultivation of literacy to the schools while simply assuming that in the universities teaching assistants would continue to populate the seminars in literature. "A majority of college students," the association's representatives complained,

> do not speak, write, or read their own language well. Graduate instructors who direct master's essays and doctoral dissertations are shocked at the extent to which they must become teachers of 'hospital' English. Yet we are aware that many of these candidates are already engaged in part-time teaching of freshman English. If they cannot recognize and correct their own egregious errors, what is happening to the end-products of their teaching? (138)

The cap to this mass of evasions was not today's demand for more research in *advanced* composition but the time-worn proposal to pass the buck of elementary composition to the schools. "Whatever the causes" of students' ineptitude, the committee said, "correction must come at the lower levels, since by the time students enter college, any bad habits in speaking, writing, and reading have become so fixed and ingrained that colleges can do little more than stress 'remedial work'" (138).

When enrollments have been high and when elementary courses in literature have been available to support teaching assistants, denigrators of composition and its teaching have often repeated the pretense that freshman English is indeed remedial, unnecessary for most college entrants, and therefore unfit for a college curriculum; but the pretense is dangerous, less because it is untrue (which it is) than because it invites the more exalted administrators to abolish the one course on which departments of English most depend for their existence. For the professoriate, the apparently safer argument, despite its own internal contradictions, is insistence both on the maintenance of the freshman course and on the wisdom of staffing it with the least experienced, least prepared, most poorly paid of teachers: the teaching assistants, who are essential if the research machine is to be kept rolling.

Perennial Exploitation

One constant within the incessant changes of the supposedly fundamental liberal discipline of English has been the fundamentally illiberal exploitation of teaching assistants. For example, the Teaching Assistants Association at the University of Wisconsin (Madison) estimated in 1970 that overworked and underpaid teaching assistants taught sixty-eight percent of all lower-division courses (not just English courses) and fifty-six percent of all undergraduate courses (Hamilton 346). At the University of Texas in 1975, according to George Nash, 157 teaching assistants taught ninety percent of the sections of freshman English, and the existence of the English Department "in its present form [depended] on (a) keeping the required lower-division courses and (b) using these courses to support an army of TAs who [served] the double function of sparing full-time faculty the drudge work and supplying warm bodies for the faculty's graduate seminars" (125). According to Carol Hartzog, at the University of Southern California in 1984–85, departments viewed "the Freshman Writing Program as a means of supporting their graduate students," who taught all the courses in the program (11). Hartzog provides a roll call of comparable situations in other big universities, fully justifying the conclusion of Stephen North in 1987 that "the tradition in most large writing programs is to have teaching assistants do most of the teaching" (35).

The motives for such extensive use of teaching assistants in elementary courses have been bluntly stated by Dean Jaros of the Graduate School at Colorado State. The TA system, Jaros has said in defending it, provides cheap teachers, saves "regular" faculty from teaching undergraduates, and still supports the graduate students who fill the graduate seminars and do the undergraduate teaching (Chism 369). Less damaging defenses have of course been offered, notably by William F. Irmscher of the University of Washington and O. Jane Allen of New Mexico State. According to Allen, many of the graduate students of literature whom in 1964 the MLA's committee found so incompetent are in fact accomplished researchers, skilled readers and writers, and lovers of language equipped to deal with special stylistic problems (169); and Irmscher asserts that "teaching assistants, if properly trained, can bring new vitality to the study of English" (27).

Clearly, it is possible that assistants appointed for bad reasons may still be good teachers, and no one denies that limited teaching, after careful training and under intelligent supervision, would be a useful part of a professional apprenticeship; but the facts of exploitation seem overwhelmingly against the defenders of the present system, who themselves do not accept the logical consequences of their argument. Most graduate students in English have done their undergraduate work in fiction, poetry, and drama, with little or no training in grammar, rhetoric, or logic; and graduate students from other departments may not have had even the exposure to "literature." The students' further training as teaching assistants is often surveillance, rather than instruction. As Charles Bridges and his coauthors say (citing Gibaldi and Mirollo's *Current State of Teaching*

Apprentice Activities), preparing assistants for their teaching "remains an isolated and often thankless task," which "departments often undertake grudgingly and only out of necessity" (vii, viii).

Thus, insecure, inexperienced, poorly prepared transients are called upon to teach courses which their professorial masters disdain. The conditions in which they teach do not improve their morale. Though they are normally paid (and rather poorly at that) for a twenty-hour week, their actual time on task is likely to be more nearly thirty hours; and commonly they are treated not as junior colleagues but as a kind of house-servant, assigned at the last minute to courses over which they have little control and denied the amenities which "regular" faculty enjoy. Worst of all, they are expected to teach rhetoric well while studying literature diligently with professors who dislike teaching. Wayne Booth is only a bit too vehement when he sums up the situation in one sharp sentence: "Ignorant high school graduates enter college and are taught by ignorant . . . graduate assistants working for slave wages in appallingly unprofessional conditions" (7). Defenders of the system, it should be added, have never explained why the assistants whose abilities they praise are overworked, underpaid, and regularly assigned to courses which the professors shun, not to the juicy plum courses which the professors monopolize.

Teaching assistants are not the only victims of the autocratic behavior with which we allegedly inspire students to live freely in an alleged democracy. Though the exploitation of teaching assistants has remained a constant whenever there are assistants to exploit, in the lean 1970s the supply ran short. A decline in the number of college-age students was projected, and in fact the number of undergraduate majors and graduate students in English fell off, sometimes sharply, partly because new Ph.D.'s found few job openings in the traditional literary fields. At the same time, however, the demand for writing courses, including freshman composition, remained high. The freshman English which Campbell had hoped to abolish now kept many departments afloat, and just ten years after John Fisher had spoken disdainfully of "service departments," the Delegate Assembly of the MLA was invited to resist an alleged trend "toward abolition of basic requirements in English composition."[1]

Two related developments helped English departments to maintain their primary functions of survival and reproduction. The professional compositionist emerged, supported in the push for status and privilege by the less lemming-like among the graduate students and the newly bedoctored; and at the same time, administrators aped business executives in appointing large numbers of contingent workers, the now-familiar part-timers, temporaries, hourlies, or freeway fliers. Franklin, Laurence, and Denham report that from 1972 to 1983 the number of part-timers in four-year institutions increased more than three times as fast as the number of full-timers, while the rate of increase in community colleges was even greater (16). In the mid 1980s, the number of full-timers in two-year and four-year colleges actually declined, while the number of part-timers continued to rise. Part-timers and temporaries together now constitute about one-half of all faculty in postsecondary education. Ray Kytle's remarks in 1971 deserve to be repeated. "At Southern Illinois University where I did my graduate work," Kytle wrote, "composition was taught almost exclusively by 'slaves'"—that is, by teaching assistants. "At Central Michigan University where I am now," Kytle went on, "composition is taught primarily by 'serfs'— untenured and, by present criteria, untenurable instructors" (339).[2]

Like the motives for the use of teaching assistants, the motives for the employment of contingent workers are crass. Both professors and administrators are aware that they cannot easily abolish the writing courses which public demand requires and which allow the continued existence of departments of English literature, but both administrators and professors welcome the opportunity to hire and fire cheap labor as professorial and administrative interests may demand. Concerning the use of the dollars which cheap labor saves, however, the literati and the decision-makers may disagree. The literati want to preserve their sinecures in the greatest possible comfort by continuing to evade the social duty of cultivating literacy; but administrators eager for the favor of governments, business, and the military do not consider the comfort of English professors essential to educational excellence. Star Wars excite administrators more than the wars of critical theorists. Though the literati may actually share the administrative desire to discourage unionization by dividing the faculty into opposing factions, in the long run the use of contingent labor weakens the professoriate. It is hard to argue that tenure is essential to academic freedom when half the faculty will never be tenured.

But reason rarely overcomes immediate self-interest, narrowly conceived. Departments of English literature continue to use contingent workers as well as teaching assistants to staff the freshman English course. Excuses for the abuses are feeble—for example, the plea that because the supposed literacy crisis which creates the need for elementary composition is only temporary, the staff to meet that need should be temporary as well (Lanham *Literacy* 155). Makers of that plea ignore the facts that some temporaries have now had to be reappointed periodically for a dozen years or so and that complaints of literacy crises are the hardiest of perennials, signifying the constant changes in the demands of bosses on the bossed.

The indifference of moralistic professors of literature to the exploitation of their supposed inferiors is also perennial. Part-timers and temporaries, as a group, are better educated and more experienced writers and teachers of writing than most teaching assistants and some professors; yet the part-timers and temporaries are exploited even more viciously than the teaching assistants. The contingent workers generally get low pay, few if any fringe benefits, and none of the usual academic perks. Without security in their work or a strong voice in controlling it, they are assigned to elementary courses, casually and without adequate orientation, but under capricious evaluation. No matter how well they do their jobs, they get scant recognition and are not accepted as integral members of the academic community. Their consequent bitterness is not lessened by the fact that many of them, as women, are expected to be content with "women's work" or by the knowledge that in a pinch their employers will violate an inconvenient contract rather than enforce it.

The Newly Risen Compositionists

A further irritant is the arrogance of the newly risen compositionists, who are full of praise for themselves and their freshly bedoctored students but contemptuous of mere "practitioners," the teachers who do the work that the compositionists theorize about. The current attempt to solve John Fisher's old problem is to keep composition in departments devoted primarily to literature, to placate the boss compositionists by admitting them to the worshipful company of privileged researchers, but still to assign the actual teaching of writing to the contingent workers and teaching assistants. With that solution the compositionists are apparently content, since it marks the literary establishment's acceptance of their claims to share the glory.

And the busily researching compositionists are anything but restrained in blowing their own horns. They talk glibly of old and new paradigms, though what they label with the presumptuous term of *paradigm* is only an ill-defined conglomerate of practice and belief, not a coherent set of interdependent propositions, susceptible of precise statement. They proudly maintain that they have opened a new field which "has clearly arrived at disciplinary status, complete with graduate programs, undergraduate majors, major conferences, and journals" (Berlin 217); but the content itself of that boast reveals that they have confused the externals of academic entrepreneurship with the intellectual elaboration of theory and method. Much of their research is piddling, much wildly over-ambitious. So Richard L. Larson, on the piddling hand, solemnly reports a method of "topical structure analysis":

> In analyzing a paragraph, one determines which "topic" is discussed in the greatest number of sentences, counts the number of sentences in which it appears, identifies the topics of other sentences, counts the number of different sentence topics, and counts the number of sentences with different topics that intervene between any two of those sentences that develop the topic most frequently mentioned. (80)

On the over-ambitious hand, Stephen North characterizes "the Experimentalists: in broad terms, those who seek to discover generalizable 'laws' which can account for—and, ideally, predict—the ways in which people do, teach, and learn writing" (137). Half a moment's thought should convince anyone that crutch-phrases like "the ways in which writing is done, taught, and learned" do not delimit a workable field of study but invite researchers to busy themselves with the universe—with everything from Germanic formulaic verse to Navy letter forms, from wax tablets to word processors, from blind Milton to the Beatles. Richard Lanham is restrained when he writes that "much research in composition has been trivial and jejune" (26).

But the most irritating characteristic of the boss compositionists is their contempt for the real teachers of composition. When compositionists brag about "the new professionalism" in their "discipline," they are thinking of themselves and the disciples who have sat at their feet, supposedly absorbing the principles of theory and the methods of research. According to Joseph J. Comprone, "This research and theory has [sic] yet, however, to influence the majority of English teachers, who often demonstrate superficial comprehension of the deeper relationships among literary, academic, and professional discourses" (299). Maxine Hairston, in *her* professional discourse, is even more roundly condemnatory of the pedagogues who have not joined her "in the vanguard of the profession." "The overwhelming majority of college writing teachers in the United States," Hairston declares, "are not professional writing teachers. They do not do research or publish on rhetoric or composition, and they do not know the scholarship in the field; they do not read the professional journals and they do not attend professional meetings such as the annual Conference on College Communication and Composition [*sic*]; they do not participate in faculty development workshops for writing teachers" ("Winds" 78–79). "Until very recently," Hairston says in another place, "most college composition teachers have not known what they were doing" ("Slave" 117). As Clinton Burhans puts it, they are the victims of the "knowledge gap" which separates them from the true professionals.

Such effusions are reminiscent of the scorn which now-forgotten pop linguists poured on "traditional grammar" thirty and forty years ago, and they leave one wondering how an apostle of enlightenment like Hairston can speak in the same breath of "the revolution in the *teaching* of writing [emphasis added]" even though most teachers remain untouched by the presumed revolution. Moreover, real evidence that the boss compositionists and their pupils get the best results in their own classrooms would be hard to find. When Hillocks announces, for example, that X method works three times as well as Y method (246–49), one has to ask not just how all the variables except precisely specified differences in method have been controlled but also how *better* has been universally defined and accurately measured. Most such claims, it seems to me, have no more substance than the counterclaim by Dennis Szilak that "when it comes to the teaching of composition, most area specialists, as Ph.D.'s, can not carry the pencil box of an experienced composition teacher" (26).

Listening to the trumpetings of the noisier compositionists, I have to ask, "*What* revolution?" I see clearly that a new group of academic entrepreneurs has achieved some degree of comfort and status. I see clearly that the old exploitation of temporaries and teaching assistants continues. In other words, I see what Stephen North describes when he writes,

> The field [of composition] has been driven [*sic*] by the need to replace practice as its primary mode of inquiry and lore as its dominant form of knowledge. That drive resulted in . . . a methodological landrush: a scramble to stake out territory, to claim power over what constitutes knowledge in Composition; and to claim, as well, whatever rewards that power might carry with it. (317)

That is a description of the oldest form of academic endeavor, barefaced self-seeking. It is not a description of a revolution, for there can be no revolution in the *teaching* of writing until the exploitation of teachers is ended.

Emasculated Resolutions

There has been much pious talk about that exploitation, but little more than talk. Personal experience brings two striking instances to mind. The first has to do with the Modern Language Association's literacy conferences, remarkable undertakings for an organization whose dominant literati have treated the cultivation of literacy with contempt. At the first of those conferences, I tried to encourage a little democracy through language by floating a petition:

> We, the undersigned, respectfully urge the MLA to give some practical effect to its expressed concern for literacy by prompt, strong action against the continuing exploitation of graduate students and part-timers as teachers of composition, the principal workers for literacy in higher education in the United States.

That petition, I have been told, was eventually signed by hundreds of participants, and eventually it reached MLA's headquarters; but for several months thereafter I heard nothing. When a rather embarrassed letter from headquarters did at last reach me, it reported that the staff officers had not known what to do with the petition. For dealing with petitions, the sponsors of democracy through language had no machinery. In the end, the letter informed me, my little document was assigned to some committee, and I have heard no more about it. Presumably the MLA is less concerned for literacy than for the continued use of fetal tissue in medical research.

My second instance brings me to the Wyoming Resolution, a promising bull calf which is now a steer. That resolution was from below, a *people's* resolution prompted by a spontaneous outburst of feeling from exploited teachers; and the great oneyers present at its birth seemed a bit vexed and embarrassed that so strange a beastie had pushed its way into the world of famed researchers and grand conventioneers. The resolution had three parts. The first was innocent enough. It called for yet another formulation of standards "for salary levels and working conditions of postsecondary teachers of writing." Such formulations, unless they are put into effect, are quite acceptable to the beneficiaries of exploitation, for they give the impression that action is being taken when in fact just nothing is being done. Parts Two and Three of the Wyoming Resolution, however, were of a different kind. Part Two called for a grievance procedure, and Part Three called for "a procedure for acting upon a finding of non-compliance": institutions running a slave trade were to be publicly exposed and rebuked. Dreamily, the resolution charged the Executive Committee of the CCCC to do all those good things.

I consider myself stupid for not seeing in advance what I now see *had* to happen to Parts Two and Three. They posed a threat to the system of exploitation without which English departments in their present state could not exist, the system from which administrators, literati, and boss compositionists have all thought to profit. Though all three parts of the Wyoming Resolution were approved unanimously at the 1987 CCCC business meeting, the Executive Committee first appointed a "task force" to make the innocuous recommendations of Part One and then appointed yet another committee, with James Slevin as its chair, to satisfy Parts Two and Three. That is precisely what the Slevin committee did not do. On the contrary, the committee "recommended and the CCCC Executive Committee determined that the CCCC could not at this time become involved in the censure of institutions" (CCCC Committee 65). By that one refusal to act, the two committees reduced their joint effort to more talk about exploitation which had already been talked about for many years; and though a politically adept, congenial, and industrious Slevin has indicated continuing efforts by his public emphasis on the phrase "at this time," no proof-pudding has been served to famished diners as of April, 1991.

The Slevin committee not only rejected implementation of the resolution which it had been called upon to implement; it also neatly subverted the argument that the *teaching* of composition, not just *research* in composition, should be honored and rewarded. The first word in the first sentence in Part One of the committee's report was *research,* and the first recommendation was that "in hiring, tenure, and promotion considerations, research and publication in rhetoric and composition should be treated on a par with all other areas of research in English departments." "Commitment to the teaching of writing" was to be demonstrated by "research and publication, participation in professional conferences, and active involvement in curriculum development and design." Faculty thus "professionally committed to rhetoric and composition" should have boss jobs: they "should coordinate and supervise composition programs" (62). There was no suggestion that the best evidence of commitment to the teaching of writing is just its devoted teaching.

The Slevin committee further weakened its report by its remark on graduate students as teachers. Unlike the part-timers and temporaries, from whom the professoriate might learn a great deal, graduate students keep the professorial seminars going; and the Slevin committee apparently assumed that "faculty professionally committed to rhetoric and composition" would continue to leave much of the actual teaching to teaching assistants, whom the committed professionals would "coordinate and supervise." Such vague reform of present conditions as the committee recommended would still allow the maintenance of armies of assistants (62–63).

These and other objections to the Slevin committee's "draft report" were made at the 1989 meeting of the CCCC at Seattle, but apparently without result. After a final rewriting, the CCCC official "Statement of Principles and Standards for the Postsecondary Teaching of Writing" appeared in *CCC* for October, 1989, where the voice is the voice of Slevin though the hand is that of the Executive Committee (329–36). This final statement is a current answer to the problem posed by John Fisher thirty years ago. Part-timers and full-time temporaries are gradually to be got rid of, but the armies of teaching assistants may be maintained, and quartered in departments of English, not rhetoric, so that the literati will not lose the enrollment in their seminars. Yet the research machine of the compositionists is also well cared for. In fact, if administrators were to accept the official assertion that doing a composition textbook is "a primary form of original research," compositionists would be recognized as the most prolific of all original researchers at the very moment when the quality of original research collapsed (331). The losers in all this maneuvering are just *the teachers of writing*—the teaching assistants, who will continue to be exploited, and the part-timers and temporaries, few of whom will make it to those "full-time, tenure-track positions" where research, not teaching, is the name of the game.

A Last Hope?

I consider myself stupid, as I say, because after fifty years in major English departments (precisely the fifty years that I have talked about), I still had fond hope for the Wyoming Resolution. I should have known that in English departments, for all their self-glorifying gabble about democracy through language, the exploitation of labor is systemic, the foundation of the enterprise, not to be corrected without upheaval. The privileged—whether compositionists, literati, or higher administrators—have resisted such change in the belief that it would deny them their privileges. It is consequently the height of quixotism to suggest that the continued abuse of composition teachers, however probable, is still not quite inevitable. Yet I do risk that suggestion.

One reason is that a more intelligent consideration of self-interest might prompt the privileged to deliberate, beneficent action. The foofaraw about literacy and the shortcomings of higher education does make it presently impossible to abolish college composition altogether, and when "the real world" compels the doing of a job, it might as well be done properly. Nobody profits from the maintenance of a permanent ghetto, and there would be no real gain from the gentrification of English departments by the banishment of the slum-dwellers to a new slum in another academic neighborhood. Right recognition and reward for the teachers of an admittedly important subject would put an end to the old and debilitating grievances that Campbell wrote of in 1939. To the argument that money is unavailable, the answer is that inadequate support of an essential program is the most wasteful of possible alternatives.

Quixotism, however, has its limits. Voluntary reformation from above is even less likely than reformation forced from below. A male-dominated professoriate has indeed treated composition-teaching as mainly women's work. One result has been that many competent and articulate women are among composition's best yet angriest teachers. If these mature but unrewarded professionals could make common cause with their male colleagues and with exploited graduate students, and if the two groups chose to risk really militant action, they might together do what generations of professors have failed to do. Should the example of their action prove contagious, the abuse of contingent labor in other academic departments might also be checked, and our universities might improve— far more so than by the mutterings of businessmen and bureaucrats.

A last hope is no more hope than fear. Human prophecy is fallible. "An old, mad, blind, despised, and dying king" may be the instrument of change as unintended as it is unpredictable. But quixotism has now declined into the evangelical.

Notes

1. The quotation is from the second paragraph of Item 9 in the Resolutions Committee's resolutions for the meeting of the Delegate Assembly on December 28, 1972.

2. For this and other references, I am indebted to Howard Ryan.

Works Cited

Allen, O. Jane. "The Literature Major as Teacher of Technical Writing: A Bibliographical Orientation." Bridges 69–77.

"The Basic Issues in the Teaching of English." Supplement to *College English* 21 (October, 1959): 1–16.

Berlin, James A. "Writing Instruction in School and College English, 1890–1985." *A Short History of Writing Instruction from Ancient Greece to Twentieth-Century America.* Ed. James J. Murphy. Davis, CA: Hermagoras, 1990. 183–220.

Booth, Wayne. "Reversing the Downward Spiral: Or, What Is the Graduate Program For?" *The Future of Doctoral Studies in English.* Ed. Andrea Lunsford, Helene Moglen, and James F. Slevin. New York: MLA, 1989. 3–8.

Bridges, Charles W., ed. *Training the New Teacher of College Composition.* Urbana: NCTE, 1986.

Bridges, Charles W., Toni A. Lopez, and Ronald F. Lunsford. Preface. Bridges vii–ix.

Burhans, Clinton S., Jr. "The Teaching of Writing and the Knowledge Gap." *College English* 45 (1983): 639–56.

Campbell, Oscar James. "The Failure of Freshman English." *English Journal,* College Ed., 28 (1939): 177–85.

CCCC Committee on Professional Standards for Quality Education. "CCCC Initiatives on the Wyoming Conference Resolution: A Draft Report." *College Composition and Communication* 40 (1989): 61–72.

CCCC Executive Committee. "Statement of Principles and Standards for the Postsecondary Teaching of Writing." *College Composition and Communication* 40 (1989): 329–36.

Chism, Nancy Van Note, ed. *Institutional Responsibilities and Responses in the Employment and Education of Teaching Assistants: Readings from a National Conference.* Columbus: Center for Teaching Excellence, Ohio State University, 1987.

Comprone, Joseph J. "Literary Theory and Composition." *Teaching Composition: Twelve Bibliographical Essays.* Ed. Gary Tate. Revised and enlarged ed. Fort Worth: Texas Christian UP, 1987. 291–330.

Fisher, John H. "Remarks for Allerton House Seminar." United States Office of Education. *Proceedings of the Allerton Park Conference on Research in the Teaching of English, December 2–4, 1962.* Cooperative Research Project #G-1006. N.p.: n.p., n.d. 17–22.

Franklin, Phyllis, David Laurence, and Robert B. Denham. "When Solutions Become Problems: Taking a Stand on Part-Time Employment." *Academe.* (May-June 1988): 15–19.

Hairston, Maxine. "On Not Being a Composition Slave." Bridges 117–24.

———. "The Winds of Change. Thomas Kuhn and the Revolution in the Teaching of Writing." *College Composition and Communication* 33 (1982): 76–88.

Hamilton, Andrew. "Wisconsin: Teaching Assistants' Strike Ends in Contract Signing." *Science* 168 (17 April 1970): 345–49.

Hartzog, Carol P. *Composition and the Academy: A Study of Writing Program Administration.* New York: MLA, 1986.

Hillocks, George, Jr. *Research on Written Composition.* Urbana: NCRE/ ERIC, 1986.

Irmscher, William F. "TA Training: A Period of Discovery." Bridges 27–36.

Kytle, Ray. "Slaves, Serfs, or Colleagues—Who Shall Teach College Composition?" *College Composition and Communication* 22 (1971): 339–41.

Lanham, Richard A. *Literacy and the Survival of Humanism.* New Haven: Yale UP, 1983.

————. "One, Two, Three." *Composition and Literature: Bridging the Gap.* Ed. Winifred Bryan Horner. Chicago: U of Chicago P, 1983. 14–29.

Larson, Richard L. "Structure and Form in Non-Narrative Prose." *Teaching Composition: Twelve Bibliographical Essays.* Ed. Gary Tate. Revised and enlarged ed. Fort Worth: Texas Christian UP, 1987. 39–82.

Nash, George. "Who's Minding Freshman English at U.T. Austin?" *College English* 38 (1976): 125–31.

North, Stephen M. *The Making of Knowledge in Composition: Portrait of an Emerging Field.* Portsmouth, NH: Boynton, 1987.

Report of the Commission on the Humanities. New York: American Council of Learned Societies, 1964.

Robertson, Linda R., Sharon Crowley, and Frank Lentricchia. "The Wyoming Conference Resolution Opposing Unfair Salaries and Working Conditions for Post-Secondary Teachers of Writing." *College English* 49 (1987): 274–80.

Szilak, Dennis. "Teachers of Composition: A Re-Niggering." *College English* 39 (1977): 25–32.

Published Writings by James H. Sledd

Books

Dictionaries and THAT Dictionary. 1962. Chicago: Scott, Foresman. With Wilma Ebbitt.

Dr. Johnson's Dictionary: Essays in the Biography of a Book. 1955. University of Chicago Press. With Gwin J. Kolb.

The Elements of English Grammar. 1951. University of Chicago Press. Pamphlet edited by James Sledd. With George J. Metcalf, W. H. Meyer, John P. Netherton, and Richard M. Weaver.

English Linguistics: An Introductory Reader. 1968. Chicago: Scott, Foresman. With Harold Hungerford and Jay Robinson.

A Short Introduction to English Grammar. 1959. Chicago: Scott, Foresman.

Articles

"After Bidialectalism, What?" 1973. *The English Journal* 62: 770–773.

"And They Write Innumerable Books." 1982. *The Writing Instructor* 2: 69–76.

"Anglo-Conformity: Folk Remedy for Lost Hegemony." 1990. In Harvey A. Daniels, ed., *Not Only English: Affirming America's Multilingual Heritage.* Urbana: NCTE. 87–95.

"An Argument for the Abolition of English Departments as They Presently Exist: Banalities II." 1980. *Conference of College Teachers of English of Texas* 45: 61–66.

"Baret's *Alvearie,* An Elizabethan Reference Book." 1946. *Studies in Philology* 43: 147–163.

"Bi-Dialectalism: the Linguistics of White Supremacy." 1969. *English Journal* 58: 1307–1315; 1329. Rpt. in 1972 in David L. Shores, ed., *Contemporary English: Change and Variation.* Philadelphia: Lippincott. 319–330.

"Biloquialism." 1973. *English Studies Today* 10: 95–122.

"Breaking, Umlaut, and the Southern Drawl." 1966. *Language* 42: 18–41. Summary in 1966, *English Studies Today* 4: 91–96.

"The California Experiment: An Essay in Disbelief." 1960. *College English* 21: 491–496.

"Can These Bones Live—And Should They?" 1978. *Texas College English* 11: 2–5. Rpt. in 1979 in Ernestine P. Sewell and Bili M. Rogers, eds., *Confronting Crisis.* Arlington, TX: University of Texas at Arlington Press. 63–72.

"Canterbury Tales, C 310, 320: 'By Seint Ronyan.'" 1951. *Mediaeval Studies* 13: 226–233.

"A Canterbury Tell." 1987. *American Speech* 2: 185–186.

"A Case for Linguistics—In Temperate Terms." 1966. *The English Leaflet* 65: 3–11.

"'Chamfred Browes' in Spenser's February Ecologue." 1945. *Notes and Queries* 188: 34.

"The *Clerk's Tale:* The Monsters and the Critics." 1953. *Modern Philology* 51: 73–82.

"Comment for Comment." 1968. In Howard C. Zimmerman, ed., *Educational Comment/1968: Ideal Designs for English Programs.* Toledo, OH: University of Toledo Press. 10–19.

"A Comment on 'Social Construction, Language, and the Authority of Knowledge' and 'A Polemical History of Freshman Composition in Our Time.'" 1987. *College English* 49: 585–588.

"Comments." 1967. In Fred Householder and Sol Saporta, eds., *Problems in Lexicography.* Bloomington: Indiana University Press. 143–150.

"Coordination (Faulty) and Subordination (Upside Down)." 1956. *College Composition and Communication* 7: 181–187. Rpt. in 1958 in Harold B. Allen, ed., *Readings in Applied English Linguistics,* New York: Appleton-Century Crofts, 354–361; and in 1964 in *English Teaching Forum* 6: 10–16.

"Cultural Monism and Linguistic Diversity: The Attack on Dialects in the U.S.A." 1976. In Robert Eagleson et al., eds., *Language and Literature in the Formation of National and Cultural Communities.* Proc. of the XIII Cong. of the Fed. Internationale des Langues et Litteratures Modernes and the XVII Cong. of the Australasian Univ. Lang. and Lit. Ass. Sydney, Australia: Australian University Language and Literature Ass. 126–127.

"Dead Cat Drifting." 1984. *Conference on Language Attitudes and Composition (CLAC)* 11: 2–6.

"DeWitt T. Starnes." 1967. *Studies in Honor of DeWitt T. Starnes.* Austin: University of Texas Press. 1.

"Dictionary Treatment of Pronunciation: Regional." 1973. In Raven McDavid, Jr. and Audrey R. Duckert, eds., *Annals of the New York Academy of Sciences.* New York: NY Academy of Sciences. 134–138, 141–143.

"*Dollars and Dictionaries:* The Limits of Commercial Lexicography." 1972. In Howard D. Weinbrot, ed., *New Aspects of Lexicography.* Carbondale: Southern Illinois Press. 119–137.

"Dorigen's Complaint." 1947. *Modern Philology* 45: 36–45.

"Doublespeak: Dialectology in the Service of Big Brother." 1972. *College English* 33: 439–456.

"'Doublespeak': Rebuttal to Criticisms." 1973. *College English* 34: 584–585; 591–593.

"A Dream for a Free World." 1983. *Alternativas* 1: 18–19.

"The English Department as Literacy Crisis; or, The Hypocrisy of Educational Reform." 1989. In Benton Burdine et al., eds., *The Victoria College Social Sciences Symposium.* Victoria, TX: Victoria College. 66–89.

"English for Survival." 1975. *The English Record* 26: 11–21.

"English Form Classes." 1958. *Language Learning* 8: 79–87. Rpt. in 1959 in *English Grammar* 12: 8–19. Excerpt from "Some Linguistic Problems in the Preparation of Teaching Materials" (cited below).

"The English Language in American Education." 1964. *The Texas Quarterly* 71: 70–86.

"The English Verses in the Huloet-Higgins *Dictionarie* of 1572." 1948. *Modern Language Notes* 63: 251–254.

"English Word-Wild: Some Obstinant Questionings of Predominate Views." 1983. *American Speech* 58: 280–284.

"An Excerpt from *Dr. Johnson's 'Dictionary.'*" 1955. *The Language We Speak: The University of Chicago Round Table.* University of Chicago Press (May): 1–17.

"A Footnote on the Inkhorn Controversy." 1949. *Studies in English* 28: 49–56.

"Go and Catch Spiders!" 1977. *The Nebraska English Counselor* 22: 3–9. Rpt. in 1978 in Edward Jenkins, ed., *Selections from the Journals of NCTE Affiliates* 3: 10–15.

"Grammar or Grammarye." 1960. *The English Journal* 49: 293–303.

"The Great Train Robbery: University of Texas IS the People." 1983 (Sept). *The Texas Observer.*

"Handmaiden of the Business Barons." 1987 (May). *The Texas Observer.*

"'Hang Your Clothes on a Hickory Limb': Comment on David Eskey." 1975. *College English* 36: 699–703.

"*Hause* and *Slaves* in *King Lear.*" 1940. *Modern Language Notes* 45: 595–596.

"Heroes, Drudges, and Word-catchers: Notes on Some English Lexicographers and Their Attitudes Toward Language." 1948. *Emory University Quarterly* 4:22–31.

"Hirsch's Use of His Sources in *Cultural Literacy:* A Critique." 1988. *Profession 88.* New York: MLA. 33–39. With Andrew E. Sledd.

"How We Apples Swim." 1991. In Mark Hurlbert and Michael Blitz, eds., *Composition and Resistance.* Portsmouth, NH: Boynton/Cook. 145–153.

"In Defense of History." 1963. *College English* 24: 608–612.

"In Defense of the *Students' Right.*" 1983. *College English* 45: 667–675.

"Johnson's Definitions of Whig and Tory." 1952. *PMLA* 67: 892–902. With Gwin Kolb.

"Johnson's Dictionary and Lexicographical Tradition." 1953. *Modern Philology.* 50: 171–194. With Gwin Kolb.

"[kũt] [kũt] BE [kũt] [kũt] IT?" 1993. *American Speech* 68: 218–219.

"Language Differences and Literary Values: Divagations from a Theme." 1976. *College English.* 38: 234–241.

"Layman or Shaman; or Now About That Elephant Again." 1985. In Sydney Greenbaum, ed., *The English Language Today.* Oxford, England: Pergamon. 327–342.

"The Lexicographer's Uneasy Chair." 1962. *College English* 23: 682–687. Rpt. in 1963 in Leonard F. Dean and Kenneth G. Wilson, eds., *Essays on Language and Usage.* New York: Oxford University Press. 93–101.

"Like Gag Me with a Spoon." 1984. In Jerome B. Angel, ed., *Test Your Own Word Power.* New York: Ballantine. 111–112.

"Linguistic Relativism: The Divorce of Word from Work." 1979. In Sidney Greenbaum, Geffrey Leech, and Jan Swartick, eds., *Studies in English Linguistics: for Randolph Quirk.* New York: Longman. 256–263.

"Linguistics and Literature Again: or, Gettysburg Revisited." 1976. *Publication of the Missouri Philological Ass.* 1: 1–13.

"Linguistics, Obeah, Acupuncture, and the Teaching of Composition by That Bastard Sledd." 1981. *Journal of Advanced Composition* 2: 147–152.

"The Literacy Crisis: Or If Johnny Can't Write, Must Teachers Walk on Water?" 1981. *Publication of the Arkansas Philological Ass.* 7: 1–17.

"Lynching the Lexicographers." 1963. In Viola Garfield and Wallace Chafe, eds., *Proceedings of the 1962 Annual Spring Meeting of the American Ethnological Society.* Seattle: American Ethnological Society. 69–95.

"Medice Teipsum." 1976. In Norman J. Betz, and Robert C. Jones, eds., *Doublespeak: A Book of Readings.* Central Missouri State University: Warrensburg, MO. 11–24.

"The Myth of the Classless and Unchanging Grapholect." 1988. In Joseph Klegraf and Dietrich Nehls, eds. *Essays on the English Language and Applied Linguistics.* Heidelberg: Julius Groos Verlag. 450–467.

"The Nasty Old Man Replies." 1972. *Journal of Advanced Composition.* 12: 214–215.

"Negative Metaheuristics: The Oldest Paradigm." 1984. *Conference on Language Attitudes and Composition (CLAC)* 12: 9–11.

"New and Newer English Grammars of English: Remarks on Their Present Status." 1964. *Illinois English Bulletin* 51: 1–11.

"A Note on Buckra Philology." 1973. *American Speech* 48: 144–46.

"A Note on the Use of Renaissance Dictionaries." 1951. *Modern Philology* 49: 10–15.

"Notes on English Stress." 1962. *Studies In American English.* Proceedings of the "First Texas Conference on Problems of Linguistic Analysis in English, 1956." Austin: University of Texas Press. 33–44.

"Nowell's *Vocabularium Saxonicum* and The Elyot-Cooper Tradition." 1954. *Studies in Philology* 51: 143–148.

"Nugae Academicae: Some Remarks on the 'Alvearie' of John Barret." 1944. *Library Chronicle of The University of Texas.* 1: 19–26.

"Old English Prosody: A Demurrer." *College English* 31: 71–74.

"On Not Teaching English Usage." 1965. *The English Journal* 54: 698–703.

"Or Get Off the Pot: Notes Toward the Restoration of Moderate Honesty Even in English Departments." 1977. *ADE Bulletin* 52: 1–7.

"Permanence and Change in Standard American English: The Making of 'Literacy Crises.'" 1986. In Gerhard Nickel and James C. Stalker, eds., *Studies in Descriptive Linguistics, Vol. 15: Problems of Standardization and Linguistic Variation in Present Day English.* Heidelberg: Julius Groos Press. 59–70.

"A Plea for Pluralism." 1961. *College English* 23: 15–20.

"Prejudice—In Three Parts." 1961. *Northwestern University TriQuarterly* 3: 21–26.

"Product in Process: From Ambiguities of Standard English to Issues That Divide Us." 1988. *College English* 50: 168–176.

"The Profession of Letters as Confidence Game." 1966. *Michigan Quarterly Review* 56: 51–54.

"Prufrock Among the Syntacticians." 1958. *Studies in American English. Proceedings of the "Third Texas Conference on Problems of Linguistic Analysis in English."* Austin: University of Texas Press. 1–21. Panel discussion with Noam Chomsky, Anna Granville Hatcher, Archibald Hill, Henry Lee Smith, and Robert Stockwell.

"Reflections." 1980. *Language Arts* 57: 8–9.

"Reply to E. D. Hirsch, Jr." 1988. *Profession 88.* New York: MLA. 80–81. With Andrew E. Sledd.

"Response to Criticism of 'In Defense of Students' Rights.'" 1984. *College English* 46: 822–829.

"Response to 'Language, Politics, and Composition: A Conversation with Noam Chomsky.'" 1991. *Journal of Advanced Composition* 11: 443–446.

"The Reynolds Copy of Johnson's Dictionary." 1955. *The Bulletin of the John Rylands Library* 37: 446–475. With Gwin Kolb.

"Rope-Dancers, Magi, and Grammarians." 1966. *Conference of College Teachers of English of Texas* 31: 10–25.

"See and Say." 1987. *English Education* 19: 133–145.

"The Seminars in Language and Literature at the Linguistic Institutes." 1956. *Harvard Newsletter.*

"Snafu, Fubar, or Brave New World? National Trends in the Teaching of Grammar." 1966. *The High School Journal* 49: 162–172.

"Soap for Burnel's Head." 1964. *College English* 25: 337–343.

"Some Linguistic Problems Involved in the Preparation of Teaching Materials." 1958. *Language Learning: A Journal of Applied Linguistics,* Special Issue—Proceedings of "Linguistics and the Teaching of English as a Foreign Language" (June): 79–87.

"Some Notes on English Prose Style." 1966. In J. V. Cunningham, ed., *The Problem of Style.* Greenwich, CT: Fawcett. 185–204. Excerpt from James H. Sledd, 1959, *A Short Introduction to English Grammar,* Chicago: Scott, Foresman.

"Some Questions of English Phonology." 1958. *Language* 34: 252–258.

"Something About Language and Social Class." 1986. *Halcyon, A Journal of the Humanities* 8: 25–46. Rpt. in 1987 in Phillip C. Boardman and Robert Gorrell, eds., *The Legacy of Language: A Tribute to Charlton Laird.* Reno: University of Nevada Press. 59–70.

"Standard English and the Study of Variation: 'It All Be Done for a Purpose.'" 1983. In Wayne Glowka and Donald M. Lance, eds., *Language Variation in North American English.* New York: MLA. 275–281.

"Standard Is a Trademark." 1963. *Consumer Reports* (May): 551–552.

"Success as Failure and Failure as Success: The Cultural Literacy of E. D. Hirsch, Jr." 1989. *Written Communication* 6: 364–389. With Andrew E. Sledd.

"Superfixes and Intonation Patterns." 1956. *Litera* 3: 35–41.

"Syntactic Strictures." 1962. *The English Leaflet* 61: 13–23.

"A Talking—For the Love of God." 1968. *The English Record* 18: 2–11.

"Teaching Prose Style to College Freshmen." 1950. *The Journal of General Education* 5: 31–37.

"Three Points of View on Teaching Assistants." 1976. *Alcalde* (April): 11–13.

"Three Textual Notes on Fourteenth-Century Poetry." 1940. *Modern Language Notes* 55: 379–382.

"Two Comments on 'Beyond Anti-Foundationalism to Rhetorical Authority: Problems Defining Cultural Literacy.'" 1991. *College English* 53: 717–721. With Andrew Sledd.

"Un-American English Reconsidered." 1973. *American Speech* 48: 46–53.

"We Have Met the Enemy—And He Is Us." 1977. In Dexter Fisher, ed., *Minority Language and Literature.* New York: MLA. 65–70.

"What Are We Going to Do About It Now That We're Number One?" 1978. *American Speech* 53: 171–198.

"'Who Are You?': Assignment and Commentary." 1985. In William E. Coles and James Vopat, eds., *What Makes Writing Good?* Lexington, MA: D. C. Heath. 33–37.

"The Whoming Pigeon." 1987. *American Speech* 62: 379–380.

"Why the Wyoming Resolution Had to Be Emasculated: A History and a Quixotism." 1991. *Journal of Advanced Composition* 11: 269–281.

"World Dimensions of American English." 1974. *American English and The Bicentennial,* Conference of College Teachers of English of Texas. Commerce, TX: East Texas State University Press. 23–26.

Selected Book Reviews

"Bidialectalism: A New Book and Some Old Issues." 1973. *American Speech* 48: 258–269. Review of Johanna S. DeStephano. 1973. *Language, Society, and Education: A Profile of Black English.* Worthington, OH: Charles Jones Pub.

"Essay Review: As in Itself It Really Is." 1966. *The School Review* 74: 341–352. Review of James J. Lynch and Bertrand Evans. 1963. *High School English Textbooks: A Critical Examination.* Boston: Little, Brown.

"High Principle and Low Behavior." 1991. *The Texas Observer* (Feb). Review of Peter T. Flawn, 1990, *A Primer for University Presidents,* Austin: University of Texas Press; and John Silber, 1989, *What's Wrong with America and How to Fix It,* New York: Harper & Row.

"Language Planning in the USA." 1983. *American Speech* 58: 42–46. Review of Charles A. Ferguson and Shirley Brice Heath, eds. 1981. *Language in the USA.* Cambridge: Cambridge University Press.

"Review." 1949. *Modern Philology* 47: 135–140. Review of Vera E. Smalley. 1948. *The Sources of "A dictionarie of the French and English tongues, by Randale Cotgrave (London, 1611)."* Baltimore: Johns Hopkins Press.

"Review." 1955. *Language* 31: 312–345. Review of George L. Trager and Henry Lee Smith, 1951, *An Outline of English Structure.* Norman, OK: Battenberg Press; and Charles C. Fries, 1952, *The Structure of English: An Introduction to the Construction of English Sentences,* New York: Harcourt, Brace. Rev. rpt. in Harold B. Allen, ed., 1958, *Readings in Applied English Linguistics.* New York: Appleton-Century Crofts. 80–92. Also rev. rpt. in R. Eagleson, R. White, and C. Bentley, C., eds., 1976, *Language and Literature in the Foundation of National.* Sydney: Australian Language and Literature.

"Review." 1957. *Litera* 4: 93–97. Review of Henry Lee Smith, Jr. 1954. *Linguistic Science and the Teaching of English.* Boston: Harvard University Press.

"Review." 1957. *Language* 33: 261–271. Review of Harold Whitehall, 1956, *Structural essentials of English,* New York: Harcourt, Brace; and Donald J. Loyd and Harry R. Warfel, 1956, *American English in its cultural setting,* New York: Knopf; and Roberts, Paul, 1956, *Patterns of English,* New York: Harcourt, Brace.

"Review." 1958. *Language* 34: 139–144. Review of Robert C. Pooley. 1957. *Teaching English grammar*. New York: Appleton, Century-Crofts.

"Review." 1958. *Language* 34: 134–138. Review of R. W. Zandvoort. 1957. *A Handbook of English grammar*. London: Longmans, Green.

"Review." 1960. *Language* 36: 173–180. Review of Roger Kingdon. 1958. *The Groundwork of English Intonation*. London: Longmans, Green.

"Review." 1963. *Language* 39: 299–304. Review of Ralph B. Long. 1961. *The Sentence and Its Parts*. Chicago: University of Chicago Press.

"Review." 1966. *Language* 42: 797–810. Review of H. A. Gleason. 1965. *Linguistics and English Grammar*. New York: Holt, Rinehart & Winston.

"Review." 1982. *English World Wide: A Journal of Varieties of English* 3: 239–247. Review of Geneva Smitherman, ed. 1981, *Black English and the Education of Black Children and Youth: Proceedings of the National Invitational Symposium on the King Decision*, Detroit: Center for Black Studies, Wayne State University; and Marcia Farr Whiteman, ed. 1980, *Reactions to Ann Arbor: Vernacular Black English and Education*, Arlington, VA: Center for Applied Linguistics.

"Review." 1986. *Dictionaries: Journal of the Dictionary Society of North America* 8: 268–271. Review of Peter H. Fries and Nancy M. Fries. 1985. *Toward an Understanding of Language: Charles Carpenter Fries in Perspective*. Amsterdam Studies in Theory and History of Linguistic Science 40. Amsterdam & Philadelphia.

Credits